FORTY ILLUSTRATORS

AND HOW THEY WORK

FORTY ILLUSTRATORS

And how they work

by

ERNEST W. WATSON

With Chapters by
MATLACK PRICE
NORMAN KENT
AND
GUY ROWE

Essay Index Reprint Series

BOOKS FOR LIBRARIES PRESS
FREEPORT, NEW YORK

INTERNATIONAL STANDARD BOOK NUMBER:

0-8369-1899-1

LIBRARY OF CONGRESS CATALOG CARD NUMBER:

76-121510

PRINTED IN THE UNITED STATES OF AMERICA

DEDICATED
TO THE FORTY
AMERICAN ILLUSTRATORS
REPRESENTED
IN THIS VOLUME

AUTHOR'S PREFACE

ILLUSTRATION is almost the only art known to millions of Americans who have never even looked upon an original painting, and who only occasionally see reproductions of easel pictures. Obviously, it must be counted among the nation's cultural influences.

Yet illustration has received but scant notice in the art world, and very little has been published about the illustrator's profession or his practices. Art magazines, with one exception, completely ignore the men and women who paint pictures for publications. This exception is the periodical, *American Artist*. Since its beginning, in 1937, it has run feature articles on contemporary illustrators alongside other articles on painters.

The enthusiastic reception accorded these articles is responsible for the publication of this book, which is largely a compilation of interviews by the author, that have appeared in the magazine over the past several years. The stories have all been written with one intention: to reveal as much as possible of each artist's creative processes. This, of course, involves a study of his personality, his particular talents, his training, his philosophy of life and, of course, his technical procedures.

The approach to the study of each artist has differed with the subject. Some chapters focus upon purely technical practices; others emphasize training and experience; still others present a single important phase of the artist's work. Viewed as a whole, this book endeavors to give a comprehensive picture of contemporary illustration in its various ramifications.

The forty artists here presented are among the most distinguished in their profession. But there is no implication that they are *the* forty best. There are so many excellent illustrators working today that another, and yet another, selection of forty might be equally impressive. What we have here is a series of interviews written for *American Artist*, before there was any plan for a book. These magazine articles were so avidly welcomed, by professional artists and students alike, that the publishers decided to bring them together in permanent form, providing invaluable instruction not to be found elsewhere.

One of the interesting developments of recent years is the removal of the stigma that formerly damned as "commercial" any artist who drew or painted pictures for advertisements. Today, practically every illustrator is selling his art to merchants and manufacturers and no one thinks less of him for it, not even directors of our museums. Several of the illustrators here represented have pictures hanging in the Metropolitan Museum of Art.

Even *fine* artists, so-called, dare "prostitute" their art in the sale of soap, jewelry, automobiles, cosmetics and underwear—a corruption that is highly profitable; the sums paid for high-class advertising art are enough to tempt all but the most holy.

Industry has indeed made the profession an extremely lucrative one, though by no means can the illustrator's income be considered "easy money." By and large, the big money goes to men who have fought hard for their position and who, even in the glow of success, find their occupation about as unrelenting in its demands upon their time and energy as that of a successful surgeon. They are mercilessly haunted by "deadlines," and even though they could well afford to take things easy it is just not possible to escape the demands of art directors that increase in direct ratio to success.

Although the emphasis in this book is upon the men who are in the heyday of their careers, a few of the chapters are devoted to members of the old guard, men like Walter Biggs and Harvey Dunn. They are included because their contribution to the profession has been noteworthy, and it is wholesome to be reminded today of certain ideals and practices that created a great tradition of illustration in years gone by.

Some of the veterans—Wallace Morgan, for example—continue to work in both the spirit and practice of that tradition, but the camera, which is foreign to it, has engendered a kind of competition that is difficult for them to counter.

Photography, the new tool, is found in the studio of nearly every contemporary illustrator. It has revolutionized the profession, introducing a new approach to illustration and substituting new ideals for old. In the hands of lesser artists, it actually takes the place of creative ability—many a magazine picture has been literally traced from photographs. For others, it is an incidental tool, expedient but not requisite. Whether for better or worse, the camera is an inescapable influence upon the work of all who employ it.

For one thing, the artist comes to rely on his model's ability as an actor. A good model, posing for the camera, supplies something that the old-time illustrator had almost wholly to create. In present practice the model, who is first briefed, is directed to act his part over and over while the camera records his performances.* From the photographs thus produced, the artist selects the action and the expression that best suit his purpose. Some illustrators go so far as to bring together a group of models, carefully cast for the characters of the story,

---

* Briefing, under another name, was of course practiced before the advent of photography. Models of earlier days have often insisted upon knowing the action and episode and some of the best of them certainly made creative contributions to the work in hand.

and rehearse them repeatedly in the required action until photographs have been secured that can be faithfully followed in the painting.

As a result of this practice, the modeling profession has acquired caste; models frequently earn as much now for an hour's posing for the camera as they formerly made in a week. Even if an artist can afford to pay these high-priced models for long hours of posing, while he paints, he will find few candidates for the job.

Photography is responsible, also, for the skyrocketing to quick success of many a young artist, who, had he been born in an earlier day, would have been obliged to reach his goal by way of the more traditional and slower path of learning. Time, only, will discover whether success thus cheaply bought rests upon a permanent foundation.

All of this is not by way of implying that photography is surely leading illustration down the road to perdition. On the contrary, we in America can boast of the excellent quality of illustrative genius at work in our country today. No tool, no matter how enticing, can seduce the genuinely creative mind. However, the aspiring young illustrator well may pause and consider the dangers inherent in the camera. The world seen through a camera's lens is not the world that is comprehended by an artist who depends wholly upon his own eyes and his own imagination. The more he relies upon photography, the greater the danger of atrophy of his own creative powers. This threat is clearly seen in the work of many contemporaries who produce illustrations as devoid of individual character as photographic prints.

The reader will, I think, find it interesting and profitable to note the influence of the camera upon the men here represented. For some it will appear to be a negligible factor in their work; for others it will be seen to be a rather essential tool.

Photographic illustration—that is, illustration created entirely by the camera—while not represented in this book, has become very important in advertising art. In the 23rd Annual Exhibition of Advertising Art, held in 1944, forty-three per cent of the three hundred and sixty pictures shown were produced by the camera.

In advertising there are many illustrative problems where the camera obviously is indicated; others are as definitely dependent upon the artist's brush. Still others comprise an arena of competition between the two. It is challenging for the brush-man to examine advertising pictures reproduced in the magazines and ask how many of the "hand painted" ones might have been as effectively produced photographically. He might profitably inquire, "What has the camera got that I haven't got?" Or its corollary, "What have I got that the camera hasn't got?" If he has allowed himself to lean too heavily upon photography, he may discover that his productions are as good as, but no better than, photographic prints. As color photography comes into more general use, the painter's need for using his own eyes, plus all the feeling and creative responsiveness in his being, will be even more urgent. Perhaps the more abundant use of photog-

raphy and of art work of a photographic nature is a blessing in disguise. Will it not challenge really creative artists and intelligent art directors to experiment daringly along lines totally divorced from camera realism?

A few of our mass magazines are using photographic story illustrations. But in the field of fiction there seems to be little likelihood of a serious threat to the supremacy of the artist's brush. In fiction an ostensibly fictitious character is more generally satisfying than a real person. Experiments in photographic story illustration to date have been unconvincing.

How to "break into the game" is uppermost in the minds of all young artists embarking upon careers as illustrators. Time was when the black portfolio and aching feet were the only answer. Some believe that is still the best answer. But, in recent years, illustration—particularly for advertisements—has become highly organized as an art-producing business, and it is getting increasingly difficult for any other than top-flight artists to compete successfully with those associated with organizations known as Art Services or Studios. These are cooperatives of a sort. They assemble under one roof all the personalities, skills, business experience, equipment and services involved in the creation and marketing of art for advertisers and publishers. Models, photography, research, mechanical details, shipping and billing are some of the principal functions that such organizations supply, in addition to selling their artists' work.

The biggest art services are impressive plants with individual studios for member artists, photographic studios with professional photographer, costume room, research library, conference room and salesmen's room with files of artists' samples. In such studios illustration functions on an assembly line basis.** Illustrations—principally for advertisements—are usually the work of several specialists. Studios maintain a staff of designers, letterers, and mechanical experts who assist artists in technical correctness. No matter how adept the illustrator, he occasionally will have difficulty handling mechanical details. The artist may be engaged on a job that calls for the collaboration of several specialists; he himself may do the figure work, another man a perspective layout, someone else the lettering, still another the mechanical elements—a washing machine, perhaps, or a wrist watch. All these elements are assembled and coordinated by the production manager who is commandant of the "bull pen," the heart and core of the whole shop. The biggest studios may have fifty or more artists on their staffs.

What must especially appeal to the artist member of such an organization is a sales service that relieves him of all selling effort and the irritations of business

** The "assembly line" basis is not new. It had reached an efficient high three decades ago in the organizations of the Etheridge Company, Charles Daniel Frey and others. In 1913, for example, a poster for the New York Telephone Company was fabricated by a hardy crew in a few hours, and billed just as quickly for $500—big money in those days.

dealings. Artists seldom see clients; the studio salesman not only sells the artist, but sees his job through the shop completely, relaying client's instructions to artist, and acting as intermediary between artist and client when questions arise.

The young artist who is invited to membership in such an organization is likely to feel very fortunate. But he may be warned by some of his seniors that in escaping the irritations of direct dealings with clients he is missing something important. Much that an advertising artist should know can best be learned through personal contact with buyers. It is highly instructive to get at first hand the client's reaction to one's work and to become personally acquainted with art directors.

Another selling agency is the artist's representative. He acts as business manager—soliciting commissions, showing samples, following up on jobs and attending to the details of delivering work and billing all orders. For these services the representative usually receives 25% commission on gross billing. There is no work done on the agent's premises, where only such office space is maintained as is needed for consultations, the filing of artists' samples and for clerical work.

Many successful artists have put themselves in the hands of these representatives, but others, who prefer a more intimate and personal relationship with their clients, deal directly with advertising managers or with advertising agencies who handle the client's accounts.

Illustration is the goal of a great majority of students in our art schools. Its allurements are many. Not the least of them is the fabulous income that awaits the winner of a top place in a very lucrative profession. Even those who do not reach the highest peak know that there are good incomes for thousands on the lower levels. What is not sufficiently appreciated is that the gold in illustration, like the ore in the depths of the earth, is not so easily brought to light. If the stories of the illustrators in this book demonstrate the extent of training, industry and fanatical devotion that lies hidden behind their facile art on the printed page, I shall feel that one very useful purpose has been served in their publication.

CONTENTS

AUTHOR'S PREFACE ix

ALAJALOV, CONSTANTIN 1

ARTZYBASHEFF, BORIS 7

ATHERTON, JOHN 15

BAKER, ERNEST HAMLIN 23

BIGGS, WALTER 33

BOBRI, V. 43

CADY, HARRISON 51

COOPER, FRED 59

COOPER, MARIO 67

CORNWELL, DEAN 73

D'ALESSIO, GREGORY 83

DAVIS, FLOYD 89

DOHANOS, STEVAN 97

DORNE, ALBERT 105

DUNN, HARVEY 115

ERICKSON, CARL 121

GANNAM, JOHN 129

GROHE, GLENN 139

Contents continued overleaf

xiii

CONTENTS CONTINUED

GIUSTI, GEORGE 147

HAY, STUART 153

HELCK, PETER 161

HURST, EARL OLIVER 171

KLETT, WALTER 179

LAWSON, ROBERT 187

METZL, ERVINE 195

MORGAN, WALLACE 203

OBERHARDT, WILLIAM 211

PITZ, HENRY C. 221

PRICE, GEORGE 227

PROHASKA, RAY 231

RIGGS, ROBERT 239

RAGAN, LESLIE 247

ROCKWELL, NORMAN 253

SAWYERS, MARTHA 263

SCOTT, HOWARD 269

SEWELL, AMOS 277

TEAGUE, DONALD 285

WATSON, ALDREN A. 293

WORTMAN, DENYS 301

WYETH, N. C. 309

COLOR PLATES

ALAJALOV . . . Tempera painting for *New Yorker* Cover 2

ATHERTON . . . Tempera painting, *Koppers Company* advertisement 16

BAKER . . . . . Tempera drawing of *Eisenhower* for *Time* Cover 25

BIGGS . . . . . Watercolor painting, *A Street in Salem, Virginia* 36

BOBRI . . . . . Brush, airbrush and cutpaper, *Taurus* 44

COOPER . . . . Watercolor demonstration, *Painting a Head* 68

CORNWELL . . . Oil painting, *Fisher Body* advertisement 77

DAVIS . . . . . Watercolor painting for *American Magazine* 90

DORNE . . . . . Painting in colored inks, *Anheuser-Busch* advertisement 106

ERICKSON . . . Watercolor drawing, *Coty* advertisement 123

GANNAM . . . . Watercolor painting for *Good Housekeeping* 133

GROHE . . . . . Tempera painting, *Spring and Autumn* 143

HAY . . . . . . Wash drawing illustration for *This Week* 154

HELCK . . . . . Tempera and gouache, *Caterpillar Tractor* advertisement 163

HURST . . . . . Drawing in colored inks, *Jantzen* advertisement 173

KLETT . . . . . Oil painting, *Woman in Padre Hat* 180

PROHASKA . . . Tempera and oil painting for *Good Housekeeping* 233

RIGGS . . . . . Tempera painting, *Capehart Collection* advertisement 243

ROCKWELL . . . Oil painting for *Tom Sawyer* 254

TEAGUE . . . . Watercolor for *The Saturday Evening Post* 287

WATSON . . . . Color illustration for *Walden on Life in the Woods* 294

WYETH . . . . Oil painting for *Drums* 311

WYETH . . . . Egg tempera painting, *Summer Night* 315

WYETH . . . . Detail of *Summer Night* 315

Constantin Alajalov

ONE OF ALAJALOV'S BRILLIANT COVERS FOR THE NEW YORKER

From Conversation Pieces by Alajalov   Studio Publications   Copyrighted   Reprinted by Permission The New Yorker

2

The Labor Pains of a Cover Design

This is the story of an artist's creative processes in the designing of one of his brilliant, satirical covers for The New Yorker.

It is, also, the story of **Constantin Alajalov** who, though best known for his *New Yorker* covers—he has done them for nearly 20 years—has other strings to his bow. And the adventurous days of his youth add up to a tale that ought to be told; and *is* told in *Conversation Pieces by Alajalov*, a new *Studio* publication. In this book Janet Flanner's account of those years, when Alajalov lived by his wits in revolutionary Russia, reveals a colorful background for a rather unique career. We have permission to quote from this story later in our text. But first let us look in upon the artist just after he has had an inspiration for a Thanksgiving cover.

Like most of Alajalov's cover ideas, this one sprang from nowhere. Once in a while the editors hand him one, but 95% of them are his own. He plucks them out of his subconscious. Occasionally they are based upon episodes actually witnessed but more often they just pop.

An idea, in the artist's mind, is a mental picture. This quickly takes graphic form in a pencil drawing, somewhat sketchy at first yet sufficiently developed for editorial consideration. And we mean *consideration*; anything seen in *The New Yorker* has run the gamut of an editorial staff in conference assembled.

With the editor's O.K. the real fun begins. The labor pains of a cover design are not always so protracted as they proved to be in the creation of this Thanksgiving assignment. Perhaps the simile applied to this period of gestation is a bit misleading; but, if an exaggeration, it is useful in emphasizing the downright seriousness of being funny. The documentation of a humorous picture has to be just as authentic as any illustration. This often involves extensive research, and all good illustrators go to unbelievable lengths to insure the accuracy of every detail. Furthermore, the most effective dramatization of an idea—especially a humorous one—exacts patient study as well as wit. The idea itself is merely the starting point; only those who have tried know what artifice is needed to put it over. A detailed examination of Ala-

jalov's pencil studies, on following pages, will illustrate how subtle changes in expression, action and stage-setting control the reader's reaction and deliver the desired punch.

Coming back to research, let us accompany Alajalov as he begins work on his Thanksgiving cover. The scene is set in the kitchens of an Army camp. What does such a place look like? One can guess, but Alajalov takes nothing for granted; he must see with his own eyes.

Now one doesn't just walk into an Army camp. First comes a call at New York's Army Headquarters at 90 Church Street. The Public Relations Officer is a nice man, but one has to reach him first and then persuade him that such a thing as a cover design really matters. It took Alajalov just two days to do that.

Fortified at last with his credentials, he journeyed a hundred miles into New Jersey and was admitted to Fort Dix with pencil and notebook. He had passed Scylla, but there was still Charybdis, in the person of an obdurate mess sergeant who insisted upon an order from his own captain. This, in time, was forthcoming.

The interior sketch reproduced on a following page is one of many which filled Alajalov's notebook that day. It is typical of his documentary drawings; sketches which have but one purpose—information. Such sketches, by the way, carry much more information than their few lines suggest to others. They serve to sharpen the artist's powers of observation and instruct his memory so that the drawings themselves may never need to be consulted.

Back home, Alajalov began the series of pencil drawings shown herewith. These were made the exact size of the finished painting which is but slightly larger than the cover itself. The development of the idea, seen in successive studies, demonstrates what has already been said about the importance of seeking just the right dramatization through experiments in expression, action and stage-setting. The changes made in these studies grew out of conferences with the editors as well as the artist's own awareness. It will be seen that slight changes occurred between the accepted drawing and the finished cover painting.

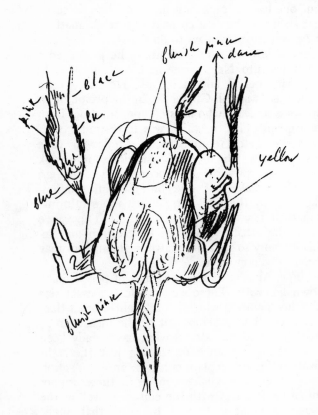

ILLUSTRATING THE LABOR PAINS

The turkeys, important *dramatis personae* in the cast, gave the artist more concern than might be expected. They led him first into the cold storage room of a neighboring butcher shop where, with numbed fingers, he drew from a frozen specimen. Afterwards he realized the inadequacy of this brief contact with turkey anatomy; the composition called for turkeys seen from many angles. His problem was solved by a sympathetic weekend hostess. She ushered him to her refrigerator and introduced him to a turkey in the pink of condition. The bird soon was posing on the kitchen table.

One step in the creation of Alajalov's covers—and an important one—cannot be shown in our demonstration. That is the black and white underpainting over which the final painting is done in color. After a careful pencil layout on illustration board he brushes in the picture with tones of transparent, bluish-gray watercolor—a complete neutral study that permits him to develop his pattern without reference to color. This underpainting is in a relatively high key. In the final color phase he works with transparent washes as much as possible but does not hesitate to use opaque pigment to intensify color and to bring out his highlights.

Although many of Alajalov's covers demand far less research and are more easily produced, the procedure here described is fairly typical of his creative processes. He will do a cover over three or four times if in so doing he can improve it. He sometimes spends weeks on them. He also does drawings for advertisements and various publications. He has painted many murals, chief among them are three large ceil-

OF A COVER DESIGN FOR THE NEW YORKER

ings for the S. S. *America*, a commission won through competition.

Alajalov is wholly self-taught—the Russian Revolution saw to that. But he is a great student and is continually drawing and painting from the model. He has painted many portraits. Both his drawing and painting, outside his professional work, are academic. Under that sophisticated technique of his lies a foundation of traditional study not even suspected by his admirers.

And now we shall let Janet Flanner take over. In *Conversation Pieces* she has written so effectively about Alajalov's adventurous youth that our readers ought to hear it in her own words:

"No one surprises us Americans more than a stranger who comes to our shores and sees us as we know we are not—except a stranger who comes over and sees us as we had not suspected we were. Constantin Alajalov is an artist at, and in, this second category.

"He is a Russian who was born in 1900 on Rostov-on-the-Don, a Cossack city. . . .

"Most painters aim at immortality. Alajalov has been willing to settle for seven days at a time as his scope. For years he has been painting some of the most brilliant covers for the weekly, *The New Yorker*. Few artists with so much talent have been willing to lay it out on so fleeting a series of significant satires. As a result no other artist has created such an accurate album of comic and contemporary Americana. Our grandparents were not the only generation who looked funny.

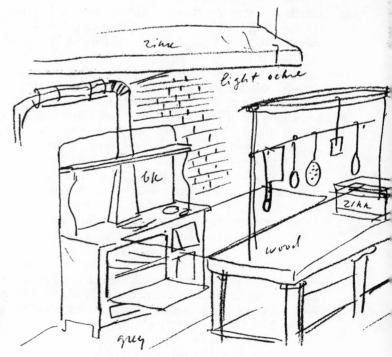

5

"As a European, Alajalov was able to catch the essence of a certain kind of American face and its form of life because Europe had rolled him around too fast for him ever to concentrate on what Europeans looked like. He was comfortably brought up in the Tzarist bourgeois tradition of Russian novels and food, English poetry, and a French governess. As an indigestible result, at the age of fifteen he illustrated Beaudelaire's Parisian poems, plus the lives of the Italian reformer Savanarola and the Spanish torturer Torquemada in the pictorial style of the Victorian decadent, Aubrey Beardsley. The Communist Revolution put a stop to all such internationalism. Alajalov was seventeen and a student at the University of Petrograd when the Revolution broke. A few months later he was a member of a new government artists guild then roving the land and as the youngest, least experienced, member was painting the biggest portraits of Marx and Lenin and the tallest proletariats on the walls of the workmen's clubs, then springing up and open to decoration all over Russia. In the southern resort town of Piatigorsk where the artists were detailed to do a rush job painting pictures on the outside of a propaganda train which was to go steaming over the provinces like a moving picture book, in three weeks Alajalov painted art all over four entire freight cars. . . .

"Eventually the artists' guild job took him to Resht, in northern Persia, where our present allies, the British and the Russians, were then disputing with arms and bombs over the matter of Persian oil. Here, to the thud of cannon, the artists used as a studio the abandoned harem, still full of its elderly female inmates, of an old Persian prince who had fled. Here also Alajalov received the honorable offer, without salary, to become court painter to the town's leading revolutionary, a beautiful and bearded idealist, Governor Usunala Khan, who had no court. However, he had a dead grandfather whose portrait Alajalov painted from imagination. Soon the grandson joined his ancestor in the Moslem Paradise. As the result of a border misunderstanding with a Persian conservative, Usunala Khan was hanged, by way of explanation.

"What with one thing and another, such as hunger, despair, and not enough money to buy paints with, it was the summer of 1921 when Alajalov finally reached the shores of the Golden Horn and Constantinople. Constantinople was then the great metropolis of refugees. It was the first European capital after World War I to become what most capitals have become in World War II—an uneasy gathering place for the homeless. Cast up in a polyglot tide by sieges, revolutions, famines and fears, every kind of Near East merchant, Levantine ship broker, Balkan mountaineer, Armenian orphan, Circassian, Georgian and Slav, Red or White, or Anatolian peasant and pasha roamed the streets if male, or hid modestly in doorways if female. Penniless Russian princes, wearing gray flannel pajamas donated by the American Red Cross, tried to sell each other Russian cakes on street corners. Russian princesses, then still real like their pearls, served as waitresses, wearing their necklaces, in side street restaurants.

"Starving in any language was easy in Constantinople in 1921.

"Alajalov, with more difficulty, lived on borrowed bread and olives. He did pencil portraits in bars in exchange for a glass of goat's milk. His first big art job was a life-size painting of Georges Carpentier and Jack Dempsey for use as a sidewalk advertisement for a Grande Rue de Pera movie house that was showing the famous fight film, still the sporting event of the Golden Horn. His painting stopped the traffic. The movie manager paid him four Turkish lire (about two dollars) for both portraits but grandly advised him to say the price had been ten when he recommended him to other motion picture palace keepers. Alajalov always told them ten but they always gave him eight, which was still twice as much as he was used to. He painted a whole foyer for the great German horror fantasy film, The Cabinet of Dr. Caligari, then showing as the sensation of civilized Europe. Alajalov lived in one slat-shaped small room in the Taxim section of Istamboul, the poor and native section of the Golden Horn city. The room was so narrow that he had to paint standing on the bed with the drawing paper tacked to the wall.

"His success in Constantinople, as later in New York, began with his nightclub murals. Constantinople nightclubs were all Russian in décors, even if owned by Greeks and run by boys from Harlem. Alajalov began with murals for Maxim's, one of the smartest, most costly spots, decorated a Taxim Cabaret and was soon eating at their tables. He took food as most of his pay.

"He also made a fine private series of drawings. He sketched the Turkish cemeteries with their carved turban headstones and the veiled Turkish women and children invariably quietly picnicking among the male dead. He drew portraits of the monstrously fat oriental women who lolled in the windows of the terrible waterfront dives. His drawing paper was the cheapest in the city—fine heavy paper watermarked with the Romanoff double eagle and intended, until the White Russian cause finally collapsed, to be used for the printing of Romanoff Restoration rubles.

"By 1923, after two years' hard work, Alajalov had saved one hundred dollars. At that time an intelligentsia organization was offering free transportation to any Russian students willing to attend universities in Germany, where, in inflation, his hundred dollars would have fed and housed him for one year. But Alajalov, world-weary at twenty-three, felt Europe was old and might never recover and that only the United States could live to be young and new. He arrived in New York with five dollars.

"The first person he met was a Russian childhood friend who was also Isadora Duncan's secretary. Russian nightclubs were also booming in Manhattan. Alajalov started painting murals in Russian nightclubs again. While the nightclub patrons looked on, he painted the murals in Countess Anna Zarnekau's Bi-Ba-Bo Club. Three years later he heard of The New Yorker magazine. It was than a year old. His first cover appeared on the September 25, 1926 issue. It showed a polite American male suffering while a musical American female sang at the piano. It also showed a strong cubist influence. Alajalov's drawings have showed up the various stoical relations between the American sexes ever since. . . . "As a satirist Alajalov paints, quite kindly, what in words would be too cruel to say. As an artist in his genre, what he really draws are conclusions."

Boris Artzybasheff

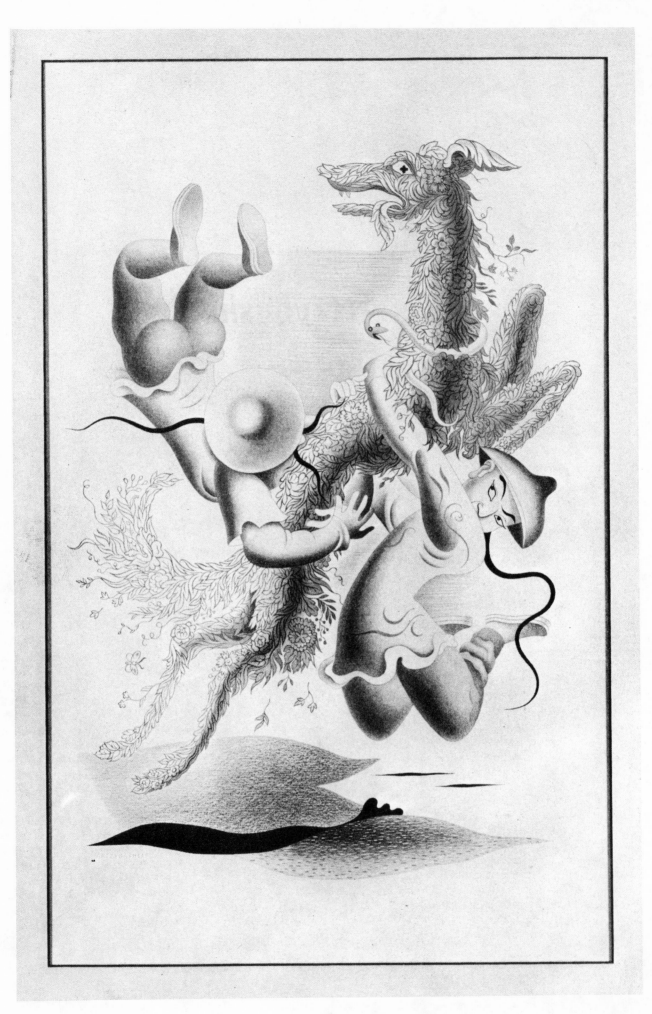

THE ART OF BORIS ARTZYBASHEFF

THE LION is Boris Artzybasheff's favorite animal. He likes lions because the king of beasts, among all denizens of the forest, has a face peculiarly adapted to the expression of human emotion. If you doubt that, you don't know Artzybasheff's lions. A lion's countenance in some hypnotic way takes on a human aspect whether one's pencil wills it or not. Artzybasheff's pencil completely exploits its possibilities. The dejected lion below, for example (from "Poor Shaydullah"). That lion is the artist's special pet because, as he says, "I feel like that so often."

As a matter of fact, Artzybasheff sees all things, both animate and inanimate, in terms of human personality. Call it fantasy. But his fantasy is most often the naked truth about things that, in the confusions of our workaday world, hide their absurd or terrible realities behind masks which camouflage their real significance.

Thus, in his remarkable drawings reproduced in *Life* (November 3, 1941), Artzybasheff employed fantasy to unmask the face of Mars, showing us what we already know, yet don't quite see: that tanks, planes and battleships are the same bloody hands, and the radio—in war—the same in-

sidious voice with which man has always warred upon his fellow man.

But this preoccupation with a serious theme is not at all characteristic of the artist; it is a momentary interlude in a career chiefly devoted to drolleries and purely decorative adventures with pen and brush. These have filled a long sequence of volumes that are as entertaining as they are beautiful.

He cannot be thought of as an illustrator in the usual sense because he has little interest in realism, and less in the obvious. You'll never find him in *The Saturday Evening Post*, and seldom in any situation where he is not allowed to indulge his bizarre imagination. If the story is dull, Artzybasheff will manage to carry the author on his back by drawings which are never dull. Indeed the books he illustrates are most likely bought for his drawings rather than the text. He is really a collector's item. And that is because he is both a designer and a wit. Design. Now we have come to the motivation of the man's genius. He is first and always a designer. Even if the edge of his wit were less keen, his drawings would still be sought by connoisseurs; he would still be a highlight in the graphic arts.

Page Opposite: Drawing for "The Circus of Dr. Lao" by Charles G. Finney. Viking Press.

Lion from "Poor Shaydullah"

9

It might also be said that his humor likewise is strong enough to stand alone. Take, for example, the story of "Poor Shaydullah," written and illustrated by him for *Macmillan* in 1931. Shaydullah, the lazy and foolish beggar, embarks upon a pilgrimage to find Allah, who, the wise men have told him, is the only one who can set his feet upon the path of prosperity. After many adventures on land and sea he nearly meets his end in a great storm on the desert which is called the Garden of Allah. As he cries out, "Where art thou, Allah?" there appears before him "a whirling ball of fire which was like unto the morning sun, but which came nearer and grew larger until it burst open like a wondrous rose. And out of the light there came a voice as strong as thunder, yet harmonious. And it said, 'I am Allah! I am the First and the Last and the world is mine, etc.'" This episode in the illustration shows Allah in all his might and wisdom to be none other than G. Bernard Shaw.

But Artzybasheff does not rely upon idea content for his humor. It springs automatically from a pen which, it would seem, can scarcely draw a line that is not pregnant with sly and subtle comedy. And because it is always enriched by good design it has a substance which the usual run of humorous drawings lack. In short, it is art.

Those who are only acquainted with this phase of Artzybasheff's work will perhaps be surprised to learn that the same mind which today soars in such flights of imagination as his illustrations for "The Circus of Dr. Lao" can tomorrow become absorbed—and pleasantly so—in a problem of statistical illustration: the making of charts, graphs and maps such as he has done for *Fortune*.

Yet this artist undertakes such tasks with the same zest that he applies to his fantasies. Give him the assignment of demonstrating what happens to the brain of a dive-bombing aviator. He will enjoy the days of patient research and the search for a dramatic presentation of the facts, a technique for telling the story in a colorful, pictorial chart which is sure to be both beautiful and statistically accurate. He does a lot of this sort of thing and loves it. It is, after all, a problem in design to which statistics, he has discovered, are intimately related. The rhythms of cause and effect very often have graphic counterpart which gives direction to the designer's graphs and charts. The movement of a statistical graph may well offer a basic line for the designer of a pictorial graph.

So, it appears, Artzybasheff's imagination is animated

Cover for Fortune

Color diagram for Fortune illustrating "The Backlog of American Aviation Industries"

Brush-drawn decoration for "Droll Stories by Balzac." Heritage Press. Reproduced at exact size of original.

Illustration by Boris Artzybasheff for "Poor Shaydullah." Written by the artist for Macmillan

by a mathematical problem as effectively as by a penciled doodle on a telephone pad. His fantasy representing the voice of the radio (see illustration on a following page) actually started with a doodle, although the idea itself preceded the doodle and there was nothing accidental in that.

Illustrative, again, of Artzybasheff's versatility was his fling at architectural design several years ago. It came quite by accident. Asked what he thought of an architect's design for an altar to be erected in the Lady Chapel of St. Patrick's Cathedral, he gave such a convincing criticism that the donor requested him to submit a rough sketch embodying his own ideas. This was in Paris where the artist was living at the time. Artzybasheff spent a month studying all the important Gothic churches in Paris and poring over books in architectural libraries.

His "sketch" was a detailed drawing such as might have come from a professional architect's office. The design pleased the donor, who proposed that it be submitted to an architectural engineer for whatever revision might be necessary from the structural angle. Artzybasheff's sense of craftsmanship rebelled at the delivery of drawings which might not be functionally correct. For several more weeks he devoted himself to the engineering problem and finally presented drawings which were wholly approved by a consulting engineer.

Artzybasheff was born in Kharkov, Russia, in 1900. At eighteen the Revolution interrupted his schooling and brought tragedy into his life. He was separated from his father, Michael Artzybasheff, the noted novelist, who later died in Warsaw, in exile. His mother, a refugee, died alone and in poverty in Turkey. The young man served in the White Army.

In 1919 he signed as a seaman on an ammunition ship bound for New York to pick up a cargo of munitions. That was a one-way voyage for the lad who had determined to become an American. Unable to speak English and with fourteen cents in his pockets he was a stranger in the land where in a few years he was destined to become famous.

Through the help of an immigration official he secured a job in a New York engraving shop. That was

Woodcut illustration used as an advertisement by The New York Times

One of a series of caricatures made by Artzybasheff for the Wickwire Spencer Steel Company

Artzybasheff's portrait covers for Time show this artist to be as skilful in realism as in the world of fantasy.

the start of his professional art career. It didn't look especially promising at the time. For fifteen dollars a week he designed ornamental borders, did lettering and the usual hack work that is entrusted to beginners. Once he displayed such genius in painting a medicine bottle that all bottle painting was thereafter entrusted to him. It was his first distinction, he had become a specialist. This honor, however, brought neither financial reward nor security, as he found when his demand for a three-dollar-a-week raise was refused.

Seeing no hope of advancement he determined to quit, a decision not lightly to be made since he had been able to save nothing from a wage which had barely kept body and soul together. But he had one asset: he was an able-bodied seaman. So he soon found himself aboard a Standard Oil tanker bound for South America.

Upon his return a few months later his accumulated savings were sufficient to establish him as a free-lance artist. In this capacity he successively designed ladies' wear, a Russian restaurant, a night club and theatrical stage sets. His first illustrations for a book of Russian fairy tales, published by E. P. Dutton, set him upon the path he was to follow. Since then he has done considerably more than fifty books. Many of these he has written and he has frequently been asked to design them too.

Artzybasheff invariably starts his designs in charcoal, whether working in mass or line. With his pencil he draws right over the charcoal, establishing lines desired for the outlines. The soft charcoal is then brushed away. To transfer these outlines to a fresh paper for the final ink or color drawing he covers the back of his sketch with graphite rubbed on from a large square stick. Saturating a wad of cotton with benzene, he rubs it over

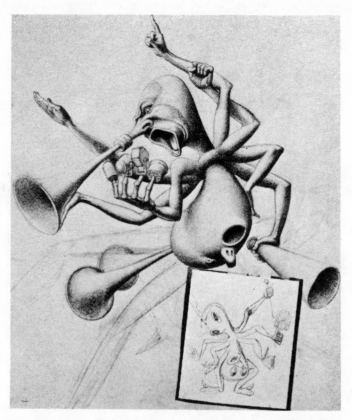

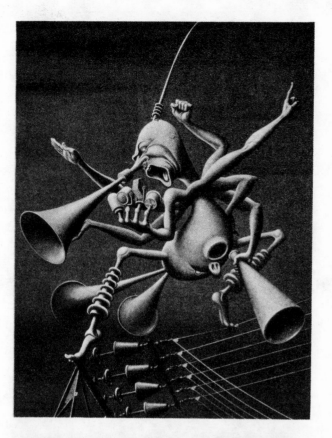

The upper-right halftone is reproduced from Boris Artzybasheff's color drawing which appeared in Life. It is one of a series of grotesques: cartoons which remind us that tanks, planes and battleships are the same bloody hands, and the radio — in propaganda — the same insidious voice with which man has always warred upon his fellow man.

The pencil drawing above is a study (18 x 24 inches) and the insert is a telephone doodle which became the basis for the bizarre impersonation.

A glance at Artzybasheff's work cabinet shows that the artist is a neat and orderly craftsman.

the graphite to produce an even tone. This makes an ideal transfer medium, giving a thin, easily erased line when a sharp, hard pencil is used for the tracing. The benzene fixes the graphite sufficiently to prevent rubbing off in contact with clean papers but not enough to interfere with the transfer.

Artzybasheff has a neat recipe also for transferring white lines on a black ground such as scratchboard which has been blackened preparatory to scraping. He discovered that A. W. Faber's silver *Colorex* when rubbed on the back of the sketch and spread with a benzene pad, as previously described for the graphite process, produces a perfect transfer surface.

Artzybasheff uses scratchboard for a great many of his drawings. He also engraves on wood. Both techniques, quite naturally, are similar under his hand. He blackens his wood blocks, as well as the scratchboard, by spraying india ink with the airbrush.

To obtain a sharpness of contour and extreme precision of line, and to more closely simulate woodcut, Artzybasheff invented the use of celluloid (technically "pyrolin sheeting" about an eighth of an inch thick) as a substitute for both paper and wood block. After spraying this with black he takes out his white lines with engravers' tools. This is one of several craft methods he has devised to give his work a technical perfection that is unique. He does not hesitate to use rags, pieces of wood, fingers or any other odd means (sup-

plementing his pen and brush) to secure different textural effects. A rough turkish towel, for example, may be employed for a certain stipple-like tone. Most of his ink work is done with long-haired sable brushes. These respond sympathetically in the production of those graceful lines so characteristic of his technique.

One knows without asking that Artzybasheff makes but casual use of a model. He has not had a model in his studio for many years, though he has a small mirror attached to his work table to reflect the pose of his hand now and then. His approach to drawing is through design rather than anatomy, though design could not function here without a thorough knowledge of anatomy. This, to be sure, is seldom displayed in any literal way but it is clearly evident even in his most fantastic versions of the human form.

John Atherton

Tempera painting by John Atherton for the Koppers Company

JOHN ATHERTON

IT IS NOT OFTEN that an artist majors both as an easel painter and an illustrator. It is a commonly held prejudice—having considerable foundation—t h a t the practice of commercial art spoils a man for painting. It is likewise assumed that no easel painter is temperamentally fitted to apply his art to the dictated demands of publishers and advertisers.

John Atherton is an exception to this rule. He has two sets of brushes: with one, he earns his livelihood—and a very good one; with the other, he paints canvases that have brought him considerable acclaim in the world of paint. From the very beginning he has been ambitious to be a painter, but, at the outset, he discovered that manufacturers of automobiles, radios and eyewash were more interested in his pictures than were the art critics. And they had the money—a circumstance that few young artists can afford to ignore.

So Atherton hired himself out to advertisers. His work had the qualities they liked, and he soon found himself in growing demand. Magazine editors in due time sought him out, too, competing with advertisers for his meticulously rendered drawings and decorations. His pictures began to appear on the covers of *Fortune* and *The Saturday Evening Post*.

In addition to his advertising drawings and illustrations, Atherton has done many posters that in themselves have brought him distinction. He first attracted attention in this field through his prize-winning poster for the New York World's Fair. Shortly after, he won both a first and second prize in the Museum of Modern Art War Bond Poster Competition. The first prize design—the clasped hands, "Buy a Share in America," was widely distributed in a war bond campaign.

Atherton, through all these successes, has become a "big name" in the commercial art world. Amazingly enough, he has also arrived as an easel painter, and at about the same time. His determination to become a professional painter has survived the temptations of the business world. All the time he has been producing his illustrations and posters, he has kept his creative painting going. His canvases began to appear in exhibitions; his name grew familiar on 57th Street, and found frequent mention in the art journals. In 1942 his painting, *The Black Horse*, won a prize in the big *Artists For Victory* competition, and was purchased by the Metropolitan Museum of Art for its permanent collection. Such an honor seals the success of any painter.

Atherton is a surrealist in his painting. One critic labeled him a "sure realist" because his dominant interest seems to be in detail rather than in mystical implications usually seen in weird combinations of unrelated objects in surrealist canvases. Yet, when we look at *The Black Horse*, we are struck by its sombre mood, its poetic atmosphere. Here, at least, mysticism subordinates such an interest in mere texture and detail as we see in *Still Life With Feathers*.

In all his work, Atherton is first of all a designer. He has a native genius for order and organization that expresses itself in everything he does, whether it be an advertising drawing, a poster or an easel picture. Nothing in his work is left to accident. Every detail and color note is as necessary to the functioning of the design as is every tiny part in the design of a complex machine. An Atherton design "works" perfectly.

How does this versatile artist go about his work? I asked him for some preliminary sketches that I might reproduce here, along with finished work, to give at least a hint of his creative processes. These processes, it seems, take place almost wholly within the recesses of his mind where none but he can observe them. They do not require experimental studies in line and color. This is true of his illustrations and paintings alike. He dreams over the composition: lets it develop in his subconscious without much analytical planning. Then he starts to draw on paper or canvas with a careful line that registers all the forms of the picture. By the time he begins to paint, his design has been quite completely visualized. This does not mean that his painting is a "filling-in" process. Color, tonality, detail and all those qualities that create what we call "expression" must, of course, wait upon the brush.

While Atherton, as I have said, does little planning on paper, preparatory to his painting, he does make very careful pencil drawings—from life or nature—of figures and objects that are to appear in any size in his design. (Typical of these studies is the drawing shown on page 20.)

It is interesting to note that, when Atherton turns from illustration to painting, he does not have to make a right-about-face. His technical approach to both is the same: both receive the same perfections of craftsmanship; both profit equally from a rare genius for design. He is one of those fortunate artists who is able to function happily in the two disparate worlds of "fine" and "commercial" art. For him, the dual role seems both natural and agreeable. He says: "I am convinced that (for me, and essentially for many who feel as I do) a decent life has greater bearing on the caliber of the work done than the so-called loss of face in making compromises. To do good work, it follows reasonably that to eat regularly, live in pleasant surroundings and have enough independence to be able to devote oneself principally to the creation of art is a more intelligent solution than the opposite of the

Advertising drawing for the Container Corporation of America

The original is 12 x 16 inches

Above —

Illustration for The Curtis Publishing Company. The original tempera drawing is 12 x 20 inches.

Right —

One of a series of covers for Fortune. Atherton has also designed several covers for The Saturday Evening Post.

Pencil drawing by Atherton, preparatory to its use in a painting

This is about one-half size of the original

starving artist, freezing in his garret with pride intact. The point is to be able to recognize when the income from commercial art has reached a reasonable figure, and not let greed overcome the urge for self-expression.

"I shall probably always do a certain amount of commercial art—for two reasons. One is that certain things are fun, and I like to do them. The other is that the life it enables me to lead is the best, for me, and I have no desire to change it for the worse."

John Atherton was born in Brainerd, Minnesota,

June 7, 1900. After serving in the Navy in World War I, he settled in California, where he studied at the College of the Pacific, San Jose, and the California School of Fine Arts, San Francisco. He began commercial art in 1926, was married the same year, and moved to New York in 1929. He now lives and works in Arlington, Vermont. His paintings hang in the Metropolitan, Whitney, Chicago Art Institute, Hartford Atheneum and the Albright Gallery.

Above —

"The Black Horse"

This oil painting by John Atherton won a prize at the 1942 Artists For Victory Competition and was purchased by the Metropolitan Museum of Art for its permanent collection.

Right —

"Still Life with Feathers"   Oil 20 x 24

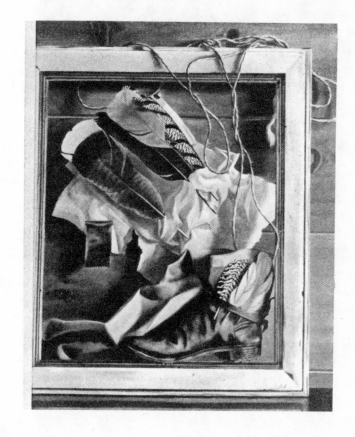

Ernest Hamlin Baker

by Guy Rowe

Working Drawing for
Baker's Time Cover
of General Eisenhower
Reduced from
the 10 x 11 inch original

Ernest Hamlin Baker's TIME Covers

Described by Guy Rowe

EDITOR'S NOTE—*Ernest Hamlin Baker's portraits of men prominent in world affairs have been appearing on the covers of "Time" for years and have set a style that has been reflected in the work of other artists. Believing that the story of this accomplishment would be of great interest to our readers, we have asked the well-known artist Guy Rowe to tell it to us. He is unusually well-equipped for the task, having known Baker intimately for a good many years. He has watched him at work, observed his methods and thrashed out scores of art problems with him. Rowe will be remembered by many of our readers for his internationally-known still life paintings made for "Jello," some years back, which brought the highest prices ever paid for paintings in that field.*

ERNEST HAMLIN BAKER is made-to-order for *Time*. This unequivocal statement is based on the credo (and its faithful performance) that Baker set for himself when they gave him his first assignment, a head of Paderewski. Here in his own words is the approach he decided upon.

"A good cover should not only help sell the magazine, but also reflect its character. Therefore, in the same sense that *Time* tries to bring out the true significance of world events in terms of personalities through its use of complete news coverage, it should be my job to try to bring out the subject's true character through a complete coverage of his facial forms—forms that tell of minor Munichs, Dunkirks, heedings of integrity, yieldings to expediency, forms that have been stamped into his face by numberless deeds and intentions, good, bad and indifferent.

"These untold tales will emerge automatically and add up to the subject's total character, provided only that I do two things: first, report unflinchingly every

perceptible form; second, weave and integrate these forms into a living unity. If it works, I will then be telling *Time* readers not only what the man *looks* like, but also what he *is* like—a really good reporting job."

All thoughts of fine art, conventional portraiture precepts, or the subject's reactions to this uninvited scrambling over his facial mounds and probings of his facial crevasses—went out the window. Baker felt bound only by considerations that made for newsstand sales, such as strong design, simplicity of large patterns, characterful expression and (later on) attractive color. Without at the time realizing it, Baker was on the verge of some interesting discoveries, one of which was that while his facial reporting was winning a quick response from the public on the basis of its sheer honesty, it was at the same time being recognized by discerning critics as a new approach to creative art.

In arriving at this new approach, Baker was responding to a demand even as the designers of modern skyscrapers responded to the demand of limited ground space. In this case the demands of limited time compel *Time* cover artists to work almost exclusively from photographs. Instead of bemoaning that limitation (or is it really?) with the preciousness typical of so many orthodox portraitists, Baker, in an honest appraisal of the camera's value, decided to make photographs go to work for him. He pored over them, first with the naked eye, then with a magnifying glass. His efforts were well

General Dwight D. Eisenhower
Time Cover — By Ernest Hamlin Baker

rewarded. Among other things he found that the sharper the print, the more valuable it was for his purpose, by virtue of the wealth of small detail it revealed—small detail, that it had for so long been the fashion deliberately to ignore. "Work for the large forms," by all means, but why not arrive at them via the small for a change. He also found that in such sharp photographs an amazing interweaving of these small forms invariably occurred. He found that all the shapes of a face are eventually rhythmic, that they move one into the other in a truly fascinating way. The human face became for him a vast landscape to be explored as by a traveler, sketchbook in hand.

In these penetrating searchings for detail Baker seeks to understand exactly and completely what is going on as to form in the subject's face. There seems to be no effective shortcut in arriving at this understanding. Once as an experiment he tried making an exact tracing from a large-sized photograph. It was no use. He could not progress until he understood the face, and he could not understand the face until he had integrated every mound and depression into a true and rhythmic relationship with the rest of the head. The up-shot was, he had saved no time. In fact he has come to believe that the tortuous labor by which he builds up his first map-in-the-round of the subject's head somehow invests his work with a living quality. I have seen him discover and run to earth, with the fierce concentration of a man-hunt, discrepancies in drawings that many an artist would regard as too small to count. In fact he continues his corrections right up to the last stroke of his rendering.

Before I came to understand the real significance of his amazing labors, I asked him if there were not some easier way of solving his problems of facial forms. He said he knew of none that would at the same time give his heads the deep intensity for which he has since become famous. It is almost as if the intensity of his effort to arrive at the stark truth about a man's face carries on through comparative measurements and meticulous checkings back and forth, and is finally transmuted by some magic into character-intensity in the subject. In any case it is certain that the utter integrity of Baker's approach and workmanship is felt by the observer, and contributes greatly to the power of his finished work.

Baker makes photographs work for him in another important way. By using as many shots as Time can supply of each subject, selected for their variety of angles, expressions, and lightings, he is able to track down practically every shape that can occur in the subject's face. And here he feels he has found an answer to that much-mooted and much-booted question of likeness or "spittin' image." Naturally, every good portrait must satisfy portraiture's first essential—"It must look like" the subject. But right here the question becomes exceedingly moot. Just what does anyone look like? The subject himself can never know, because the only self-image he ever sees is mirror-reversed. None of his family or close friends really knows, as witness the bitter difference of opinion when any portrait is shown to a group of intimates.

And certainly the still camera holds no greater hope of success. Compare 24 different photographs of anyone, and you'll find yourself looking at a dozen different persons, and that's being conservative. These variations in likeness are due in part to differences of moods, expressions, shooting angles, lighting, and perspective distortions, but most of all, thinks Baker, to the camera's inability in any one shot to throw into perceptible relief all of the forms of a man's face. Right here he believes is where the artist leaves the camera standing still in its tracks. For, by discreet emphasis and arbitrary lighting, the artist can incorporate into any given head every form, large or small, that could possibly occur in that pose. So it is that from the many photographs supplied by Time, Baker gathers all the form data possible, then builds them into a basic pose. When this has been done, the correct proportions followed, the shapes bound together rhythmically, and stated in their just relationship, the result, he believes, will give the truest likeness possible in a still picture. It should here be noted that, to Baker's mind, a close-up motion picture of the subject in color tops anything known when it comes to showing what a man actually looks like. He ranks his own method second only to that.

This then, to me, is the contribution Baker is making to portraiture. By the study of camera shots in multiple he locates all the facial forms. These he amplifies and binds into a structural unity, thereby achieving a remarkable intensity and quality of life. "Working from photographs" has for too long implied some sort of artistic foul play. Baker has once and for all tossed that connotation onto the ash heap. Since seeing him work, my own ideas of drawing from photographs have changed considerably. And I might here add that it is no job for an amateur to tackle. It's disaster, if you don't know what you are doing. But when, like Baker, the artist recognizes the true and dignified worth of the camera, and uses it with artistic intelligence and skill, he can greatly increase the scope and efficiency of his work. In this connection, I like to imagine Da Vinci, in fact all of those giants of the Renaissance, making the marvelous use of the camera that they surely would have. They were big enough and efficient enough to have utilized any mechanical aid to research as is shown by such devices as artificially stiffening garment folds for study purposes. They would have had no fears of jeopardizing their creative processes thereby. Research is one thing whether it be face to face observation or gazing at a glossy print. The creative act is quite another thing, having to do only with the decisions the artist makes in utilizing the data he has gathered.

In line with these thoughts on artists and the camera an account of the part played by Baker in Time's outstanding covers will be of interest. It all started in 1939 when Ralph Ingersoll was publisher of the news magazine. When the Paderewski assignment came along, Editor Dana Tasker, casting about for new blood, went to Ingersoll, who, remembering the variety of assignments Baker had done for Fortune, said, "Send for Baker, he can do anything." By permitting himself only two hours' sleep out of the forty-eight allowed for the job, Baker managed to merit Ingersoll's appraisal, but not without first ripping off an unlatched door from his station wagon as he and wife Ernestine skinned the roadside birches surrounding their woodland home, in their first mad rush in months to meet a delivery date.

But Baker wanted this to be more than one isolated

job. So he drew up a letter in long-hand, in which he emphasized, among other things, that a well-drawn portrait is superior to a photograph in every department save possibly that of authenticity in the mind of the reader, due to a definite camera-mindedness resulting from the widespread use of photography (and even this reservation was later to be invalidated by the authentic quality of his work). This letter found its way to the desks of several editors and Baker likes to think that it may have helped to crystallize some of the cover-thinking the editors were engaged in at the time. At any rate, within a week they gave him Hearst to do and with Hearst he really did ring the bell. From then on they used him more and more frequently, with the result that for more than a year Baker did the bulk of *Time's* drawn covers. Meanwhile, tired of door-ripping delivery rushes (he actually did rip off a second door and nearly a third) from his birch woods to New York, sixty miles away, Baker took a room in New York, one block removed from *Time*, from which retreat he now stages his delivery rushes entirely on foot.

Finally the deadlines came too thick and fast and Baker had to ask for one week's respite out of every four. Other artists were called into or attracted by this expanded market, and *Time* swung into its present 52-painted-covers-a-year policy.

For the greater part of the first year the backgrounds of Baker's portraits received a minimum of attention. Toward the end of the year Circulation Manager Perry Prentice and Tasker decided to have Baker try a black and white background with figures behind the head of Kenneth Roberts. This turned out so successfully that when Christmas came and Baker was given Niemöller to do, Prentice had a full-color inspiration for a background that really went to town. Since then backgrounds in *Time* covers have been standard practice.

Baker feels that during these years of working for *Time* much of the success of his work can be directly attributed to the highly intelligent and appreciative at-titude of its editors. They allow their artists the greatest leeway possible and never make a criticism that does not have a sound basis. And in portraiture that means an awful lot to an artist, as any experienced portraitist will testify. In their cover portraits they prefer character to flattery—another godsend to the artist. Dana Tasker, with whom Baker has all his dealings, particularly reflects this attitude in his gift for dealing with artists and inspiring them to their best efforts. He has excellent taste and is an amazingly keen critic, yet always open to conviction. Baker says he is as intelligent an art buyer as he has ever known, seeming always to recognize that *Time's* interests are best served when those who create for it are given a set-up that is understanding and stimulating.

So much for the practical side of Baker's *Time* covers. A word now about his actual working procedure. After making a careful cartoon in black and white similar to the one of Gen. Eisenhower, reproduced herewith, he traces the drawing down onto a piece of illustration board. Then he mixes, in separate pans, all the colors he plans to use, having brought them into "tune" as he calls it. With a kneaded eraser he taps off all the surplus pencil dust from his tracing and begins painting. He works only in tempera but he uses it in very thin washes, blotting out the excess constantly with linen handkerchiefs. He first covers the entire surface with very pale washes of color. Through this underpainting all the light gray lines of his drawing show. From then on he builds up slowly from light to dark, always transparently and always blotting. As soon as the modeling begins to take shape he establishes his darkest darks, as a sort of anchor to swing his values around. Then he finishes completely the background, shoulders and everything except the face itself, leaving that always to the very last. It is a long, hard, and unusual process; but it has produced as fine a series of heads as has yet been seen in journalistic portraiture.

It is seldom that the illustrator as reporter has either the time or the opportunity for working directly from the person to be portrayed. Baker's assignment by Fortune to do a painting of John L. Lewis, however, afforded both time and opportunity. On the following pages the artist gives an account of his procedure in this interesting project.

Portrait of John L. Lewis by Ernest Hamlin Baker

*Painted from life for Fortune, and
reproduced in color in that magazine*

Ernest Hamlin Baker

Tells How He Painted John L. Lewis' Portrait

With the order from *Fortune* for a portrait of John L. Lewis, to illustrate an article in that magazine, came a couple of dozen photographs of the czar of the C.I.O.

It had been arranged that Lewis would pose for me in Washington, but he had consented to give no more than an hour of his time. The photographs therefore were invaluable as preparation for the most effective use of that precious hour. I pored over them, studying facial forms, recurring muscular phenomena, checking one pose against another and getting as thoroughly acquainted with the man's external aspect as one can by such means. At the same time I read whatever articles of a basic nature I could find that would not only throw light on his character, but also give me a talking acquaintance with the two conflicting theories that animate C.I.O. and A.F. of L.

There was a two-fold purpose in this. Being able to speak the man's language during that sixty minutes of posing was as important as an acquaintance with his character. The ability to put his sitter at ease and keep him alert is no less vital to the portrait painter than a control over his tools of expression. If you have ever sat for your portrait, even for a short time, you know how quickly you become drowsy. Certainly *Fortune* didn't want a *drowsy* Lewis—anything but. In fact they had quite definitely said that, of all the types of looks that lurk behind his dramatic visage, the menacing look was the one I was to go after.

By the time of my arrival in Washington, I felt confident of my ability to talk with Lewis in terms of his own interests, and had enough questions at the tip of my tongue to start (start, mind you) twenty conversations about the union problems of the American worker. Incidentally, I might here add that during this preliminary peek into the labor split, I found myself becoming very genuinely interested in the subject aside from its being an aid to the gathering of portrait data. I doubt if, prior to the occasion, Lewis had similarly prepared himself for conversation on the subject of portraiture; but then—why should he?

When I telephoned Lewis' office the next morning, his secretary-daughter, whose keenness and pleasantness must represent no small asset to him, told me I could have thirty minutes—it turned out to be forty-five. I found Lewis most personable, simple, direct, gruff in exterior, distinctly likeable, and sort of quietly terrific. I at once realized that in trying for that menacing look I would not have to resort to fantasy. At first he appeared a little stiff and ill at ease over the experience in prospect. He called attention to his newly-laundered collar that he had donned for the occasion—which I wished he hadn't. He first took a strained, tilted-back attitude which, had I drawn it, would have given the readers of *Fortune* a perfect worm's-eye-view of his nose and chin. So I manœuvred him back to the vertical, into a state of semi-relaxation, and went to

On-the-spot pencil sketch (one-half size) preparatory to the final painting

work. I was glad enough of all that study of his photographs; it gave direction to my efforts and served as a short-cut to my notations. Curiously enough my "conversation-starters" at first drew no better than cautious monosyllabic replies. I think he suspected me of doing a reporting job as well. Later on, however, he grew reassured as to the singleness of my status, and waxed quite polysyllabic. Towards the end we were getting along famously, as is shown by his finally asking me if I'd like to have him rumple his hair for me, the which I most certainly did, and the which he most certainly did—with both big hands. What a shot for the newsreels! He explained with almost boyish naïveté (which I later came to learn was not a little flavored with showmanship) that he had smoothed his hair down in anticipation of the sitting, but that, actually, his hair was for the greater part of the time in a tousled state. Naturally I was delighted over the result because it not only tied in with his shaggy, gruff exterior, but also contributed greatly to that menacing look *Fortune* had requested. The two pencil sketches (reproduced

at one-half size) show the before and after effects. And right here I want to go on record as saying that, be his labor theories what they may, and his methods however autocratic, there is no denying the power and magnetism of the man's personality. About the first words I said to my wife, upon return to our hotel, was, "There's one swell guy!"

Back in my studio I made a very rough color-sketch in miniature (1)—reproduced half-size—to establish the pose and the four main colors. Next came a charcoal study (2) of the facial forms, trying chiefly to express power and movement. Then I made a charcoal study (3) to solve the dark and light problem. This drawing (16 x 20 inches) was made on tracing paper over sketch No. 2, as was the stylized form study in line (4). The final painting was done on illustration board which had previously been prepared with a ground of Titanox B, mixed with some thinned white shellac. In applying Titanox B in the future, I think I would either add a twentieth part of castor oil to avoid subsequent brittleness, or mix it with damar varnish. This ground, when dry, gives a velvety, pure white surface, quite resembling gesso, and I must confess makes it difficult to control transparent color. Further use of this ground might lead me to try isolating it with some sort of thin size—before applying color. For the information of those interested, Titanox B is a trade name for titanium dioxide and now can be obtained, as I understand it, in its powder form in good paint shops.

The line drawing (4) was then laid down upon this board and transferred. The color (oil) was applied with a bristle brush, first charged with thinned pigment. On

Rough color sketch in miniature to establish pose and four main colors. Reproduced one-half size of original.

Below: Charcoal study (16 x 20) of the facial forms trying to chiefly express power and movement

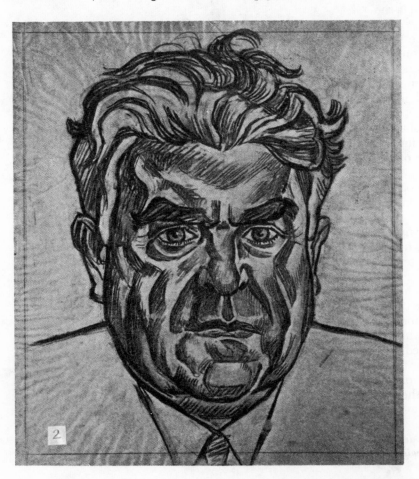

that surface it is necessary to keep the brush wiped very dry and to use very light strokes. All the colors of the painting were quite arbitrarily chosen, with due regard of course to their generic truth. For instance, Lewis' skin presented a half-hidden mottled effect. This effect I tried to suggest in the facial textures. Then too, many people—including myself—have labored under the delusion that his hair and eyebrows are black. This they are not; unless forty-five minutes of intense observation at a distance of six feet can be wrong. Of course I deliberately overstressed their underlying note of grayed-sandy-red, in order to add to the effect of power, aliveness, and, shall we say, the volcanic potentialities of the man. After all, in a subject like Lewis, color is relatively unimportant. To my mind the thing that makes or breaks such a portrait is whether or not one reveals through the forms of his face his fearlessness, his ruthless sincerity, his sheer power. How he uses that power, and with what results, are beyond the concern of the portraitist.

*Charcoal study (16 x 20) for a solu-
tion of the dark and light problem*

*Stylized form study in line made
over sketch 2 on tracing paper*

31

Walter Biggs

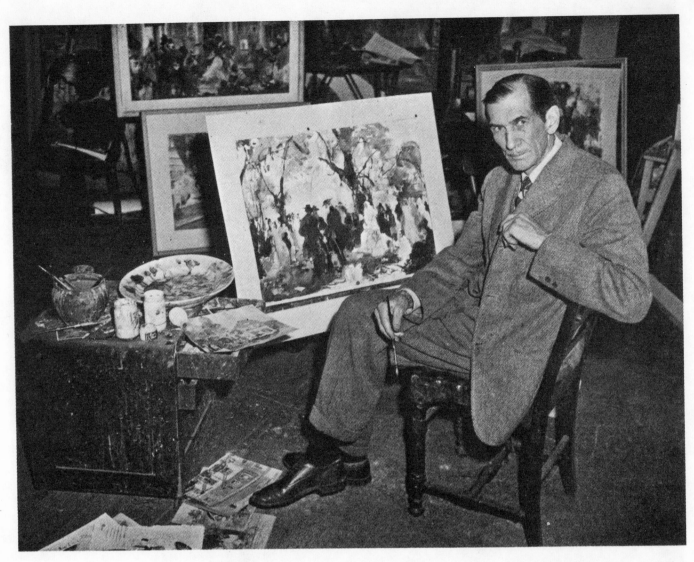

Here we see Biggs working on a final rendering of the "Dunkards' Foot-Washing Day," which was preceded by the studies on pages 38 and 39. His palette is a porcelain platter. The jar is tempera white with which he mixes his watercolors when he desires a gouache effect. Three or four rather worn brushes complete his painting equipment.

WALTER BIGGS

From a tempera drawing about 10 x 20 inches

AN HOUR of good conversation with Walter Biggs in his studio projects from the past a pleasant picture of a mellow illustrator's world. For Biggs began his career in horse and buggy days when even artists could enjoy the amenities of a more graceful era.

That was before the building of the great wall, the wall that divides all art into two parts—"fine" and "commercial." To be on both sides of that wall at the same time is a feat few have accomplished. Biggs, since the wall sprung up, has managed it; the painters have claimed him as one of them even in the days when he was devoting so much of his time to magazine illustration. They made him a member of the National Academy of Design and invited his pictures to the national exhibitions. Of late he is more prominent in the painters' world than in publication circles—most of his illustration work appears in a single magazine, the *Ladies' Home Journal*—and he enjoys the privilege of painting pretty much what he pleases.

He always painted in the way he pleased. He was fortunate of course in working principally at a time when editorial policies were not controlled by the man in the street, through reader surveys; when publishers were naïve enough to put more stock in the opinions of art editors than those of the delicatessen man who answers questionnaires. Biggs recalls those early days with nostalgic pleasure. "You have no idea how different they were," he says. "Going to see an art director was like visiting him in his home. You could drop into his office without an appointment and be received like a guest. He seemed to have plenty of time to talk with you. All of us older chaps like to remember such men as Drake of *Century*, Meers of *Harper's*, Chapin of *Scribner's*, and, more recently, Henry Quinan of the *Companion*—men who really loved pictures. I should add that the type even now is not extinct, for Frank Eltonhead, art editor of the *Ladies' Home Journal*, is one who retains the old-time graciousness in spite of present-day pressures.

"Imagine a thing like this happening today," continued Biggs. "I was walking home one winter evening long ago, when I passed the door of the building where the old *Metropolitan* had its offices. It was dark, about six o'clock, and it was snowing. I had a portfolio of samples under my arm. On the spur of the moment I thought I'd take a chance and go in. The office was dark except for a drop-light over a desk at which a secretary was still working. She told me, what I suspected, that everyone had gone home.

"Suddenly from the dark a voice called: 'Have you some pictures there to show?' A gentleman came out of the gloom into the circle of light. He led me across the room to his office and asked me to show him what I had. I spread out my pictures. He looked them all over. 'Do you want to sell these?' he asked. I answered him that nothing would please me more. 'I'll take this one,' he said, standing a painting against his wall. 'And this,' picking another. Two more were selected for purchase before I went, and manuscript for a story was thrust into my hand.

"My patron, I learned, was not Homer St. Gaudens, then art editor of *Metropolitan*, but R. H. Russell, the owner. For several years I did quite a bit of work for the magazine and always through Russell himself."

Biggs chuckled as he recalled his first meeting with Drake. "Drake was a great fellow," he said, "and everybody liked him immensely, but he had one peculiarity that I discovered that day when I sold him my first picture. I was just out of art school and was dead broke; in fact I had actually spent my last nickel for carfare to get to the *Century* office. You can imagine my joy when Drake said he would buy that picture! 'How much do you want for it?' he asked. 'Fifty dollars,' I replied. 'That is too much,' retorted Drake. 'I'll give you $47.50 for it.' He saved $2.50 for *Century*, and by following this practice day in and day out the sum total saved for the publishers must have been considerable. The deduction was always so slight that no one ever got peeved. We looked upon it merely as an amusing foible of a very lovable man."

It was natural that the magazines should turn to Biggs when there were stories of the South to illustrate. Biggs was born and brought up in Salem, Virginia, and though he has always spent most of his time in his

"A Street in Salem, Virginia"   *Watercolor by Walter Biggs*

A story illustration for the Ladies' Home Journal painted by Walter Biggs. The original, in color, was on a 30 x 40 canvas. Courtesy the Curtis Publishing Co.

New York studio, he returns as often as possible to his old home where he loves to paint the familiar scenes and the people with whom he grew up. No one, of course, can portray the colored folk with greater understanding. No one can better translate the color and the spirit of the Southland.

Biggs is a genuine Southerner, a gentleman who unconsciously does the right thing at the right time—not because he has been taught to do it, but because it is utterly natural for him to act that way. I don't imagine you could hurry Biggs much. He is deliberate, takes enough time to do things properly. He would rather do a picture over again than feel dissatisfied with any detail. When he delivers his illustration to the *Ladies' Home Journal* office in Philadelphia, likely as not he will raise some question about the picture with art editor Frank Eltonhead. "Do you think maybe I've subordinated that figure a bit too much?" he may ask. If in discussion both think the point well taken, Biggs will carry the picture back home and start an entirely new one. He never stops on any work until it "feels" right. He has no quota of so many jobs for such and such a financial result. His only quota is his own satisfaction in each piece of work he finishes.

Walter Biggs is one of the few illustrators extant who owes nothing to the camera. He draws and paints directly from the model. After playing around with small sketches in pencil and gouache, he calls in models and makes careful drawings. Then, without the models he begins to develop his pictures in color, experimenting with composition until he gets what he wants. After that, the models are again summoned, and in the final rendering of the figures he paints directly from them. There is no photography at any point.

Biggs used to paint his illustrations principally in oil. Now he prefers gouache, having come to the conclusion that this medium does better in reproduction. His painting equipment is amazing. His palette is a large, white porcelain platter. On the raised rim of this he squeezes tube watercolors; mixing is done in the depressed area. A large jar of white tempera and three or four rather scrubby-looking brushes complete his outfit.

His painting procedures would terrify technical purists. Biggs once gave a watercolor demonstration at the National Academy of Design, on an evening when several artists were painting pictures for the edification of visitors to the annual show. Many who watched were aghast at his unorthodox methods.

38

On these facing pages we see how Walter Biggs studies his pictures. The charcoal sketch below was his first graphic visualization of an idea that he had long been mulling over. The three large halftones were reproduced from three separate studies in gouache on 26 x 36 inch sheets of water-color paper. His gouache technique permits considerable experimentation on each study. He uses a minimum of water and, consequently, is not much bothered by the buckling of the sheet. The final painting is mounted on heavy illustration board.

In the picture for which these four sketches are preliminary studies Biggs depicts the annual "Foot-Washing Day" of the Dunkards, a non-conforming religious sect adhering to the primitive simplicity of the early Church. The foot-washing ceremony occurs in a tent, vaguely seen in the background.

Watercolor exhibited in National Academy of Design in 1945

Walter Biggs' studio probably has the distinction of being the most disorderly one in town — a cleaning woman's nightmare. But he knows where everything is!

First he washed-in large areas on his Whatman board. Then began a series of scrubbing, scratching and even rubbing his wet painting. His brush was dipped now in opaque white, now in his colors. He appeared to be floundering, but it was soon seen that the rather chaotic looking masses gradually emerged into a well-ordered pattern which, with a few deft finishing touches, ended in a rendering having great technical charm.

Biggs' gouache technique permits of limitless experimentation; he makes even radical changes in his composition on a single sheet. But he also likes to paint various versions of the same subject, as he did with the illustration of the *Dunkards' Footwashing Day* reproduced on preceding pages. He has always made considerable use of charcoal, a medium of great flexibility and expressiveness.

Biggs' studio is without doubt the most disorderly one in New York. In spite of its size—it is unusually large—the visitor does well if he finds his way to a chair without stepping on the litter of sketches that almost cover the floor and have already received the footprints of former visitors. Every corner is cluttered with such stuff as only an artist's studio can boast—costumes,

40

Study in charcoal and wash (12 x 16) for an illustration

Biggs' illustrations frequently begin with small sketches in wash and charcoal like this one of a Negro church scene. In them he projects the essential design of the picture.

draperies, properties, screens, mirrors, cabinets, files of magazines, old canvases, a lay figure and some broken-down furniture. Biggs simply never gets around to straightening things out. On the balcony is a collection of some 600 costumes, principally of the century following the American Revolution. A thick layer of dust overlays the entire conglomeration—a cleaning woman's nightmare.

Well, it doesn't matter. In the midst of that confusion many handsomely conceived pictures are produced. Symphonies in color spring from the all-enveloping dust.

Biggs came to New York in 1904. He studied at the old Chase School under Robert Henri and Kenneth Hayes Miller. For a time he roomed with George Bellows who was also enrolled in the school. There was no teaching of illustration as a special subject, nor did Biggs ever have a course of training elsewhere, in what was to be his livelihood. He has carried on Henri's tradition. Classes he has taught have produced some of our best illustrators. He has always looked upon illustration as just another application of a painter's skill to which he owed all the resources at his command.

Bobri

TAURUS

One of a series of twelve designs for "Signs of the Zodiac"

by B O B R I

The original drawing (tempera on colored paper) is 18 x 20 inches

bobri

A TALL, scholarly-looking gentleman stepped up to a ticket window in Grand Central Station and shoved a bill under the brass wicket. "Let me have a five-dollar ticket please." Surprised, the ticket agent looked up, asked, "Where to, sir?"

"Oh, nowhere in particular—anywhere," came the astonishing reply.

Other travelers awaiting their turn at the window craned their necks. The ticket man's eyes blinked, "Beg pardon, sir; afraid I didn't understand you. You wish a ticket for . . ."

"I've got no special destination in mind," smiling patiently, "just anywhere five dollars will take me."

The agent turned to his ticket rack, ran his hand dubiously over the pasteboards, faltered: "This is most unusual sir, if I understand you, I'm really at a loss, can't you . . ."

The traveler interrupted. "Five dollars will take me to any number of interesting places. Just let me have any five-dollar ticket that comes first to mind and—please—there are other passengers waiting."

Bobri, unpredictable in his art, is original in his be-

havior which, contrary to the implication of the incident at the ticket window, is actuated by highly intelligent purpose. That ticket to "anywhere," for example, is a device to grasp the hand of fate, to be led into new and unpremeditated experiences. Arrived at his chance destination, Bobri will wander about, with or without his sketchbook, according to his mood, and in due time will return with something consciously or unconsciously added to the drawing account of an exceptional background.

Background. Keep that in mind when studying the work of V. Bobri. Not the background of accidental environment—though that is a considerable factor—but the background of self-directed experience and culture. That background is an indistinguishable component of his creative genius. To arrive at some acquaintance with it let us turn to an excellent, though brief, biographical sketch by S. Yalkert, a friend of the artist, who outlines the prominent events in an unusual career. It gives more than a hint of an appetite for adventure which in the more tranquil environment of later years finds outlet in graphic innovations.

45

Above —

From a drawing in color for Avon Products, Inc.

On page opposite —

1. **Drawing for Koret handbags**

2. **Drawing for Avon Products, Inc.**

3. **Advertisement for Matson Navigation Co.**

BOBRI

1

2

3

"Bobri," writes Mr. Yalkert, "was born Vladimir Bobritsky, in Kharkov, Ukraine. He was a pupil in the Kharkov Imperial Art School, where the curriculum was an admixture of penal servitude and antique exaltation. All professors were admired, respected. Students goose-stepped in uniform and were proud of it. All wore hair shirts for the Muse. In an atmosphere of self-flagellation and voluminous output those who could not pass were forever disgraced. Those who remained learned anatomy, the old masters, the moderns, manners, style, how to draw and how to argue.

"At seventeen he was already designing sets for the Great Dramatic Theatre (as distinguished from the Small) of Kharkov, and was one of the first to introduce Gordon Craig's methods.

"He fought during the Revolution in several armies, with and against. After the Revolution, came a long and enforced period of travel and a kind of montage of activity. As a refugee he traveled on a handmade passport, eight closely printed pages in Polish, so skilfully wrought that it left no doubt as to his talent and feeling for calligraphy, since it successfully passed the expert examination of the English, French, Italian and Greek consular authorities. With it he fled to Feodosia, thence to Constantinople. In the mountainous, peninsular Crimea he worked as a wine presser for the Tartar fruit and wine growers. Later he came in contact with Russian, Hungarian and Spanish gypsies, studied their lore, the peculiarities of the different tribes. Having met with a band of gypsies in the Crimea he earned his way as a guitar player in their chorus. It is his long love for the guitar which makes him today a finished musician (secretary of the Society of the Classic Guitar) and composer (*Danza En La*, performed in New York's Town Hall in 1936).

"Wandering through the Greek islands he was hired to do ikon painting for a Greek monastery on the Island of Halki. In Asiatic Istanbul he painted signs. In Pera he played the piano in a nickelodeon, lectured on art— free lance, unknown to the museum's administration but to the complete satisfaction of button-holed tourists. In an abandoned Turkish mosque he made an important archaeological find, a Byzantine mural, which later was restored by the Turkish Government. It was in Constantinople that for two years he did the *decors* and costumes for the Ballet Russe of Constantinople in order to earn his passage to America.

"Through all those wanderings his knapsack always had a watercolor box, a drawing pad. The record was kept with constant sketching of people, stories, folklore, folk music and crafts. And there were always the museum and the gallery, the theatre and the cafe. Art school had not ended in Kharkov. It is this scenario which has yielded its many parts to the concentrated, contemporary field of design."

That is Bobri's background prior to his coming to New York. His experiences in America, if less dramatic, have been consistent with his flair for adventure. Soon after his arrival he was operating his own textile printing establishment. In 1925 he was called in by the art director of Wanamaker's in an experiment with modern advertising. His radically different newspaper layouts were more than the management could stomach and both artist and art director were dismissed. But Saks Fifth Avenue saw, admired and beckoned. Bobri here found enthusiasm for his innovations.

Bobri's more recent work is well-known to all whose interests embrace the field of commercial design. It is always prominent in the Annual of Advertising Art.

So much for factual information. What can be learned of Bobri's creative processes?

That can best be answered by saying that today's problem was solved yesterday, perhaps way back in those Constantinople days, or even in the gypsy wanderings in the Crimea. Putting it another way, he works from background to foreground. He asserts that often his approach to a design is as unpremeditated as the purchase of a ticket to "anywhere." Out of the sub-conscious— isn't that the same thing as background?—comes an idea. The pencil begins to play with it. The embryo grows. Memory, imagination and skilled hand are all at work. Can Matisse help, or Picasso—or Goya? I think we see him in one of our reproductions. Originality, after all, is a matter of fertility; fertility comes from soil that has been fertilized. Bobri draws upon the great out of the past: unhesitatingly borrows from Constantin Guys; the Persian miniaturists; also the classic Greeks, and thus avoids the limitations of an uninstructed imagination.

A good commercial artist is a fine artist in the marketplace. Such an artist is continuously replenishing his esthetic storehouse against the recurrent grind. Bobri spends hours at his easel; he does wood carving; he draws from the nude model; he sketches incessantly; he engages in cultural pursuits not directly related to graphic art but none the less inspiring as sources of design ideas.

Bobri's New York studio, naturally enough, is a busy place. He carries on his work with the assistance of two or three artists who, like himself, are Americans by adoption and who likewise have been trained with characteristic European thoroughness. Whatever comes from Bobri's studio is as meticulous in technical execution as it is original and effective in design. Behind it all is a canny sense of merchandising without which no amount of artistic genius is useful in the field of advertising art.

On page opposite —
Drawing by Bobri for Koret handbags

Koret

bobri

Harrison Cady

A typical Peter Rabbit feature reproduced from the color Sunday section syndicated by the New York Herald Tribune. Harrison Cady has been producing this strip for over twenty-three years.

Harrison *Cady*

WHEN HARRISON CADY was a wee lad his father took him out into the fields and upturned a stone with the toe of his boot.

There, in the dirt, lay buried treasure. A fortune really! A tiny black beetle—priceless legacy as it turned out, for a boy with the strange genius of Harrison Cady.

There must have been something humanly suggestive in the antics of the creature scurrying about to find sanctuary in the damp earth. At any rate, years later, a whole family of beetles, grotesquely garbed in human habiliments, hopped right out of Harrison's subconscious in the hour of his greatest need. He reached for his pen in this crisis, made a batch of beetle cartoons. These, submitted to the old *Life* magazine, started the struggling young artist upon a highly successful career. The beetle, henceforth, and all the humble creatures of field and forest were to become the comical inhabitants of a graphic world created for the entertainment of two generations of children—grown-ups too.

Young Cady was quite at home in the company of his entomological and mammalian actors for he had received almost his entire education from an ardent naturalist, his father. The great outdoors was his classroom, all its wild life, the curriculum. The master could hardly have dreamed that this fresh air university was fitting his pupil for both fame and fortune.

But that is precisely what was happening. Cady, in time, took his place in a galaxy of stars in the illustrative firmament, to remain virtually constant throughout a long lifetime. Not a star of first magnitude perhaps, yet a luminous one, still twinkling in the heavens today after the peak of greatest brilliancy—the years when he drew for the old *Life* magazine.

Cady, to date, has made over 10,000 illustrations for Thornton Burgess' *Nature Stories* now seen as a New York *Herald Tribune* syndicated feature. He has illustrated many books on the adventures of Peter Rabbit, Reddy Fox, Johnny Chuck, et al. Weekly, for over twenty years, he has done a Peter Rabbit page for the *Tribune's* colored comic section. It is not strange that Harrison Cady is known to the millions merely as the "Peter Rabbit Man," or that only in the limited reaches of professional art he is esteemed as a talented and serious artist who etches, paints, exhibits in the big shows and is represented in museum collections.

Harrison Cady was born in Gardner, Massachusetts, in 1877 and lived there throughout his boyhood and adolescent years. He was provided with a grammar school education. That appears to have been quite adequate since his father, as I have said, was a kind of Mark Hopkins University.

In addition to those walks in the fields where the boy was introduced to the insects, birds and animals that were to become his stock in trade, there were enchanted hours spent with his father's library of over 1,500 volumes behind a counter in his general store. Here he got on speaking terms with the heroes of history and literature and developed an enduring passion for reading.

Of art influence or instruction the town of Gardner was barren, although Parker Perkins, a local artist, did supply a measure of incentive by allowing the boy to visit his studio and copy pictures. But Cady never set foot inside an art school.

By the time he was eighteen his savings amounted to thirteen dollars, a sufficient sum, he decided, to grease the ways for the launching of a career. With this capital

Typical Harrison Cady illustration from the old Life magazine

Old Professor Owl: I'M GREATLY SURPRISED, WILLIE SNAKE; YOU HAVE BEEN
IN THE CLASS THREE MONTHS AND YET YOU ARE UNABLE TO MULTIPLY.
Willie: WELL, YOU KNOW, TEACHER, I AM ONLY A LITTLE ADDER.

in the pocket of a new store suit, he set out for New York wearing a flat-crowned derby and carrying a telescope bag. At New London he got the Sound steamer that, the next morning, set him down on the Canal Street pier.

A newspaper advertisement directed him to a rooming house on Ninth Street, where he was welcomed by a slatternly woman and domiciled in a small attic room without windows other than a skylight cut in the ceiling. Of heat there was none except that which came up the stairs, flavored with stale cooking odors.

Cady's first professional work was done for *Truth*, a magazine that competed with the then popular *Life*. This commission, a set of decorative initial letters, netting sixty dollars, was followed shortly by a connection with McLaughlin Bros., publishers of children's books. The work included a set of silhouette decorations and other drawings for a Mother Goose and paid what Cady considered a princely sum.

By dint of frugal living—Harrison was now able to deposit $500 in a bank on the corner of Eighth Avenue and Fourteenth Street—he moved to Greenwich Village into a $16-apartment that provided sufficient quarters for two, his mother having come to him upon her husband's death.

The McLaughlin connection came to an end at the beginning of the 1907 depression, when free-lancing was hazardous, and Cady had some anxious moments. But an opening on the *Brooklyn Daily Eagle* came in the nick of time. He went to work at $20 a week as a newspaper artist covering crimes, fires, dog shows and social events with his facile pen. No better school for draftsmanship has ever been devised.

After four years of this grueling work—there were only three holidays during a year—he got pretty well fed up with the job. And those fascinating beetles of boyhood

memory started creeping around in his imagination. Finally they took graphic form in that series of pen sketches which were submitted to *Life*. The magazine bought three of them for $90 and continued for five months to accept occasional drawings. Then, at the age of twenty-four, Cady was invited by John A. Mitchell, the editor, to join the publication's staff.

It is characteristic of the man that, elated as he was by this triumph, he was fearful of giving up his salaried job on the *Eagle*. He knew the discomforts of insecurity. Suppose the well of his imagination should dry up, or at least flow but meagerly!

But the decision he made was a foregone conclusion. It led to a felicitous connection with one of America's great magazines. He found himself in a company of such illustrative notables as C. D. Gibson, T. S. Sullivant, Wm. H. Walker, Otho Cushing, Angus MacDonald and Orson Lowell.

Cady's contributions to *Life* were by no means limited to the comical antics of bugs and rabbits. He has been crusader as well as comedian. His pictorial commentaries upon serious problems of the day were frequent full-page, sometimes double-page features. During the first World War he enlisted his pen against the Kaiser in a series of powerful cartoons. Many drawings of this period also reveal his alarm at the despoiling of the countryside by billboards and hot-dog stands that, with the advent of the automobile, were springing up along the highways.

But Cady is, fundamentally, a humorist. He is at his illustrative best when there is a twinkle in his eye and nonsensical fantasies are talking shape on his board. It was his zoological extravaganzas that brought him fame. They were widely reproduced in many publications, often in full color on magazine covers and on children's pages in *Good Housekeeping, Ladies' Home Journal*,

"A Family in Germany that hasn't lost a member"
Double-page cartoon by Harrison Cady drawn for Life magazine in 1917

Country Gentlemen and *The Saturday Evening Post.* Those of us who were brought up on *St. Nicholas* will remember Cady as one of our great pen heroes.

Cady's cartoons, all his drawings indeed, have been characterized by the most meticulous execution, elaborate scenes being filled with infinite detail—something going on all over the place. He loved to represent an entire town or countryside alive with insects garbed and acting as foolish as their human prototypes.

These drawings, it can be seen, represented prodigious labor. "That is what Mr. Mitchell wanted and was willing to pay for," said Cady. " 'You put the work in,' he often told me, 'and I'll put the money in.' And he did. He kept upping payments for my drawings."

Although Cady's income was now in the five-figure bracket, prosperity did not tempt him into extravagance. He continued to live modestly and his savings were carefully invested. All his life Harrison has been money-conscious. Since boyhood, when he tasted poverty, he has thought things out in terms of what they cost. When, as a young man, he was startled to learn that a wealthy acquaintance had spent $2,000 merely to welcome a new baby into the family, he asked his mother about his own C.O.D. charges. Dr. Parker's fee, he learned, was seven dollars. A neighbor who came in to help for one week was paid three dollars and keep. Harrison, ever since, has lost no appropriate opportunity to brag about being a "ten dollar baby." That, by the way, will be the title of an autobiography upon which he is leisurely working.

Cady estimates that his father did not spend over $800 on him altogether. Comparing notes with a younger man whose education alone had cost $10,000, he reminded the youth of the tremendous responsibility for yielding a return commensurate with such an investment.

"Poverty was my legacy," says Cady, "and I have ever been grateful for it. Poverty teaches great lessons so many fail to learn. To an eager mind it reveals that most of the best things in life have no price tags on them. When as a lad I arrived in New York, I was at once impressed by the pleasures and opportunities that were to be had on an empty purse in the great city. There were the wonderful museums filled with the wealth of the world; there were the art galleries and the fine shops. In the auction rooms one could sit without a dollar in pocket while pictures, sculpture, objects of art—many and sundry products of men's genius—were exhibited for everyone's inspection. And in New York with its cosmopolitan population one could watch the world go by. The poorest boy could stroll in Central Park and gaze at the fine turnouts—prancing horses, grand ladies, liveried coachmen with highbred dogs running behind. Yes, New York was, for me, the land of heart's desire, an inexhaustible treasure house to be explored and possessed. And most of it to be had for the asking."

As a result of continuous exploration throughout the years, the great metropolis has indeed been possessed by Cady as few possess it. He can talk for hours about

its history, its famous men and women, its opportunities. His memory of all he has read and experienced is phenomenal: the past appears to be as vivid for him as the present. A walk with him up Fifth Avenue is a historical travelogue. Central Park and its environs he calls his front yard. Its wonders, ranging from wild flora and fauna to the cultural achievements of all mankind—seen in the museums—he recites with guide book thoroughness. And sums it all up with a cash valuation which, if you are interested, is, or was in 1942, exactly $859,941,000. And this is not merely a guess!

Cady, to get back to his work on *Life* magazine, was enjoying prosperity. But those golden days were numbered. Editor Mitchell died in 1918 and, although the magazine lingered on a few years, Cady's connection with it came to an end.

But he had already begun his illustrations for Thornton Burgess' adventures of Peter Rabbit in the "Old Briar Patch," "The Smiling Pool" and "The Green Forest," and in 1922 he was invited by the New York *Herald Tribune* to contribute a Peter Rabbit series to their syndicated Sunday comic section. He was persuaded also to write a few books himself. "Caleb Cottontail," written for Houghton Mifflin, 1921, was followed by several others and by stories for *St. Nicholas, Good Housekeeping* and *Ladies' Home Journal.*

For many years, as previously noted, Cady has been an able practitioner in the fine arts. He has exhibited his etchings, watercolors and oil paintings in the national shows—and won prizes: Honorable Mention at the Allied Artists Show and the *Edwin Palmer Memorial Prize* at the National Academy 1945 Annual. His etchings are owned by the Metropolitan Museum of Art, Library of Congress, New York Public Library and

"Pittsburgh Snow"   Oil   24 x 30

*"Wounded
Whale"*
25 x 30

other noted collections. He is prominent in the art circles of New York and Rockport, Massachusetts, where he has spent some part of every year since 1901. He is a member of various societies, including the Society of Illustrators, Society of American Etchers, American Watercolor Society, Dutch Treat Club, Ship Model Society and the Salmagundi Club.

In 1915, Harrison married Melina Eldredge, daughter of a prominent Brooklyn family living on Dean Street, and the Cadys made Brooklyn their home until 1939 when they moved to their present studio apartment on 67th Street.

Twenty-five years ago Cady bought the old Headland House in Rockport, built in 1781. His precaution in "endowing" this, his summer home, is testimony to his inability to forget that there is a wolf lurking out there somewhere—though he may be out of sight at the moment. He says: "I have never been one who believes it will always be fair weather. I made up my mind that this was to be our permanent home, a fortress, a safe refuge to which we could always retreat, come what may. Accordingly, I decided to 'endow' it much as one endows an institution. I made careful estimate of taxes, insurance and maintenance; then invested a sum in an annuity that would finance the place in perpetuity."

Chief among Cady's hobbies is a collecting propensity that has filled both his homes with a polygenetic assort-

ment of art objects. As a result of his wanderings at home and abroad he has gathered together a treasured miscellany of old Italian, Flemish and Chinese paintings, Venetian cabinets, porcelains and jade carvings. There are Spanish varguenos, Persian palace doors and brasses from Holland. Drawers in an Italian cabinet are filled with miniatures. Scattered about the home are pieces of armor and a considerable number of ship models, remainder of a larger collection, most of which

"Eastern Point Light"   *Watercolor*

57

A Harrison Cady Christmas card

went up in flames during a fire in the Brooklyn home some years ago. It is evident, as Harrison discusses his trophies, that his Yankee trader instinct salts his satisfaction in any treasure bought at a bargain. He claims that his native perspicacity was whetted by a bit of advice he once got from Alexander Drake, art director of the Century Company when he began selling drawings to *St. Nicholas.* Over the door of Drake's office was a handsome ship model of an American Frigate. Harrison openly admired it, expressed the hope that some day he might come into possession of such a treasure. Said Drake, "Well, Cady, just keep a sharp eye and you can have almost anything you want at your own price." Harrison, ever since, has had his ceiling price on every coveted trophy. One of his proudest exhibits is a model of the Constitution that hangs at the head of his balcony stairs. Formerly in the possession of Captain Clark,

Commodore of the Cunard Fleet, it is a beautiful five-foot replica of the famous fighting ship.

Ask Cady what, among his collections, he values most highly and he quickly answers: "my friends."

His capacity for collecting friends is indeed his greatest charm. He is a good conversationalist, loves to talk and is well served by an astonishing memory. His fun-loving nature, capital investment of his career, prefers whimsical topics to sober ones. He is "a man with a quick relish for pleasure" as Macaulay would put it. He loves to spin fantastic yarns and is especially fond of ambushing a new acquaintance with tall tales having just enough plausibility to assure polite attention until the final denouement. Every yarn is likely to be punctuated with his characteristic period "—and that's that." Which might as well serve for the final biographical note on a rather remarkable career.

Fred Cooper
by Matlack Price

at the Auto Show

that's what
they *all* say!

at the Auto Show

that's what
they *all* say!

at the Auto Show

that's what
they *all* say!

at the Auto Show

that's what
they *all* say!

at the Auto Show

that's what
they *all* say!

at the Auto Show

that's what
they *all* say!

at the Auto Show

that's what
they *all* say!

at the Auto Show

that's what
they *all* say!

at the Auto Show

that's what
they *all* say!

Drawings by

FRED G. COOPER

Arthur Kudner, Inc., Advertising Agency

C. G. Christensen, Art Director

Mr. Christensen, commenting on this series, said:

"Each year at Automobile Show time, we try to find some way to keep Buick before the eyes of the general public and Auto Show visitors in particular.

"Last year we conceived the idea of small space 'reminder' ads, liberally scattered through the newspapers, and having a high attention value for the small amount of space used.

"We had decided on the slogan, 'Better Buy Buick!' In selecting this phrase, we had chosen it as the simple 'net' of what we hoped the whole buying public would be saying after seeing and trying this fine car.

"It occurred to us to put this phrase literally in the mouths of various types of people — and thus the idea for the series of cartoons was born.

"The ads were reproduced in space a single column wide, and their strong blacks gave them good visibility on the printed page. We feel they did a good job in creating the impression that all sorts of people were saying 'Better Buy Buick!'"

"fgc" or FRED COOPER

(to those who may not remember the old familiar monogram)

By MATLACK PRICE

PROBABLY all art students and beginner artists whose circulation is normal have their heroes. It was so in the Renaissance, and it has been going on ever since. It keeps up standards and gives the comers-on something toward which to aspire. Perhaps, at first, as the well-known "sincerest form of flattery," they imitate their hero. Then they get over that, but always remember how much his influence helped them.

I wish that it were possible, statistically, to give even an approximate figure that would show how many artists (now practically grown up) have been inspired and influenced by the work that so long appeared with the lower-case monogram f.g.c. To some of the younger ones that vintage work signed f.g.c. seems of such classic antiquity that they are sure the sprightly new work signed FRED COOPER must be by some new man, or possibly by the son or grandson of f.g.c. Not so: let me here testify and depose that it is the same man, for it has been my very great pleasure, over a period of years, to know both of him, and to have counted him, over all the years, one of my most esteemed friends, among the goodly fellowship of artists.

Fred Cooper came to New York in 1904, after five years in San Francisco, where he journeyed from his birthplace, McMinnville, Oregon (*natus est*, 1883). His first noteworthy achievement was the now famous figure of the quaint little Colonial character which he did for the New York Edison Company. This figure keyed most of their advertising, posters, and promotional work for years. At about the same time, he painted the surviving sign for the Tap Room of the Prince George Hotel, and was soon doing covers for *Life* and *Collier's*, along with countless (and very funny) little black and white topical decorations for *Life* editorials. The worded gags which Cooper lettered in as a part of the drawings (often like an *ad lib* "aside" by the artist) made them doubly funny.

Then there was the series of brilliant posters for vaudeville at the old Keith & Proctor's Fifth Avenue Theatre, from 1907 to 1910, and later, his New Year's posters. These were an annual joy to his friends, being a privately printed edition, usually autographed, and always embodying a new and unexpected idea.

It is a fortunate thing for American graphic arts, lettering, and poster designing that there have always been a few really first-rate artists setting and maintaining a standard. Before Cooper became an influence of con-

spicuous importance there was Edward Penfield, followed by C. B. Falls—both of whom influenced and inspired the younger artist—and so a certain continuity goes on.

It is not easy to pin down in words exactly wherein lies the peculiar quality of the work of such artists because it is a composite of several things. It begins with inventiveness and imagination and gives the impression, always, of a certain fine integrity, a kind of conscientiousness that would scorn to deliver a careless, unstudied drawing. There is subtlety of technique, though this isn't at first apparent. Much of the work of all three of these men has seemed almost obvious, though you have only to compare it with the work of their nearest imitators to see how far from obvious it is. One quality that might be observed is a certain *directness* of approach, creating a sense of authority.

One of the happiest incidents of Fred Cooper's genius for lettering has always been his extraordinary flair for designing monograms.

And, speaking of monograms, I had a preview in the artist's skyscraper studio, in downtown New York, of a book of monograms done by f.g.c. over a period of years. Without breaking into superlatives, when this book is published it will be the book on monograms that the world has been waiting for. There will be plenty of people, then, who will discover for the first time what a monogram can be and what they have been missing all their lives.

Somewhere I have a newspaper clipping that says, in all seriousness, that a certain psychological investigation has proved, beyond peradventure, that there is a distinct connection between the human possession of a sense of humor and intelligence. If this be so (and I, for one, heartily believe it to be) then Fred Cooper is super-super intelligent. And I think that his work, with its attendant success, proves it. He has consistently believed—and demonstrated—that the whimsically humorous manner in a poster, an advertisement, a decoration for an editorial, will break down the resistance and aloofness that so many people have for the printed word or the selling message. And why not? Humanly, it is so in conversation. The popular chairman

Fred Cooper as he sees himself
Courtesy N. Y. World Telegram

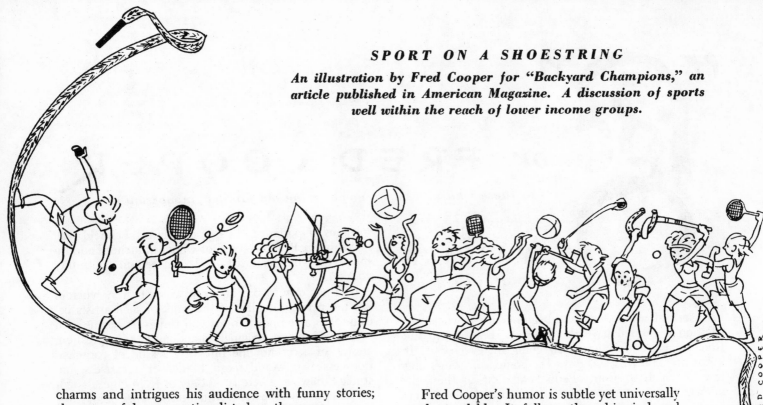

charms and intrigues his audience with funny stories; the successful conversationalist does the same.

Humor has never been looked for in school textbooks —but why not? There should be no essential connection between education and boredom. In a series of textbooks called "Growth in Using English," published by Harcourt Brace, you will find a liberal and very stimulating seasoning of funny drawings by Fred Cooper, whose wit, here, conspires with the text for attraction, attention, comprehension and memory values.

LINES TO A GIRL'S HEAD

Dear girl Dear of mine, thy hair girl of mine, is like the Summer, thy hair is like so soft, so sweet, so pleasant the flowers, so to my touch; I always was plumb rich, so exquisite dippy over such. I love you, dear, you against my lips, really are a hummer. If love were dumb like luscious gold I'd keep on getting dumber. That's how I love spun out in fairy you, dear, but not how much. Should I tell all strips. Why, dear, I'd rate the booby-hutch and then I'd lose you to I just could chew some darned newcomer. Such precious hair! So silken the stuff for hours. and so blest! I know its roguish magic in my dreams. (The cat What though the was up here sleeping on my chest.). How fine and irresistible sky be all smear- it seems! (I never would in all this world have guessed how ed up with showers? much you owe to permanents and creams.) Dear girl of mine, Thy captivating thy hair is sheer perfection, so fresh, so fair, so ravishing and mane with sunlight bright; so captivating, dear, so full of light, my heart is up- drips, and thus side-down with genuflection. If I'm all wrong I'll bow to your correc- I hold it in my tion, but you're too modest, dear; I know I'm right in every line and finger tips; I'll word that I recite. You see, I wrote the book in this connection. take it as the best Such pleasing hair! So bonny, so benign, so absolutely right in. of wedding dowers. tone and form, that mop of yours, sweetheart, is just divine! Why Such comely hair! all these words of love that surge and swarm if I don't think Dear Entrancing as your dome a supershrine? Huh? I'm not ranting just to keep me girl of the breeze can- warm. Dear girl of mine, thy hair is like the singing of mine, thy essing gently some clear brook play-dancing down a glen and flinging face is oh! some far sunlight every now and then, its sparkling waves with so pretty; the southern happy laughter ringing. All this is on the level, throne of beauty; isle, that dear, and I'm not stringing, mine is an ab- dimpled, winsome, sweet. threads solutely truthful pen. You think I'd Its lines are so symmetrical and its velvet spill this stuff to any wren? neat; the fairest in our large and grow. magic There's truth in every drop of ink city, I'll tell the universe that reads through ink I'm slinging. Enchanting my ditty. What though thy nose got mussy—the trees hair! Incomparably right! in the heat, the red upon thy lips too and brings Its luring, subtle gla- nearly meat? I know the drug store's closed, dear dreams mor has me hypped. and more's the pity. A pleasing face! When- to ravish and I dream about it ev- e'er I see its smile my spirit soars on wings beguile. (Sit ery blessed night. of pure delight. A face of such extraordinary quiet, dear! (What's this I hear style, with eyes so wonderful, so dreamy bright, You twist about peroxide dipt? and lips that I could kiss mile after mile. and make They say that lack- (Why is it when I kiss I want to bite?) Dear me sneeze. ing that your hair's girl of mine, thy face is like a jewel; a Your tres- a sight. Crabap- priceless pearl is every priceless tooth! ses itch my plesauce! I don't Thy face is radiant with the glow of nose and believe I'm truth; my soul's aglow with fire and you're cramp my gypped.) the fuel. You're kinda mean at times but style.) never cruel, so full of all the sorcery of youth; I'll spill the word you're absolutely couth! I'll get you yet, by theft or heck or duel. A charming face! So gentle and so dear! Delightful lips! Bewitching, velvet skin! The best in all this world; not one compeer. Your smile's a smile, sweet- heart, the rest just grin~ I'll kiss thy smiling lips right now and here and chuck my darling underneath her chin-

From a full-page drawing in the old Life magazine, this fantasy by Cooper reveals a lithesome literary proclivity which rounds out the genius of this irrepressible humorist.

Fred Cooper's humor is subtle yet universally understandable. It follows the whimsical and plays more often on the funny implications of things than on the obvious. Though we can guess from our own experience, there is no knowing how many thousands of subway riders have had their boredom, and even their acute misery happily mitigated by Fred Cooper's posters in the Interborough cars under the masthead of the "Subway Sun." This was a long and noteworthy series, and one in which the artist's unfailing wit and whimsicality went far to offset the banality of the prevailing advertisements. The series ran for four years, involving a fresh poster nearly every week —and that meant a demand on the artist not only for the character and quality of each poster but for consistency in character and quality over the whole long period.

I feel that I ought to recall some anecdotes that would reveal Fred Cooper as vividly as his work reveals him. I do remember one very typical remark: A young and rather forward artist I knew, with samples, had called on Fred Cooper one time when he was art editor of the old *Life* magazine. I was interested to know how the young artist's work was received, for he seemed a little subdued and thoughtful. "How did Mr. Cooper like it?" I asked. "What did he say?" The artist answered: "He said that he could resist it."

Robert E. Sherwood—who was editor-in-chief of the old *Life* magazine—once described Cooper's inimitable genius in the following words:

"Our subject's intellect is parted in the middle. On one side of the Great Divide is the right frontal brain lobe, which is mathematical, exact and scientific. Opposite to it is the left frontal brain lobe, which is completely cuckoo.

"The left frontal brain lobe might be called the production department. It is here that the ideas are born and given their first nourishment. When large enough to shift for themselves, they are permitted to swim across to the right frontal brain lobe, which is the distribution department. Here they are measured, ap-

INTERBOROUGH RAPID TRANSIT COMPANY

The Subway Sun

OUR MEN KNOW THEIR JOBS

THE SAFEST RAILROAD IN THE WORLD

VOL. XII No. 1

— THOMAS E. MURRAY ~ Receiver —

194?

I'm at the Bronx ZOO!
Come up and see me!

☞ TAKE 180TH ST. BRONX PARK TRAIN

"The Subway Sun," pasted on the end windows of the Interborough Rapid Transit trains, publicizes New York's educational and recreational opportunities. After Cooper's whimsical presentation of the free Symphony Concerts at the Metropolitan Museum of Art, recorded attendance jumped from 2,000 to 14,000.

This trade-mark for the New York Edison Company was designed by Cooper way back in 1904.

praised, charted, diagrammed, bundled and delivered to the public. . . . If the left frontal brain lobe were to be atrophied, and the right frontal brain lobe were compelled to operate on its own, then Mr. Cooper would be no more than an expert engineer and would probably be elected president of the United States. Whereas, if the right frontal brain lobe were thrown out of commission and only the left or production department were functioning, then Our Subject would have to be quietly put away somewhere in a room upholstered with soft pads.

"For instance: The verses in 'Lines to a Girl's Head' are in sonnet form, there being included no fewer than six sonnets for a total of eighty-four—count 'em (or, better yet, take my word for it)—eighty-four lines. The Master spent several months of agitated mental activity deciding that this would be worth the effort. Then he exhausted three weeks composing the sonnets, using several dozen terms of endearment, all different. . . . The next step in the laborious process was the division of the six sonnets into typewritten lines, each line exactly 50mm in length. After this, Mr. Cooper outlined the girl's head on a sheet of drawing paper that he had subdivided into quarter inch squares. Then he counted the squares in each section of the design, compared his total of squares with the total mileage of the typed copy, found that he would have to multiply the latter by 1.3 . . . and at this decimal point I hereby give up. Suffice it to say that 'Lines to a Girl's Head' was ultimately delivered in good condition to my desk at Life's office."

A member of the Society of Illustrators and the Dutch Treat Club, Fred Cooper has long been one of the mainstays of their annual shows. Because he thinks that life and people are amusing, his art looks as though it had been fun to do. It is easy to look at and easy to smile at.

Remember Victor Hugo's classic reply to his questioner who asked the great litterateur if it were not very difficult to write epic poetry? "No," replied Hugo, "easy or impossible." So it is with Cooper's particular kind of art. But easy as it must be now, it would be a mistake

This sheet of pen sketches, picked up in Cooper's studio, shows how the artist employs an odd moment sharpening his capricious pen.

BASE
BALL
TODAY

abcde
fghijk
lmnop
qrstuv
wxyz

*This is the famous Cooper lower-case alphabet.
It falls to the lot of few artists or type designers
to create an alphabet fine enough and distinctive enough to find its way into universal use, to
acquire the classification "Standard" and to bear
the name of its designer*

**The drawing by Fred Cooper which surrounds this page was originally
used in Collier's on a page carrying a sports article by Grantland Rice**

to assume that Cooper's art just happened. Behind it are years of discipline and at first plenty of drudgery. His first job, for example, was the illustration of a 1,400-page hardware catalog in San Francisco. Probably that task was one of the real foundation stones of a career marked by a consistent respect for good, sound, work; vigorous, substantial drawing and studied design. I don't believe that Fred Cooper ever turned out a careless drawing in his whole prolific career, and the apparent "ease" of his work is deceptive. It rests on a conscientiously built-up foundation of thought and technique.

Everyone who knows anything at all about lettering, beginning with the classic vigor of Edward Penfield, knows that no finer standard has been set or maintained than that of Fred Cooper's lettering. He was one of the first to prove the bold effectiveness of lower-case letters, and while he is a master at any kind of letter, he will live on in the annals of lettering as one of the greatest exponents of the lower-case. Along with his other work for the Division of Pictorial Publicity in the first World War, there stand the famous food conservation posters, still cited as examples of the finest poster lettering we have ever had. It characterized Fred Cooper's work from the start and carried over into the "Subway Sun" posters. These topical, local-interest stickers on the end windows of the cars were originally the idea of the late publicity-counsel, Ivy Lee, but it was not until the advent of Mr. T. E. Murray, as receiver for the line before the amalgamation, that cartoons replaced type-set text.

You hear a lot about "sales appeal" in posters, and if you are at all critical-minded your impression from most posters is that there is more talk about it than there is appeal. Not so with the sprightly "Subway Sun" graphic skits by Fred Cooper. One example proves the point. After his whimsical presentation of the free symphony concerts held at the Metropolitan Museum of Art, recorded attendance jumped from 2,000 to 14,000.

Artists, or anyone else, for that matter, may draw whatever conclusions they wish from the circumstance that Fred Cooper had no formal art training. This proves nothing about art training but a lot about Fred Cooper, who is that *rara avis*, the "natural," as Hollywood might say. His art, like his wit, is spontaneous— so much a part of him that it can't be analyzed, explained or copied. Certainly one of the reasons for its wide popularity over a period of years is the simple fact

Designed by F. G. Cooper for the English Speaking Union, in 1918. Printed from two wood blocks in dark blue-green and tan, by Hal Marchbanks.

that it doesn't need to be analyzed or explained.

Humor that is always in good taste, integrity of craftsmanship that has never made any compromise with sound standards, place Fred Cooper's work in a unique niche in the long-time record of essentially American art. And it will live long beyond the popularity of most of the literal art of our time because there is, in it, so much of the compelling, human, friendly personality of the artist.

Mario Cooper

1

2

3

4

MARIO COOPER SHOWS HOW HE DOES IT

After having traced on the illustration board the faintest outline of the figures, they are developed in pencil (Fig. 1). All the subtle drawing is done in this way, making sure with pencil shading where the heavy and light tones should go and that the intrinsic design balances. Having achieved the right drawing and the approximate balance of light and shade, the surplus pencil is removed by means of a kneaded eraser. Then the heavy blacks are painted in india ink (Fig. 2), leaving some of the fine lines until the very last. The large black areas having been painted, the first colored ink glazes are then applied (Fig. 3), putting very light tones first, in order to "feel" the texture of that particular piece of paper. Tones are gradually built up through a series of glazes. In the final stage (Fig. 4) the tones are finished and the last and final black lines are painted. These are used mostly as accents. A line is needed only when it functions as line; there is no point in using lines when the tone itself suffices.

68

Mario  Cooper

DURING one of those famous "evenings" at the Society of Illustrators Club in New York, William O. Chessman, art director of *Collier's*, introduced Mario Cooper as "a short little fellow who came straggling into my office under a tremendous bundle of drawings, leaving a trail of blood from his tired and bleeding feet." He said he felt sorry for the "poor little guy" and, seeing that he had "something on the ball," gave him a story.

That was back in 1930. Today Mario Cooper is still a "short little fellow," but he is no longer a "poor little guy." He does definitely have "something on the ball" as *Collier's* readers and the publishing world have known for some years. That trail of blood leading to Bill Chessman's office marked the beginning of a career which has been mutually profitable to Cooper and *Collier's*, not to mention other publications which occasionally have been enriched by Mario's brilliant drawings; "occasionally" because ever since Chessman gave Cooper that first story *Collier's* has adopted him pretty much as its own. No wonder! Cooper is a natural born illustrator. He has a genius for sensing the essential spirit of a story, and a creative faculty for enhancing its content and expressing its beauty and meaning.

Harvey Dunn once said, "In making an illustration, you must take poetry and song into it. You must contribute something of romance and drama to the pages of the magazine." Cooper does just that. And Cooper, by the way, was a pupil of Harvey Dunn and is one of his most ardent disciples. He studied under that master at Grand Central School of Art, later following him as an instructor there. (Previously he taught at Columbia University.) In his own work he reflects Dunn's idealism; at the same time he is the most practical of contemporary practitioners. By that I mean that he is one hundred per cent appreciative of the magazine's production problems and is ready to adjust his idealism to its legitimate demands. When he sees one of his drawings reproduced in predominant red instead of the delicate emerald green of his original he may wince—he does, but he will understand that some advertiser has gone violently red in the same form which carries his picture. If the picture is printed in black and white only he will accept that blow agreeably, knowing that it hurts the art director as much as it hurts him. There will even be times when a drawing which jumps the gutter will come out red on one side of the picture and blue on the other page. Such a situation sounds ruinous but I have seen that happen and have not been aware that it was an accident of production, until Mario has pointed it out to me.

Because of these mechanical expedients, which are unavoidable, Cooper is wise not to rely too heavily upon color. His color, in his originals, though always pleasant is not assertive. He doesn't depend too much on it. Consequently, whatever happens to the color after his originals leave his hands, his drawings are not likely to suffer greatly. He says that one of the first things he learned as an illustrator was the folly of expecting "reproductions" of original art work. " Of course," he says, "the picture seen on the printed page won't be like my drawing. All I worry about is that it will be good in itself." Quite a neat distinction there!

So we won't talk about Cooper's color. Let us rather focus upon his superb design and exquisite craftsmanship. I know it's dangerous to use superlatives, but I do not believe I'll be censured for saying his drawings are exquisite, particularly his drawings of women, whom he depicts with a grace that stems from an appreciative eye and an uncommonly facile brush. Frankly, these two merits, design and craftsmanship, especially the latter, have made me a great admirer of his work.

Before I visited Cooper in his studio I had no knowledge of his methods of work; whether he drew from models or photographs of models. Well, he uses photographs; as do most of the best men in contemporary illustration. It's an almost universal practice today. Some use them more creatively than others. To see Cooper's photographs alongside his finished drawings is to realize that about all they contribute is factual information. They certainly do not help much in the final expression. They are no substitute for the creative faculty. Cooper, without them, would still be the Cooper we admire. I

Mario Cooper's illustration for a Collier's story. The original, in full color, is 14 x 16½ inches.

3

1

2

The four preliminary studies on tracing paper, here reproduced at one-eighth size of originals, demonstrate Mr. Cooper's study methods. Fig. 1 represents a study in rhythms; Fig. 2 expresses a feeling for angular elements carried throughout the design; Fig. 3 is a careful pencil line drawing. Fig. 4, a wash drawing on tracing paper, is a study in pattern and values. There were other tracing paper studies, but these four represent the various phases in the picture's development.

4

Exact-size detail from a Mario Cooper illustration for Woman's Home Companion

think that the splendid work of Cooper and some other moderns points up the conviction that it is the man's ability, not his methods, which is important.

The close-up, borrowed in illustration from the movies, has given us, as in Cooper's drawings, some very expressive characterizations and certainly some extremely delectable renditions of the human figure. Cooper's paintings of heads, for example. He draws and paints these with such great artistry that I am directing attention to them by reproducing an exact-size detail of a girl's head from one of his illustrations, and asking him to show us his step-by-step procedure in its development. And, on this page, we are showing an exact-size halftone of two heads from another illustration. Although not in color it illustrates a kind of "old master" quality of painting. It reminds me of the canvases of some early Flemish and Italian masters, and certainly deserves worshipful scrutiny.

Cooper paints with colored inks on illustration board. Occasionally he dips his brush into his watercolor box, but only when that medium will serve better for some special purpose. His meticulous rendering of detail is done with a No. 9 sable brush and not, as one might surmise, with a No. 1 or a No. 2.

A camera stands in the corner of his studio. He is his own photographer. With his photographs before him he develops each figure separately on tracing paper, making changes on successive sheets laid over previous studies. He customarily redraws a figure many times. When all figures have been individually perfected, he puts them together in trial arrangements until they compose to suit him. Then he traces the main outlines onto his illustration board. The only preparatory pat-

tern study is a rapidly brushed-in effect such as shown— much reduced—on the opposite page. In his tracing paper studies of the figure he takes great pains with clothing and drapery—he is noted for this. But at no point does he experiment with detail until he comes to the final painting. If a detail or even a whole figure doesn't suit him when completed, he scrapes it out with a razor blade and does it over again. The razor blade leaves the paper surface very smooth. A little rubbing with an eraser gives it a sufficient tooth again.

Mario Cooper was born in Mexico City in 1905. His father was a Californian, his mother a native of Mexico. When Mario was nine, the Coopers moved to California where the boy received his education. He studied art at the Otis Art Institute and the Chouinard School. Later he studied at Columbia University under sculptor Oronzio Maldarelli. He plunged into the professional world via engraving house, art service, and advertising agencies. He became an expert letterer and layout man. He studied drawing in night classes whenever possible and copied the work of Dean Cornwell, Harvey Dunn and Pruett Carter. Finally came that trail of blood to William Chessman's office at *Collier's*.

Cooper married a Los Angeles girl, Aileen Anita Whetstine—also a pupil of Harvey Dunn. The Coopers live in Port Washington, New York. They have two children, Vincent and Patricia. Cooper's hobbies are African masks and wood working—he makes his own studio furniture. Sculpture is his absorbing art interest. He works in plastilene and has had some of his pieces cast in bronze. He looks serious in his photographs, but he is exuberant, enjoys life, and laughs a lot. He is as good a companion as he is illustrator.

Dean Cornwell

Drawing by Dean Cornwell for mural in the new State Building at Nashville, Tennessee. Cornwell's style of drawing has been evolved in part through his practice of projecting his drawings on canvas, by means of an opaque reflecting machine. This necessitates a precise line.

74

Dean Cornwell poses with his sixth canvas in the "Pioneers in American Medicine" Series painted for John Wyeth & Bro. This one depicts Dr. Oliver Wendell Holmes, in 1843, reading his paper on the cause of child-bed fever (his own discovery) before the Boston Society for the Improvement of Medicine. These Cornwell paintings are widely distributed, in reproduction, among physicians and are exhibited in drug store windows.

ONE OF THE FIRST things I noticed upon entering Dean Cornwell's studio was a large sheet of paper upon which were ten or twelve small charcoal compositions. "Those," he explained, "are analytical studies of some of Orozco's paintings."

I mention that incident at the outset because it goes far to explain the man and his extraordinary success. At fifty—and after thirty years of continuous work in illustration and mural painting—Cornwell, a recognized master of composition, is a zealous student of composition; as well as of everything else that bears upon his career as an artist. His great accomplishments and his world-wide reputation have not made him complacent. The goal, for him, is always over the horizon of today's achievement; a seven-day week of work and study is insufficient to attain it.

Cornwell is an artist of large-scale performance, and it is *scale* that first impresses the visitor to his studio. He works big, thinks big; in physical appearance he is perfectly cast for the part. Tall, well built, he is personally expressive of vigorous, creative energy. His manner, without conceit, gives assurance of complete adequacy for whatever comes his way. In conversation he comes immediately to the point, not uncomfortably with intention of hurrying it through, but for the purpose of using the time to the most profitable advantage for all concerned. That time-value sense is a characteristic of men whose capacities, no matter how great, can scarcely keep pace with the demands put upon them.

Dean Cornwell is best known by some as a mural painter, by others as an illustrator. It is the purpose of this chapter to deal principally with his illustrations, but it is impossible to write about either phase of this man's work without considerable reference to the other. His murals in the Los Angeles Library; General Motors Building, New York World's Fair; Lincoln Memorial, Redlands, Cal.; Court House and new State Building

at Nashville, Tenn.; the Raleigh Room, Hotel Warwick, and in Radio City, New York—to name a few—have through reproduction become familiar to those who have not seen the originals.

Examining a mass of newspaper clippings on Cornwell, I came across an account of his painting of the famous Los Angeles Library murals. It was written by Thomas Sugrue and appeared in the February 26, 1933 issue of the New York *Herald Tribune*. I want to quote it here because it tells so much about the man and his characteristic approach to creative problems:

"The theory that modern artists are practical men of the world who barter their wares with the shrewdness of a trader on the floor of the stock exchange received a severe jolt yesterday when Dean Cornwell, who returned last week from California, reported that he had not profited a penny on the five years of labor he put into completing the largest set of murals ever put on canvas, for the new Los Angeles Public Library at a contract price of $50,000.

"'The money I received covered the cost of the materials and transportation,' he said, 'and part of my expenses, but the labor had to be written off to personal satisfaction and love of art.'

"Mr. Cornwell, who has entrenched himself for the winter in his studio at 222 West 59th Street, thought he had put over a stroke of good business when, on his sketches and bid, he won the contract in June, 1927. He gleefully set about painting four murals 40 feet square and eight minor murals 20 feet high, containing 300 figures four times the size of ordinary men. He estimated the job would take the full five years allowed and planned to do it in America. There was no reason, so far as he could see, why $50,000 would not cover the entire cost and offer him a reasonable return.

"The first difficulty arose when New York failed to supply a studio large enough for the canvases. Mr. Corn-

This is Cornwell's first study for the Fisher Body painting. The artist discarded it because the man operating the radar device covered the most interesting portion of the gun. Cornwell then chose the moment after the firing of the gun, permitting the radar man to leave his post for a moment. (This was one of two sketches submitted to the client.)

well was forced to go to London where he rented a studio from Frank Brangwyn, England's most famous mural painter. Now and then he had to hurry to Italy to look at the work of Renaissance muralists, and especially to study the Byzantine mosaics.

"Twice he had to return to New York in search of models for a clipper ship and the gold mining period, and once in search of Indians. He had to set up shop in the Little Church Around the Corner in New York to paint a bishop, because no church would allow its vestments to go to a studio; and he was continually harassed by problems of engineering and architecture.

"First he made cartoons seven feet square. These were photographed and projected on the large canvases where they were sketched in charcoal. Smaller projections were painted in the blue and gold color scheme, and then the process was repeated again and again, as the artist reached closer conceptions of his idea.

"When he ran out of money he paused to replenish his cupboard by doing magazine illustration such as first made him famous.

" 'For five years I didn't have an hour of restful sleep,' he said. 'I know I shouldn't do it, but I worry until a job is finished. Usually it is two weeks, this time it was five years.'

"Finally, in 1931, he was ready to paint the large canvases and he again returned to the United States and set out for Los Angeles, with his trainload of materials. Once more the problem of a studio arose, and this time the cinema producers came to his assistance. A studio had been built for the special purpose of producing scenery and backdrops for large stages, and had been abandoned when the depression laid its heavy hand on the country.

" 'In the end everyone was satisfied except some artists who didn't get the job,' Cornwell said, 'and I felt like every artist who wants to do something in the way of a public utility. I nearly lost my shirt doing it, but the satisfaction of those grand figures and the realization that thousands of people will see and enjoy them made up for it all.' "

When in 1941 America entered the war, it was inevitable that Cornwell's brush would be requisitioned for paintings illustrating the drama of men and machines in action. The demand came from national advertisers who turned from the selling of merchandise to selling the war. Fisher Bodies contracted with Cornwell for a long series of paintings to run in fourteen magazines.* The one we reproduce in color appeared in the summer of 1944. This illustrates a 5″–38 gun and its crew in action.

The first study for this picture (at left) shows men at their proper battle stations preparing to fire the gun. This was not acceptable to the artist because the man operating radar, at the upper right, covers too much of the interesting part of the gun.

The accepted design (right), submitted with another view of the gun, dramatizes the moment after firing when the target has been hit and the radar man leaves his station to shake hands with his buddy, who is seen at lower right in the prize-fighting gesture of victory.

All war pictures must be approved by the War or the Navy Department, both of which, ironically enough, sometimes are loath to give the artist the information he needs to make his illustration correct. When new and secret designs are involved, the picture will not get by if it is correct in *all* details. In such exigencies the drawing has actually to be falsified to get the Department's O.K.

Asked the source of facts needed for this war picture, Cornwell said: "By nosing around and by just plain luck. Sometimes the Army, Navy and Air Corps do cooperate, but mostly the artist has to dig it out the hard way. I watch all news photographs and documentary films. Sometimes a news photograph, examined under a

---

* "In all these Fisher Body jobs," explains Cornwell, "my illustrations had to be so designed as to permit cropping on any or all sides in order to accommodate themselves to the varied page requirements of the magazines in which they were to appear."

Painting by Dean Cornwell for a Fisher Body advertisement. It appeared in the magazines in the summer of 1944

Above is a reproduction of a finished charcoal drawing for another Fisher Body painting. Drawn on thin, rag stock white paper, the exact size of the painting, it was transferred directly to the canvas with carbon paper.

magnifying glass, reveals a scrap of detail of real importance. That prize-fight gesture, for example, was picked out of a small, rather vague newspaper print. (It has since become quite common.)"

In an assignment of this kind, research consumes a great deal of the artist's time. After his preliminary studies have been completed and a "comprehensive" sketch in color accepted by client and War Department, the finished painting goes quite quickly.

A photostat, small enough to go into a projecting lantern, is made of the comprehensive. This is sometimes projected directly to the canvas and the outlines drawn on canvas with black indelible pencil and sometimes with india ink, preparatory to painting. In some instances, if there is a possibility of wishing to develop details or change the drawing as the picture progresses, then Cornwell draws with red pencil or sanguine chalk.

At other times the comprehensive is projected onto a large sheet of thin paper instead of the canvas. This gives an opportunity for corrections and further development of details, in such exacting subjects as these war pictures, before the design is finally outlined on canvas.

From this exact size, corrected drawing a tracing with carbon paper is made to the surface of the canvas, upon which painting may begin without the need of further changes in drawing. The tracing is done before the canvas is stretched, the canvas being tacked on large, hard surfaced board for accurate and clean tracing with no "give."

After the lines of the design have been drawn on the canvas with the brush, it is Cornwell's practice to make an underpainting in egg tempera, transparent without white. The colors merely hint at those to appear in the final rendering in oil, and the whole underpainting is in a very high value key. The primary purpose of the underpainting is definitely to establish the design in thin, flexible tempera medium so that there will be no considerable experimenting with the final oil painting. Any number of changes can readily be made in tempera underpainting by sponging off and quickly repainting. The medium is applied to the canvas in thin washes over which the drawing can be corrected if necessary with charcoal, pencil or brush. Figures drawn exact size on tracing paper can even be transferred if desired, this

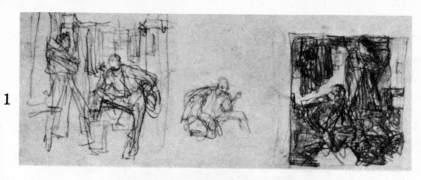

1

AN UNUSUAL CASE HISTORY
OF A DEAN CORNWELL ILLUSTRATION

It demonstrates how the hysterical demands of contemporary illustration sometimes force the artist to abandon the logical illustration of a critical episode and dramatize some minor incident which offers opportunity for spectacular visual action. The story is "Lady Said Goodby" in the February 1942 American Magazine. For explanation see text on the following page.

2

3

4

5

6

7

These are preliminary studies for the illustration reproduced on the page opposite. The halftone at left is from a charcoal and white chalk drawing on red paper. The other is from an oil color study done on illustration board. Both originals are ten inches square.

by pinholes and a pounce bag, the dry color adhering even to a wet or tacky surface.

Cornwell formerly did his preliminary composition studies on a very small scale, just a few square inches in area. He discovered that in the finished painting—perhaps 30 x 40—there were too many problems left unsolved in the thumbnail studies. Now his comprehensives, often in oil color on heavy paper, are made from one-quarter to one-third finish size. However, he points out a danger in preliminaries which approach the size of the final picture: one is likely to shoot too much energy into them, leaving less enthusiasm for the canvas itself. These larger sketches are unfortunate, from an emotional standpoint, but are necessary for advertising clients' O.K. purposes. "Incidentally," says Cornwell, "I've never seen it fail that the larger and more finished sketch will always be chosen over a better but smaller sketch that is less finished in detail."

Dean Cornwell's illustrations—he estimates he has done over 1,000—are invariably painted in oil. But he does not recommend this medium for present-day illustration. It is not suited, he points out, to the type of work editors are now demanding. For one thing, oil lacks the wide range of values and brilliancy of color offered by watercolor, particularly by the powerful aniline colors used so much today. It is all a matter of keeping in step with the times. The radio, movies, rotogravure and picture magazines—indeed the very tempo of modern life—have changed the whole aspect of illustration. When Howard Pyle a half-century ago introduced oil painting as an illustration medium, a colored picture in a magazine was highly prized. Often it found its way into a frame. The original was reproduced with loving care on a flat-bed press; it was a work of art. It seemed all the more so because it was associated with literature; only the works of noted writers were deemed worthy of such pictorial treatment. In the hysteria of modern publishing, color flashes from every page. Editors try to out-scream each other with blitzkrieg lay-

outs and raucous color. Action must be forced; pictures must almost have sound and action. On cheap paper, run through mile-a-minute presses, a picture painted with brilliant aniline dyes stands the best chance of shouting down competitors. The result is as transient as a newspaper.

A very good demonstration of this hectic demand for eye-stopping action is found in the case history of an illustration Cornwell did for "Lady Said Goodby," a story in the American Magazine, February, 1942.

The scene is laid on a western dude ranch; the story concerns a summer romance between the girl, who is a guest, and one of the ranchmen. The girl's love proves as fleeting as the changing season and, as the summer ends, approaches zero.

For his drawing Cornwell chose the moment when the girl seeks out the rancher to announce the end of their friendship. On the preceding page, 1, 2 and 3 represent his study in the development of this theme. No. 3 is from the color study submitted to the editors. This was not acceptable; it lacks action, that is, visual, arresting action—although a dramatic moment in the lives of these two people. So the manuscript was searched for a more spectacular incident. This was found in a chance meeting of the pair later on. The episode, though emphasized in the picture beyond its importance in the story, satisfies the current insistence upon violent action capable of arresting the roving eyes of restless readers. Study No. 4—in color—proved a bit too turbulent; it was followed by 5 and 6, which are the basis for 7, the colored illustration. The artist still prefers No. 3.

The modern ascendency of the camera is another factor in making contemporary illustration what it is. Many of the younger illustrators rely so heavily upon it that they become more expert as photographers than skilful as painters. They will do all their creative work with the camera and often actually trace the photographic print. Many never use the model at all.

Dean Cornwell is, shall we say, of the old school; at

This illustration by Dean Cornwell for "The Man Who Would Not Die" appeared in the January 1942 American Magazine. The original painting is 40 x 44 inches. The dramatic quality of this picture is enhanced by the device of keeping the object of the alarm out of sight. This excites curiosity and tempts one to a reading of the story.

any rate he is in the tradition of sound craftsmanship of the school which assumed that an illustrator is first of all a fine artist. He uses models constantly, the camera rarely. If the job calls for a twenty-five-dollar-an-hour glamour girl, that is different.

A man who can draw with Cornwell's facility doesn't need to rely upon photography. His sketchbook and pencil make a far more useful recording of the object than a camera. The camera, he points out, takes everything in its relative importance in nature. An illustrator's task is to focus upon details, actions and effects which are significant in a particular story. Cornwell finds a precise pencil drawing, made on location, ten times more useful than a camera shot. "Your eye goes around what interests you when you draw it," he says. "You put its real significance—to you—into the drawing. But often in referring to your snapshots you even wonder why you took them." Cornwell is always sketching. That, he says, is his hobby. It isn't quite a busman's holiday because, after an exhausting day's work in the studio, sketching from nature or the model is real relaxation. He even calls it a restorative. At any rate he is always at it: his studio is filled with portfolios of sketches of landscapes, trees, furniture, buildings, everything.

Dean Cornwell is very fond of charcoal, uses it in his drawings from models and for his composition studies. When a drawing is to go into his projection lantern for transfer to canvas he goes over the figures with a carbon pencil line to sharpen them up. Sometimes in his color experiments he paints in oil on a piece of cellophane laid over his charcoal study.

Looking through Cornwell's portfolios one is struck by the evident fact that this artist thinks out loud. As soon as an idea pops, his pencil begins to play with it, keeps pace with his mental conception as though geared to it and, following a series of sketches which start with scribbles, one can trace the growth of an idea throughout its development.

"A composition," says Cornwell, "is not just a nice arrangement with everything gracefully filling the space. No matter how satisfying it may be from an abstract point of view it is meaningless in illustration unless it is built around and wholly expresses an authentic idea that motivates the particular picture."

Speaking of color he declares that, "A great colorist is known for his grays just as a chef is known for his gravies and sauces. It really isn't very difficult to cook a good beefsteak properly; the real test of a master cook is the gravy or sauce to go with it. The grays are the sauces that flavor all other colors on the canvas."

"An important difference between the painter of easel pictures and the illustrator," says Cornwell, "is that the former goes through life painting the things that he sees before him, the things that appeal to him, while the latter is forced to paint something that neither he nor anyone else has seen, and make it appear as if he has actually been an observer on the spot." And finally, "The measure of the illustrator is his ability to take a subject in which he may have neither interest nor information, tackle it with everything he's got and make the finished picture look like the consummation of his life's one ambition."

Gregory d'Alessio

"In my joy at not having to ride in jeeps any longer
I'd completely forgotten this aspect of civilian life."

A CARTOON FOR COLLIER'S BY GREGORY D'ALESSIO

Slightly reduced from the original wash drawing

Running the Gauntlet of Cartoon Editors

AN INTERVIEW WITH

Gregory d'Alessio

Gregory d'Alessio

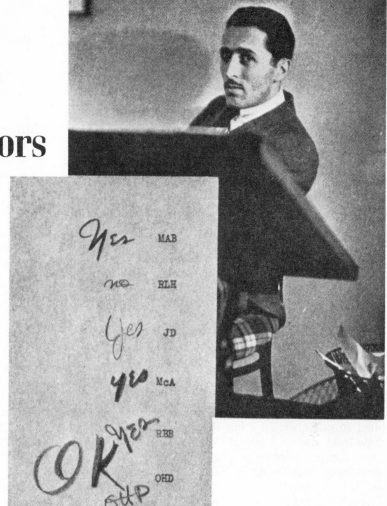

"How," we asked d'Alessio, "can a beginner break into the cartoon game?" "Well," said our host, "he's got to run the gauntlet of cartoon editors just as every comic artist does, just as I have done. There's only one thing that will land him on the pages of *Collier's*, *Esquire* or *The New Yorker*: that is a good gag with a good drawing.

"Here's what I mean by 'running the gauntlet.' Let us suppose Elmer Jones of Jonesville, Missouri, has thought up a good gag—or believes he has. Elmer draws his cartoon, shows it to his sweetheart, his sisters and his friends. They all laugh, declare that Elmer is a *card* a natural born comic artist. So Elmer wraps up his masterpiece and confidently mails it to the cartoon editor of one of the big weeklies. It reaches the editor. He looks at it. He doesn't roar with laughter as did Elmer's friends—not even if it is funny! Elmer's drawing is just one of about one thousand that come to him weekly. Well, after the obviously hopeless cartoons have been weeded out, Elmer's remains with the few survivors; it really is good. These survivors now must run the gauntlet. Some editors pass them along to five, six or seven staff members for a vote (see specimen ballot in the illustration above). A cartoon that gets by that jury of experts is pretty apt to 'click' with the public. And bear this in mind," said d'Alessio, raising his pencil for emphasis, "Elmer's name on the cartoon, or George Wolfe's or Lariar's or even Peter Arno's won't sell the drawing: the papers can't afford to play favorites. The fact that I am personally acquainted with some editors gives me no 'drag.' I compete with Elmer on even terms, day in and day out. Well, let us assume that Elmer's cartoon gets the votes and the editor's final O.K. Elmer receives a check (quite an impressive one to Elmer), and the congratulations of his friends. He throws out his chest. He has broken into the game. All right, let's see just what kind of game this is, and enquire whether Elmer has what it takes to play it. In the first place he must be able to draw. As I have already said, it takes a good drawing and a good gag to make a cartoon. The chances are that Elmer would put the gag first and the drawing second. It might interest him to know that a cartoon is sometimes purchased for its gag alone—if it is especially good—and handed to another artist to be redrawn. That is not the kind of success Elmer wants.

"Elmer will also find that while he has at last crashed his first major magazine, the trick is to repeat—again and again—or he will be one of those scores of cartoonists who, out of economic necessity, must retain his job at the local foundry or bank cage. Deflate that chest, Elmer, and look at this matter coldly and practically. Are you prepared for a long stretch of disappointment and actual unremunerative labor?"

The drawing that needs no gag line is, in d'Alessio's opinion, the highest type of cartoon. He reminds us that old-time gags were often several sentences long. Words have gradually given way to the story without words. Today, cartoons with a short line or no line at all are more compelling. Naturally the drawing itself must be more expressive, the artist more of a pictorial dramatist.

The Japs and Nazis knew the power of a picture without words. Particularly in China, where the percentage of illiteracy among peasants is high, were the cartoonists considered by the enemy the most dangerous of the intellectual elements. A crude cartoon, with no words to read, brought many a message home to the

simple peasants, as to the nature of the foe. These cartoonists when captured by the Japs were shot on the spot.

"I never use models for my cartoons," d'Alessio replied to our question, "but that doesn't mean I don't draw from models. I attend a sketch class at the Art Students League as often as possible. That gives me constant study from the figure. Then I carry my sketchbook everywhere: in restaurants, the theatre, on the subway." The artist indicated a pile of about fifty sketchbooks on a shelf. "If one knows the figure and keeps in constant practice through drawing from life he should not need a model for cartoon drawings. Indeed it is my experience that models can actually be in the way. Without them the drawing is apt to be more spontaneous and lively.

"As to gags," continued d'Alessio, "Elmer, if he is a clever fellow, may be able to create many of his own, though there are few comic artists who invent all of their gag lines. Gags have become quite an industry today and the artist can buy all his gags—if he can afford to. I buy some and create others. I have the conceit that mine are better than those I purchase. But gags one must have—lots of them. As soon as a new cartoonist breaks into print there is no dearth of gags, for the gag men are always watching newspapers and magazines for new customers. (Incidentally they expect 25% and up of the publisher's check.)" D'Alessio led me to his filing cabinet in a corner. "Here are approximately 3,000 roughs and gags. I need to have plenty of raw material at hand to turn out ten or a dozen roughs for cartoons each week—which is my average."

D'Alessio pulled a sketch out of the file. "Here is a typical rough such as I submit to the magazines. Roughs are done quickly, all 8½ x 11 inches, on ordinary typewriter paper, and, though carried only far enough to express the idea adequately, are quite well conceived as to composition. Also they are executed in a clear, sharp decisive technique. Notice that this one is in ink with a little wash, and this one in Wolff pencil No. 2 or No. 3. I never turn out 'pale' roughs. You'll never catch an editor's eye with an unimpressive rough, as if you yourself had no confidence in it when you executed it.

"When accepted, they are redrawn larger, with careful attention to details and accessories. They must be authentic to be convincing. If a rough idea is rejected, back it goes in the file; some other editor may accept it. The very magazine that first rejected it may even accept it when submitted at a later date. That has happened more than once.

"I said before that Elmer and I compete on the same terms. Of course I have this advantage: The editors know my work so I need only to submit quickly drawn roughs. It would be wise for a newcomer in the field to submit several finished drawings at first; otherwise the editors would not be sure that the cartoon would be successfully rendered—no matter how good the idea.

"It's always safe to keep ideas timely and fresh. Since a cartoonist is, in a sense, a social satirist, he must study everything and everybody around him keenly in terms of taking a playful punch at them.

"Precious time and unnecessary work can be saved by exercising a little shrewdness in connection with the marketing of cartoons," d'Alessio said earnestly, when we brought up the question of how and where to place Elmer's offerings. "Some magazines use only sophisticated jokes, others favor whimsy. Some editors prefer risqué gags, others insist upon clean, wholesome humor. Then there are *taboos*. Many editors avoid unpleasant themes: accidents, death, prison scenes. Jokes also become taboo through repetition. Once all the rage, they get worn threadbare."

It takes time, study and experience to become familiar with the market. Of course the artist should study the magazines continually to keep his finger on the pulse of the cartoon market which is constantly fluctuating. D'Alessio sells to only the top-flight publications, in person. An agent handles his roughs from there on and markets them among other miscellaneous publications. His roughs, therefore, are always on the move.

Fast action is necessary, particularly when certain ideas among the batches "in the mill" quickly lose their timeliness and therefore their meaning.

The stock market crash of 1929 was responsible for d'Alessio's career as a cartoonist. He lost his job as bank teller in Wall Street. In desperation he looked about for another job but could find nothing. He had always been interested in drawing, even when a reporter on a Brooklyn newspaper. So he started to draw cartoons. For three years he had tough sledding. But persistent struggle finally landed him in *The Saturday Evening Post* with his first published cartoon.

This is the rough—reproduced at about half size—that d'Alessio submitted for the "Your slips are showing" cartoon. Done in pencil and wash.

"Your Slips are showing, Miss Downs"
Cartoon by d'Alessio for Publishers Syndicate
About one-half size of original drawing

At the moment, d'Alessio's principal work is a panel cartoon distributed by the Publishers Syndicate to some fifty newspapers in the U. S., including a few in Canada and one in Hawaii. The panel is called *These Women* and in it he lampoons the foibles of the women of our time, particularly in relation to the war and the American scene in general.

"Creating cartoons for syndicates," says d'Alessio, "imposes the problem of choosing gags that will have a general acceptance among newspaper readers throughout the country. Gags suitable for *Esquire* or *The New*

Yorker, by way of contrast, are tailor-made for selected audiences." D'Alessio is also on the staff of *Parade*, a Sunday supplement. He draws a number of spots each week and contributes frequent pages and spreads on special timely subjects.

As this is being written, d'Alessio's magazine efforts are directed toward developing a feature cartoon for *Collier's*, based on the arrival home of our fighting men from overseas and national military centers. It is entitled *Welcome Home*. "I'm trying to make it the best work I've ever done," said the cartoonist. We saw a few reproductions and they looked pretty good to us.

D'Alessio works very rapidly, sure of himself at all times. He gets his deadline work completed quickly and turns to other things related to his profession though not connected with it. He has been on the Board of Control of the Art Students League for several years and is chairman of the Committee on War Cartoons of the American Society of Magazine Cartoonists. This Committee, since Pearl Harbor, has worked closely with different government agencies on matters pertaining to cartooning for the war effort. Its members are now concentrating on sketching wounded veterans in hospital centers and teaching and encouraging those with inclinations toward cartooning. Often d'Alessio is called upon to help out his wife, Hilda Terry, also a cartoonist, with a problem. Thus it will be seen that this particular cartoonist's life is a busy one.

```
Cartoon Idea:              No. 2463

Scene: Lingerie counter of a
Department Store. In the back-
ground is a box half open with
an article of underwear half in,
half out.             many boxes
                    Boss
Woman customer to clerk:
                     very pretty
"Miss, your petticoat is hanging.
        MISS DOWNS!"
```

This is a gag slip that was submitted to d'Alessio by his gag writer. He has edited it—longhand—according to his own opinion as to how to interpret it without changing its basic idea.

Floyd M. Davis

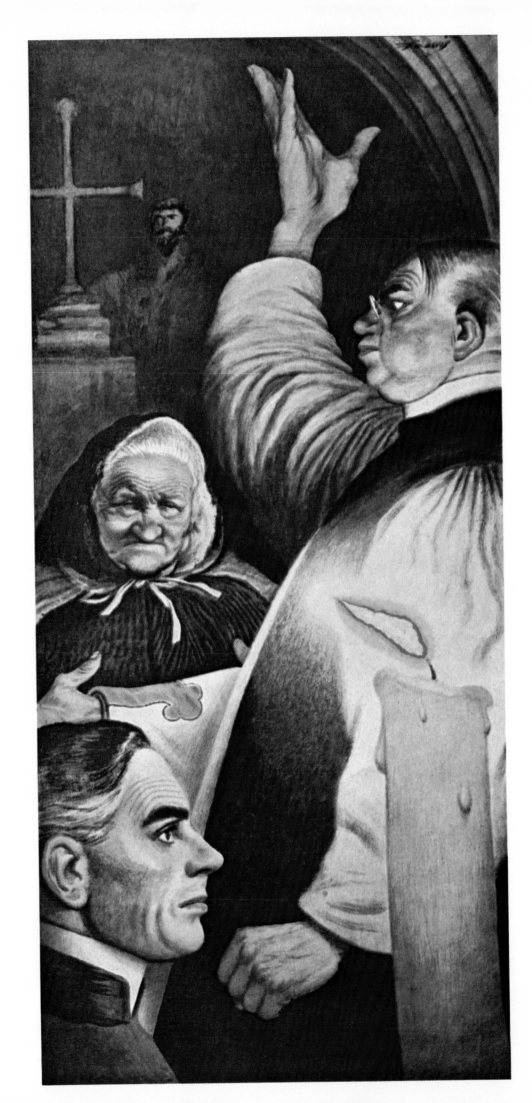

Illustration by
Floyd Davis for
"Altar Cloth"
in American
Magazine

Floyd M. Davis

"WHEN YOU APPROACH FLOYD," warned a friend, apprised of my desire to interview this popular illustrator, "you'll have to be almighty persistent. The first thing he'll say is 'Why bother with me when there is a real artist in the family?' (Referring to his wife, Gladys Rockmore Davis)."

I was prepared for that because I had already asked Mrs. Davis to be the subject of an article on pastel painting—this before I knew that the two famous artists were members of the same family. Even so, I had my troubles; first to persuade Floyd, then to get at him. My first letter brought no answer. A follow-up phone call by my secretary brought a brusque refusal, followed,

later the same day, by a remorseful apology for being so unfriendly, and a promise of cooperation if we still wanted to use him. He explained that the phone call had interrupted him at a moment when he was wholly absorbed in a creative problem; at such a time, he said, he was as snappish as a bear surprised at a feast.

It is quite a trick to get an appointment with almost any artist who is a top-flight magazine illustrator. Deadlines, in present-day publishing practice, come so close on the heels of assignments that the illustrator scarcely finds enough time for sleep. A telephone call can indeed be serious when he is striving desperately to complete a drawing that has to be put aboard the six o'clock

Right —
This penciled scribble by Floyd M. Davis is the only preliminary study, on paper, which preceded his painting of the illustration for "Greater London," a story by Roland Pertwee which appeared (in color) in the Woman's Home Companion in June 1941. It is reproduced in halftone on page 93.

Below —
Detail, reproduced at exact size, of the original drawing for the "Greater London" illustration

plane. Or when he is in one of those creative impasses so often encountered at the beginning of a new assignment.

Little wonder that Davis, answering the phone at such a time (we called him when he was starting *Heads You Lose*—a serial by Christianna Brand which ran in *The Saturday Evening Post*), was hopelessly befogged and had to be rescued by Mrs. Davis, whose studio adjoins that of her husband. It's a good arrangement when rescuing is turn about as it is with the Davises.

If it is a bit difficult to get your foot in the door of Davis' studio, once within, you meet the friendliest and most considerate of men. So it was that I was most graciously received with my photographer.

One of the pictures we got that day tells a lot about the man and his organization for work. Over the north window—it looks out on the Harlem River—is a battery of fluorescent lamps which, switched on in late afternoon, extend the day far into the night without perceptible change in quality of light. Davis does a good bit of night work; the telephone is quiet after business hours.

The mirrors seen behind him are in frequent use as he draws. He doesn't depend too much on models, though of course he has a considerable number of different types within call. Like many artists with years of experience behind them, he is less dependent upon models than upon memory and imagination.

Those are bottles of colored inks on the windowsill. In a corner, not shown, is modeling wax and an unfinished figure. The camera is only a hobby—Davis does not use it for photographing his models.

Note those heaps of photographic magazines with their wealth of scrap on costumes, customs, action and all manner of flora, fauna and miscellany from the

This is a halftone reproduction of Floyd M. Davis' illustration for "Greater London."
In the Woman's Home Companion it appeared in color and extended across two pages.

world over. No illustrator could function without reference material of that kind.

As for types, these crowd Davis' mind till there is standing room only. They come from a retentive memory which seldom loses an interesting face once seen. These he grafts onto models that come to pose for him in the flesh. He relies almost wholly upon memory and is not addicted to sketching. He seldom uses any model literally; an old lady, for example, may serve as model for a sensitive old man. "But," he asserts, "models usually conflict with exaggerated imaginative attitudes which are more truthful and far more interesting than photos or poses—caricature and some distortion is more arresting and much more fun for me in illustration than the literal."

He is particularly fond of rough rural types and decadent highbrows of smart society, though he is by no means pigeonholed in any specialty. As Mr. W. T. Martin, one-time art editor of *The Saturday Evening Post*, said, "Davis is not a 'Johnny-One-Note' pounding away at the same melody. He is equally at home with hill-billies and Park Avenue, with the interior of a small-town barber shop and the backwater in an English village.

"Like every illustrator who is worth his salt, his pictures are painted with imagination and honesty. He manages to put excitement into them and impact and a differentness born of his own originality. His style and approach are so original that they encourage imitators, and at the same time make the task of imitators insuperable. Davis has such a feeling for characterization that none of the people he draws are ordinary, and he is willing to lavish loving care upon a job and put all into it he feels it needs, regardless of time and effort."

If you are numbered among Floyd's friends you may bob up in one of his illustrations. "Frequently," he says, "I find myself creating a story character in the image of a friend or acquaintance. Sometimes it turns out to be an actual portrait." To illustrate, Davis pointed to a striking likeness of Earle Winslow, a fellow illustrator, in one of his recent drawings. This practice often comes to his rescue when he is having a difficult characterization problem. He had been struggling for a day and a half with a type in the "Greater London" illustration, until the actor Charles Laughton came to mind as the type he was trying to visualize. (See page 92.)

Asked to show steps in the development of an illustration, Davis said, "I'm afraid you'll find me a poor

93

subject for a how-to-do-it demonstration, because the whole creative business goes on in my head where you can't see it. Here's all I've got to show on paper for my study of this *Post* story"—displaying a few sheets of note paper filled with nearly unintelligible scribbles, clipped to sections of the story galley. "These hieroglyphics—to you—represent my only preliminary study on paper. From them I go at once to my final drawing, in colored inks, on illustration board. Sometimes the picture materializes quickly and with comparative ease. Frequently it 'comes off' only after a protracted struggle of two or three days; this is more likely at the start of a serial when the very first drawing establishes the story characters. These same people, you know, have to appear and reappear in the drawings for six or seven installments." Before the first drawings are delivered, Davis has them photostated for reference in doing those that are to follow. In color, too, the artist commits himself irrevocably in his very first drawing to a color scheme that will give continuity to the entire series.

Ask Floyd Davis how he composes his illustrations. All he can tell you is that he usually begins at the bottom which, when painted, gives him a sense of foundation for the rest of the picture. Generally speaking, he works from the bottom up, pretty much completing things as he goes. This in contrast to the method of working all over the canvas simultaneously. From this we must deduce that Davis has an exceptional faculty for developing his motive on an unseen canvas.

Does he do this analytically? Is he "design-conscious"? "No," he replies, "my drawings are not *composed*; that is, they are not conceived as abstract pattern, as designs. All my creative faculties are focused upon purely illustrative qualities — characterization, action, putting the story across; and adding that something to it which goes beyond a factual interpretation of the author's narrative, extending and enriching its significance. It seems to me that the artist, if suf-

Advertising drawing by Floyd Davis for the H. J. Heinz Company

ficiently endowed and adequately trained, doesn't need to give composition much thought; composition should be intuitive, just as dressing well is intuitive for the person of good taste. It happens."

As for training, Floyd Davis never had the benefit of art school instruction. He learned his craft the hard way. Forced by circumstance to quit high school at the end of his first year, he got a job in a lithograph house in Chicago. For $3.00 a week he made tusche and did every kind of manual work entrusted to an apprentice. He was brought into contact with art—didn't he carry lithographic stones about the shop?—and was given some opportunity to develop his own drawing skill. His first real art job was with Meyer Both & Co., the well-known Chicago Art Service.

His art career, interrupted by two and a half years of service in the U. S. Navy during the first World War, was resumed when he returned to Chicago and joined the Grauman Brothers' organization as an advertising artist. It was here that he met the girl who was to become his wife. Gladys Rockmore, a successful fashion artist, had been taken on at Grauman's, the only woman on the staff. It was an experiment; it didn't work. As soon as Gladys entered the studio Floyd's output

dwindled, and as the weeks went by became practically non-existent. At the end of two months the management, in self-defense, if with reluctance, invited the young lady to leave—a martyr on the altar of romance.

But for Miss Rockmore martyrdom had a happy ending: she and Floyd were married in 1925. He had left the studio and was now a free-lance advertising artist. The following year the couple moved to New York where Floyd, dividing his time between advertising and magazine illustration, soon became top man in both fields. Now, art editors compete with art directors of advertising agencies for his drawings.

It will come as no surprise to learn that Daumier, Goya, and Toulouse-Lautrec are chief among Davis' graphic heroes. These masters of caricature and characterization have influenced him consciously. They are, he says, his best clipping file.

Floyd Davis' hobby is his summer home in Barnegat Bay. Here he loves to get into his old clothes and become carpenter, stone mason or painter, according to the current needs of his place. He swims in the ocean two or three times daily and takes long walks. In the city he devotes his spare time—what little there is—to music, the theatre and his friends.

95

Stevan Dohanos

Drawing for a Saturday Evening Post Cover

By Stevan Dohanos

IF YOU should be ushered into the living room of Stevan Dohanos' home in Westport, Connecticut, you would almost immediately notice a very unusual decorative object set in a nook by the fireplace. It would puzzle you greatly, that is, if you were not familiar with the man's character and work. To Dohanos' friends and fellow artists it is a graphic symbol of his passion for a particular kind of beauty which he sees everywhere around him. It is a telegraph pole. Or rather a model of one. Planted in a mahogany base six-by-twelve inches, this miniature replica of a telegraph pole—about eighteen inches high—faithfully reproduces its stance, its structure, its texture, its color, its weather-beaten steadfastness; all the qualities that make Steve Dohanos love telegraph poles and other common objects which most people think of as ugly, if they think about them at all. Now Steve's passion for telegraph poles and fire plugs— he has painted both from Maine to Florida—is of more than incidental interest. So you can see that the miniature telegraph pole represents something more than a hobby of collecting strange things. It reveals the man.

That pole symbolizes a selective vision through which he views the world about him. One might almost call it a sixth sense which enables him to discover beauty in unexpected places and in the most trivial objects. When Steve goes out to paint, he brings back the most surprising pictures. Once he painted a twenty-foot length of rusted railroad tracks with weeds growing up between rotting—and to him, exquisite—ties. This watercolor, by

the way, happened to be a turning point in his life. The late Edward Bruce saw it at the Whitney Museum, bought it. Later, when the Section of Fine Arts of the Treasury Department (of which Bruce was the Director) was looking for artists to send to the Virgin Islands, Dohanos was among the five lucky ones selected.

Another railroad subject is a view of a steel gondola car; not the whole car, just the lower part of it showing two wheels of one truck and the short strip of rails underneath. The drab, worn colors of the car and the roadbed are accented by the bright yellow dandelions.

Looking out of a window into his backyard he found a subject there: a revolving clothes dryer silhouetted light against the green foliage. On a wall in his living room is a watercolor of a dilapidated section of hurdle fence which has slumped from old age into a rhythmic, weathered pattern. Another picture in his studio is a watercolor of a wash-basin glorified by a ray of sunlight touching its curved rim. Steve likes signs too. In his affections they compete with telegraph poles and fire plugs. He paints them into his landscapes just as the expert sign painter would have them.

In all such commonplace items of the contemporary American scene, Dohanos finds the loveliness that others must take long journeys to seek. "No matter how drab any subject may be," he says, "there can be something whimsically beautiful in it or it becomes beautiful through accidents of light and shadow. And I try to drain every last drop of interest out of it. As an example,

an old frayed broom can catch a lovely light and cast an equally dramatic shadow, and beyond that it can suggest and recall the pattern of the daily lives of people who use it."

Texture, perhaps more than any other quality, arouses this passion for rendering commonplace things. Examine Dohanos' pictures with this in mind. And look especially for worn textures which he says "are more exciting than new ones. Anything that shows wear and tear, age and neglect, has more character than bright, new and polished surfaces."

Dohanos speaks of the "attitude" and "eloquence" of such subjects as miners' shabby shacks with their crooked clapboards and broken windowpanes, or a worn pathway through an empty lot. He asks you to note the "dignity" in the drape of an old canvas thrown over a cache of a workman's tools covered for the night.

You've got to understand this passion of his for beauty in common things to explain his spectacular success as an illustrator. And you will see, as you study his work, that his feeling for the significant in incidentals is a big factor in making his illustrations convincing. You will see that he has lavished painstaking effort on every part of his drawing, in backgrounds as well as in foregrounds.

Dohanos when asked to talk about illustration will begin with emphasis upon research, not because it is the first part of every job, but because it is—for him—perhaps the most creative part. But let us ask him to tell us in his own words just how he goes about making an illustration:

"Usually," he explains, "a story carries two or three illustrations. A lot of ideas result from reading the manuscript and I jot down all of them. I eventually pick out one as the dramatic smash that portrays an important highlight in the story and the main characters. Secondary illustrations are less pretentious and may be selected more to add local color and mood to the story.

"After all, the author describes a scene pretty well and to re-create this setting is just a job of research and posing of models. To this you add your own knowledge of nature and the way things move and exist. Your technique and ability to draw what you set out to draw finally carry it from that point to its completion. The individuality of style comes into the painting at all points—from the selection of incidents to the last brush stroke.

"An important factor is research. And I can't be too emphatic about the importance of that. I never begin a painting until I have complete and authentic information for a drawing, particularly because I work so realistically that there is no covering up a bit of ignorance with a careless stroke of the brush.

"Where do I get my material? Everywhere and anywhere; the library, the museum, in the telephone booth —calling up everyone who might have been in the locality—and of course through a visit to the spot whenever that is feasible."

In the story *Man Lost*, a serial which Dohanos illustrated for *The Saturday Evening Post*, the only weapon of primitive savages who form the background of the story was an hulche—a cunningly carved stick with which they threw their arrows. Dohanos found such a stick at the American Museum of Natural History, and, to get this detail right, he sketched the original and later carved a replica to be used by the model posing for the painting. The painting of it in the illustration carried conviction.

Procedure is best explained by taking a job and describing its course from client to artist and back to client again. Take, for example, one of his Coca-Cola advertisements. The Coca-Cola Company, in this case, merely specified the locale to be Panama. The object for the artist was to tie the product in with Army life somewhere in the Canal Zone. Emphasis was to be placed on a casual friendly incident of "sharing a coke." Here the artist chose the so-called backyard of the Canal, a far-flung outpost rather than the more formal and forbidding scenes of the Locks and the usual emphasis on large ships traversing the Canal.

Since the artist could not go to the Canal Zone area to paint from life, an elaborate search was made through Army photographs and the artist's own files for all Canal Zone material. All the bureaus of information regarding the Canal Zone were contacted. Sources of research information are limited only by the patience and energy of the individual. But this is the part of the job that contributes greatly to the success of a painting.

Finally a batch of material was ready to use for the first color sketch to show the art director. This was then approved by the client and returned to the artist. Models were posed in the correct costumes and photographed. Then painting proceeded from these photographs plus actual painting from life of the more important models who were called back to pose for the final painting. In some cases models are not photographed but painted straight away into the final painting.

Stevan Dohanos, one of a family of nine children, was born in 1907, in the mill town of Lorain, Ohio. His

"Man Lost." This is one of a series of illustrations by Dohanos for the serial "Man Lost," by C. E. Scroggins, which ran in The Saturday Evening Post from October 26th to November 16th, 1940, inclusive. It was reproduced in color. The original watercolor was 35 inches long.

Photograph of a Negro model wearing a wig and armed with an "hulche"— a throwing stick for arrows. This is one of about 25 photographs Dohanos made from this model for an illustration for "Man Lost."

school days were over when he reached the legal age of sixteen, and he then became a working man. He spent several years at various jobs until he finally succeeded in getting into an advertising art studio in Cleveland. His only preparation for an art career was a correspondence course, some evening classes at the Cleveland School of Art, and such self-instruction as he could manage through drawing during spare hours. He made innumerable linoleum cuts and woodcuts and worked in every phase and medium of art. Since that time he has pursued a combination career of fine and commercial art, winning numerous awards in each. In the fine arts field he is represented with easel and mural paintings of the American scene. His easel paintings are in museums and private collections.

A Watercolor by Stevan Dohanos

This realistic watercolor, exhibited in 1940 at the Whitney Museum, depicts a black fire plug with yellow trimmings which repeat the color of autumn leaves.

In the early days in an advertising art studio he did everything that came along: lettering, still life and layouts. All of this he considers splendid training, particularly layouts, which give a sense of composition that is basic in illustration.

Dohanos migrated to a New York studio in 1934. There he did still life subjects, salads, beverages and all manner of products. He also did many landscape studies for advertisements. The various phases of art he had experienced all began to add up in New York. With the final inclusion of figure work, which he did not develop until this point, he became a fully rounded illustrator. Knowing how to plan a picture well and then putting significant, sharp detail throughout is the best answer to why his illustrations are so successful. The artist points out, however, that sharp detail in a painting must be pulled together by a broad treatment of light, color and carefully painted edges, or else everything pops out of place. Also, the main object or figure in a painting must predominate. Too many artists fill a painting full of detail but fail to pull it together. Here is where detail can trip one up.

Through the Section of Fine Arts, Washington, D. C., he has completed three Post Office mural assignments at Elkins, West Virginia; West Palm Beach, Florida and Charlotte Amalie, Virgin Islands. In 1936 the Treasury Art Project commissioned him to paint landscapes in the Virgin Islands. He designed the 1940 Christmas Seal for the National Tuberculosis Association.

At this writing, Dohanos is best known for his *Saturday Evening Post* covers. For his subjects he selects everyday incidents in the life of John Doe, portraying a present-day Americana. These make their appeal not through clever idea or "gag" but through the artist's penetrating sense of drama in the common things of life, the same genius for revealing the importance of the unimportant that is symbolized by the artist's love of telephone poles.

One of six murals painted by Stevan Dohanos for the West Palm Beach Post Office. The theme for the series was the delivery of mail by foot from Miami to Lake Worth in the early days when the beaches and swamps were the only trails.

This wash drawing by Stevan Dohanos for the Barrett Company
won an Award for Distinctive Merit at the 21st Art Directors Exhibition

Albert Dorne

Painting by

ALBERT DORNE

for an

Anheuser-Busch Advertisement

*Drawing for an advertisement
for Hiram Walker & Sons, Inc.*

ALBERT DORNE, descendant of a family many generations in New York, was born in dire poverty in the shadow of Brooklyn Bridge. In his early teens he was seized by a driving ambition—the only serious ambition he has ever entertained. He determined to become a great commercial artist and make lots of money.

His dream has been realized; he is, in fact, one of the best and the highest paid in the field of advertising illustration.

To reach this pinnacle he has overcome obstacles that might well have daunted even an Horatio Alger hero. As a boy he suffered with heart trouble and for a time was a tuberculosis patient in a city institution. His formal education was ended in the seventh grade when he was compelled to seek his fortune in the business world. For a few years he performed such menial tasks as were open to a lad without special skills. All the time he was drawing—and dreaming. His principal god in the art world was J. C. Lyendecker who, he had heard, was paid $1,000 for a single Arrow Collar illustration.

When he was seventeen he tried to apprentice himself to Saul Tepper, now a prominent illustrator but at that time chiefly occupied as a letterer. Tepper didn't want an apprentice, couldn't afford one, but Dorne, who was bent upon learning to letter, offered his services as sweep-up and errand boy for the privilege of picking up what he could in a professional way. Here was opportunity!

In order to eat, Al secured a job as night shipping clerk with a neighboring business firm. He even managed to do some professional boxing. All this left him a bit short on sleep, but that didn't matter much; he was getting his feet on the first rungs of the ladder to fame. At the end of two years he was good for $90 a week as a letterer.

The real foundation of Dorne's career was laid in the five years that followed. During this period he worked with Alexander Rice whose studio was always busy with hack work of every description, including an account with a foreign language newspaper. He put in long hours, seven days a week, and slept in the studio which was in an office building. For many years this routine was not broken by a single vacation. However, he developed an amazing drawing facility. And speed! In Rice's place deadlines chased each other around the clock with relentless urgency. Ten illustrations a day was not an uncommon stint—it was an eighteen-hour day!

A day's work! At the week's end $300 or $400. Yes, Dorne was getting on. But he wasn't getting a thousand dollars for a single drawing so he kept his eye on the future rather than the present.

During that grind at Rice's he had learned many things besides drawing. He learned how to "sell a headline" and he learned *not to change his mind*. This is italicized for emphasis because Dorne considers it particularly important. Changing one's mind implies imperfect conception of the problem or lack of well-planned strategy before one picks up his brushes. And changing one's mind wastes time; that is particularly abhorrent to a man who is conscious of the dollar value of a minute.

Most of Dorne's present attitudes and practices were acquired through sheer necessity in Rice's studio—he never saw the inside of an art school. There simply was not time for mind-changing in the rush of work there. No time for experiments or preparatory studies. "Under such conditions," says Dorne, "a fellow just has to learn to do his experimenting in his head and do it fast."

Dorne learned his lessons well. Today, so he main-

Text continued on page 112

Advertising drawing for American Airlines, Inc.

"Hot — but not bothered" was the caption for this colored drawing for Havoline Oil, a full-page advertisement for The Texas Company. The drawing was 11 inches high. The detail of the horse's muzzle, shown below at exact size of original, demonstrates Dorne's meticulous handling of the smallest detail.

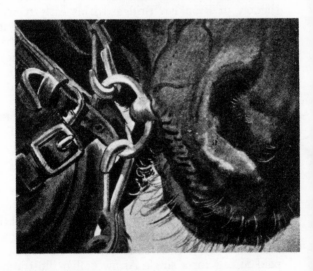

Painting (in full color) for a page advertisement for Mobilgas, Socony-Vacuum. All of Dorne's paintings are done in colored inks.

Illustration (in color) for Redbook Magazine (April 1943). The original is 6½ x 9 inches.

Illustration in color for a double-page spread in Look magazine (December 29, 1942). The original was exact size of the reproduction — 11 x 21 inches.

Sanka Coffee continuity. A full-page advertisement appearing in Life and other magazines.

Brush and black-ink drawing for an Irving Trust Company full-page advertisement. Dorne prefers a brush to pen for line work. Original drawing and line cut are 7 x 5 inches.

**Color drawing for a Havoline Oil advertisement
The original was 9 x 9½ inches**

1

Demonstrating Albert Dorne's Drawing Practice

FIRST comes the comprehensive sketch. This shown (much reduced) on opposite page (3) was made exact size of the page advertisement (10 x 14) and, of course, in full color. No preliminary studies preceded this comprehensive which was made to show the client. Lettering and type, pasted up with the colored drawing, gave the client an exact impression of the finished page.

NEXT, Dorne made a very careful drawing of the figure, table, shirt and all other properties, using an H pencil on tracing paper. For characterization he relied upon pictorial scrap of which he has plenty in his files. He dressed his assistant in the Chinaman's coat, posed him in desired action and had him photographed. The detail shown here (1) is slightly reduced from the original drawing. In illustration 6 this photograph is seen under Dorne's left hand and inseparable cigar. Slipped under the edge of his illustration board we see a photograph of the wall telephone (upper left corner) and one of the shirt and the flatiron (upper right corner). The matted comprehensive (center) lies underneath all. Dorne borrowed the iron and the spray gun from a Chinese laundry. The shirt was spread out upon a table and photographed in his studio.

2

TRANSFERRING the drawing to illustration board (2) was the next step. The drawing was blackened on the back by a soft pencil.

THE WORK was then ready for the brush. In 6 Dorne is shown painting-in the shadows with black india ink. His drawing and modeling were all done in black and gray and the color (blue in this case) was brushed over all. The effect is brilliant and the shadows are transparent, disclosing no hint of the black underpainting. Figure 5 is a reproduction of the figure as rendered in black ink, before the color had been applied. Figure 4 is reproduced from the finished painting.

DORNE scorns the use of airbrush; with his sable brush he can put the highest polish even on automobiles and other objects demanding the smoothest textures.

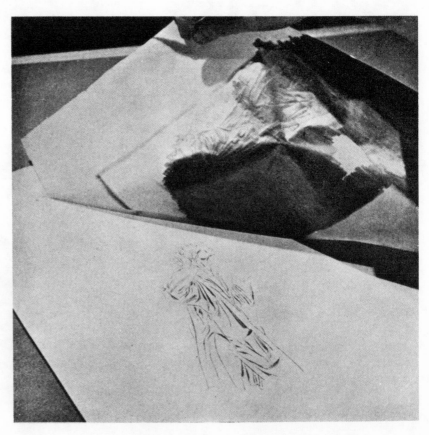

3

A FULL-PAGE
ADVERTISEMENT FOR
THE TEXAS COMPANY
Irwin Wasey & Co. Agency

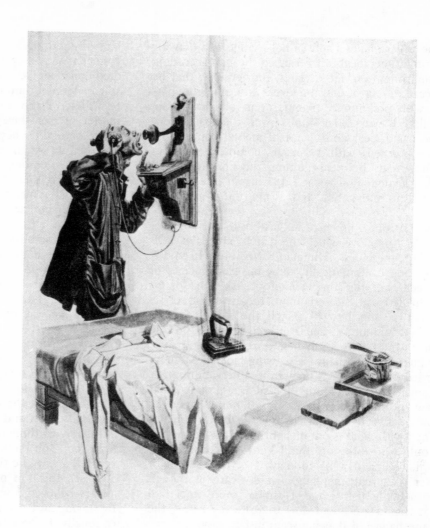

4

5

6

tains, he never makes a substantial change in a drawing or painting. Once begun it is carried through according to original intention. He declares, furthermore, that he can't recall doing a drawing over. Nor does he play around with preliminary try-outs even for those thousand-dollar drawings. He mulls over the assignment until he has a clear and complete mental conception. Then he proceeds with a careful "comprehensive" to show the client. Before beginning the final rendering he makes a meticulous pencil drawing in line. This is transferred to illustration board and the brush work begun.

Dorne attributes much of his facility to the development of his memory which, he claims, comes as near being photographic as is humanly possible. He says it now functions automatically, retaining clear images of things seen, without conscious effort. Ask him, for example, to describe the restaurant, theatre or street recently visited and he will sketch the scene with an astounding amount of detail although, while on the spot, he had not consciously memorized it. Perhaps this faculty goes far to explain his drawing facility. Memory is recorded observation. "I draw from observation rather than knowledge," says Dorne. He admits, proudly, that he knows nothing about anatomy. "I don't know the difference between the clavicle and the brain. I'm not concerned with what is out of sight. What concerns me is the outward expression; this I know by constant observation. When I want to draw a certain action or character I see that, mentally, just as clearly as though it were actually before me. I am no more uncertain about it than I am about how to write my name; the actual mechanics of drawing seem just as easy."

Faithful as Dorne's memory is, he doesn't trust it when it comes to factual details. These are checked carefully against photographic documents. He never goes out "on location" for his facts; never does he seek them at the Public Library morgue which he says he has not consulted for over a year. He has his own morgue in his New York studio, the most complete and best organized library of photographic reference I have seen in the studio of any artist. It occupies a battery of six metal, five-drawer filing cabinets. The collection is indexed in the best library cataloging manner and, needless to say, is constantly growing. An assistant, who manages Al's New York studio, spends a good part of his time clipping current magazines and filing the scrap.

Mention of this photographic library brings us to an aspect of our story which has great significance in understanding Dorne's character and his career. I refer to his executive ability.

I think I will not be contradicted by those who know Dorne, when I say that he is one of New York's most efficient business men. He himself knows this and is proud of it. "I've organized my entire life on a business basis," he explains. "I wouldn't get anywhere unless I did. Take that morgue, for example. To be sure, it costs money to maintain it, but it costs infinitely less than it would for me to spend valuable time running around looking for reference material every time a new job comes into the studio. Why, I could complete a thousand dollars' worth of drawings in the time I might lose through research for a single job."

If I have given the impression that Dorne will not look at anything less than a thousand-dollar job, I must correct it by saying that his billings include many hundred-dollar and even fifty-dollar drawings. The net result in terms of annual gross income is about the same regardless of the importance of the assignment. As a matter of fact the smaller jobs actually total to more since, naturally, they involve less study.

When an assignment comes in it is examined by the assistant, in conference with Dorne, then the assistant selects from the library all pictures he thinks Dorne could possibly need for that job. This scrap is collected in a folder and with the assignment is put in a studio cabinet, ready for use.

Dorne's establishment is otherwise well set up for the efficient conduct of his business. He employs a business manager and an accountant. The numerous details of handling orders, correspondence and billing he leaves to a secretary. "No, this is not luxury," he says, "just the businesslike way of running a business. It doesn't pay me to do anything someone else can do for me."

So Mr. Dorne sits at his drawing table all day without much interruption except for the telephone which serves to keep him in touch with clients. "I seldom call upon a client in person," he explains. "When we need to confer, there is the telephone. The client has my drawing before him and we can talk about the work just as effectively as though I were in his office. Saves a lot of time too! You know how it is when you call on a man; you tell a yarn, he tells another—a lot of time is washed away. In this I'm not thinking only of myself: I have always believed I was showing my client consideration by staying away from his office as much as possible. Occasionally, to be sure, a face-to-face is necessary; then it is apt to be a luncheon conference."

Dorne takes particular satisfaction in his versatility. He is a bit proud of his ability to hide his identity. He believes a commercial artist should, like an actor, be able to play an infinite number of roles. This is no idle boast. As I examined scores of advertisements in his studio I was surprised to discover among them many previously seen in the magazines but not recognized as Dorne's.

Another contribution to his success is his ability to execute every assignment in its entirety without calling upon some specialist for this or that detail. Many advertising drawings are the work of several specialists—one for the automobile, another for figure, another for landscape, and so on. No brush but his own touches one of Dorne's drawings, whatever the subject matter. He has appropriately been called a one-man art studio.

Dorne's originals, by the way, are rather small; some are made for little or no reduction. He believes that small scale is a safeguard against over elaboration. In small scale one is less likely to put in unessential details; the probability of faithful reproduction is greater and, in working, one has before him an almost exact impression of the effect to be seen in the printed picture.

Perhaps you haven't noticed it, but Dorne moves the sun about at will. It may be shining from several directions in the same drawing. This allows greater freedom in both composition and rendering.

For years Dorne has done all his color work with inks. His technical procedure is demonstrated in accompanying illustrations. We need only add here that he never

Drawing by
ALBERT DORNE
for the
Axton-Fisher Tobacco Co.

employs the airbrush. His trusty sables will simulate the most exactingly smooth textures; witness his rendering of automobiles.

Often Dorne is away from the city weeks on end, for he does much of his work on his farm outside Peekskill, near the Hudson River. He lives in a beautiful pre-Revolutionary house and has converted the enormous old barn into a studio. His day often begins at five in the morning and lasts well into the night. He works about as hard as he ever did. "Success," he says, "sometimes makes a man careless. You know it would be pretty easy for me to turn out work a little short of my best, I do it so automatically. I'm on my guard against that, and actually work infinitely harder and much longer on my drawings now than I used to several years ago."

However, he takes time out between jobs for shooting—his favorite outdoor sport—and for four-wall handball. He also spends many hours working in his vegetable garden, and gives even more time to his chickens, often numbering above a thousand.

If you expect to see him painting at the edge of the woods you will be disappointed. Much as he enjoys the fine arts, he has never painted an easel picture, nor has he any desire to do so. He doesn't even carry a sketchbook, has never done sketching of any kind. This is consistent with Dorne's whole attitude toward art. Drawing, for him, is a busines tool. You would no more expect to see him making a drawing for fun or for the good of his soul, than to find a plumber in his shop of a Sunday making wipe joints just because he loved to make wipe joints. Drawing and wipe joints are means to an end—the same end really.

You mustn't think from this that Dorne doesn't thoroughly enjoy drawing and painting: he is never having more fun than when bent over his drawing board. You know that, if you are at all familiar with his work. It is wholly expressive of an amazing zest for life and rollicking good humor.

Dorne's humorous drawings are well known to every one who notices the art of the nation's advertising. His humor is by no means confined to those illustrations consciously directed in lighter vein. Examine the action in any drawing where figures are incidental and you will usually discover that Dorne has had a lot of fun with them.

Examples of Dorne's work shown in this chapter are reproductions of advertising drawings. Since this story was written in 1943, Dorne's story illustrations have appeared in the Post and other magazines.

Albert Dorne is in his forties, and is five feet, nine inches tall. He has jet black hair—thinning—and bushy, black eyebrows that shadow piercing, black eyes. In physique as well as professional accomplishment our hero presents a dramatic contrast with the sickly lad on New York's lower East Side, who, without a chance in the world, set out to be "a great commercial artist and make lots of money."

Harvey Dunn

"In Search of an Eldorado"   **Illustration by Harvey Dunn for The Saturday Evening Post**

Reproduced by special permission of The Saturday Evening Post, copyright 1938 by The Curtis Publishing Company

HARVEY DUNN

Milestone in the Tradition of American Illustration

"TEACHING is the most important work I have ever done." That is what Harvey Dunn told me—with deep conviction—as we sat together in his studio in Tenafly, New Jersey.

Such a declaration will surprise many who, conscious of Dunn's brilliant career as an illustrator, can conceive of no greater satisfaction for an artist than the success and acclaim with which his creative genius might reward him. But it will come as no surprise to his many students who have learned that a great teacher is first of all a great lover of mankind.

I can hear Harvey Dunn's booming laughter as he reads what I am writing about him, and most likely he will exclaim, "As good a graveside eulogy, by the lord Harry, as any man could ask." That's how he characterized a recent biographical essay from which I am going to quote below.

It was nothing more than interest in the other fellow that prompted the establishment of that school of illustration which Harvey Dunn and Charles S. Chapman opened in an old farmhouse in Leonia in the summer of 1915.

In order to make things as easy for the boys as possible, Dunn and Chapman sold art supplies to them at cost, got them subsistence jobs in the town, found suitable rooms for them, even undertook to feed them on a cost basis.

That Leonia enterprise was the beginning of what came to be known as the Dunn School of Illustration. Although the Leonia class was short-lived, Dunn continued to teach informally in subsequent years. Students flocked to his studio, bringing their work for criticism. Many of our best-known contemporary illustrators are among those who learned much about picture making— and about life—from Harvey Dunn.

Dean Cornwell, perhaps Dunn's most famous student, was one of that first group of thirty-four to meet in the old Leonia farmhouse. Recalling his experiences there, Cornwell said: "I gratefully look back on those days I was privileged to sit at Harvey Dunn's feet. That was before World War No. 1; and Mr. Dunn was under 35 years. He taught with a view of preparing one to live happily for a long time, and to live soundly. Because in those days there was nothing but peace and contentment to look forward to; as contrasted to any attempt to study today, when a student doesn't even know whether there will be a magazine tomorrow—to say nothing of being drafted, or enlisting. [This was written in 1943.] I stress his youth and the picture of his time because he was then in a state of maximum exuberance during the rarest part of his life when, as I have said, the world was an awfully nice place to live in.

Harvey Dunn

"Mr. Dunn taught art and illustration as one. He taught it as a religion—or awfully close to such. He taught it with such reverence that he never permitted the student to view a picture resting upon the floor. He believed that if work was worth showing it was worth the ennoblement of lifting it up above the eyeline.

"He taught us to use imagination at a time when such publications as *Life*, and rotogravures were unheard of. Travel data was very scarce and when found was of very poor photographic quality as compared with modern printed matter.

"During the summers in Leonia every man was supposed to be at work at his easel at 8:00 a.m. sharp. If a man was not, the punishment was 'no criticism for that day.' Many students thought they were getting away with something by rushing down and sleepily stroking a brush across the canvas—without having had any breakfast; then when Mr. Dunn left they would sneak back into bed and get some more sleep. Curiously enough most of those boys, despite their cleverness, are not in the art business at the present time.

"In the evening (in Leonia) everyone met at one or another's studio for what we called 'composition parties.' Each of us would make, in line, what he considered the worst possible composition he was capable of producing. This was handed to the man on his right who was supposed to make it into an exciting and attractive picture by the clever placing of the source of light and the disposition of the light and dark masses— without altering any of the original lines. It goes without saying that we had many nights a week sketching from a live model, and the very presence of Dunn, who always drew, made one ashamed to just come off with an ordinary art-school-like drawing. His personality demanded one get that 'something.'

"Dunn taught dramatic viewpoints based on the truth of human existence, as against artificial, theatrical effect. He used to say, 'Take liberty, but not license.' And preached tonal values 24 hours a day! It was probably the only illustration school, since my time, where students learned to relate a human figure to truthful outdoor surroundings. A great part of our training during the short time we studied with him was still life on rainy days and landscape painting part of every other day. These landscapes were not from the viewpoint of pretty pictures to please tourists, but an attempt to understand what takes place in nature at all times and under all conditions. No good Dunn student of my day was ever without a pad or sketch box; and I think we developed an unusual memory and ability to observe.

Recently Harvey Dunn revisited the scenes of boyhood days. He made this pencil sketch of Manchester, So. Dakota, three miles from his birthplace. "It's much the same as it was," he says, "except that the whiskers have grown a little longer."

We learned to see the most complicated outdoor scene always in tonal value and to render this on a very small scale with a lead pencil, always translating into three tones that which was before us. We used to do this on small scratch pads—smaller than a postcard—and I would say it was the most valuable training of any I can recall.

"I might say that Dunn individualized all teaching. To some he'd say, 'only paint with a 2-inch brush'—if they were inclined to be too niggling. While to others, who were sloppy or too loose, he'd threaten to make them do a large drawing with a pencil point.

"Dunn, in his teaching, was more concerned with the essential spirit of the work than with technical procedures. He never taught what kind of brushes or what kind of paint to use. It was merely whether the result had anything in common with the excitement of human existence. It's true that some of his students couldn't help proceeding with a picture much in his manner, but this was never insisted upon.

"Perhaps the most valuable thing that Dunn taught us was honest dealing with our fellow men and a constant gratitude to the Maker above for the privilege of seeing the sun cast shadows. In other words Dunn taught a basic American philosophy."

Harvey Dunn is one of the vital links in the tradition of American illustration, a link joined to Howard Pyle, that founder of the tradition, whose school in Wilmington, Delaware, Dunn attended for two years. From Wilmington, Dunn brought more than the influence and instruction of his famous teacher; there he met Johanne L. Krebs whom he married in 1908.

But let Harvey Dunn tell his story in his own words as they were written in a letter to H. Dean Stallings, librarian of Lincoln Memorial Library of South Dakota State College, this in response to a request from the Library for a biographical sketch. A factual record could be contained in an inch of type, but these words of Harvey Dunn tell more about him than anyone else can write:

"A buffalo trail ran due north and south just east of the Redstone Creek, Dakotah Territory, cutting across its meandering bends and going for many miles in both directions. The town of Manchester is about three-quarters of a mile to the west of it and, between the two, the section line parallels it as far as to the jog a little ways north of Carthage. Three miles south of Manchester on this road, and one mile east, Thomas Dunn filed on a homestead, the west forty of which was bisected by the buffalo trail. Sixty rods east of the trail and about forty rods north of a section line, he built a claim shanty measuring seven by nine feet with six-foot posts. This was in 1881. Two years later this became a lean-to, attached to a much larger building, a twelve by sixteen foot structure with a not too over-sized attic.

"Cottonwood and box elders had been planted north of the house and their leaves shimmered as they danced in the summer sun.

"On the morning of March 7, 1884, before daylight, Thomas Dunn started for De Smet driving his yoke of steers. Arriving there, he made his purchases, among them a sewing machine which was carefully lifted into the wagon. Its varnished height gleamed above the wagon box before being covered with a buffalo robe, hair side in for greater protection. Snow was driving before a brisk wind on the morning of the eighth so that the stable was scarcely visible, and the hens stayed in.

"Along about ten o'clock, it is said that a great squalling and general hubbub arose in the house. For the first time, I had lifted up my voice in a new world.

"Four years later, Thomas Dunn having bought the preemption rights on the southern half of Section 29, Town 110, Range 57, and sold his homestead, moved his family and house, south, down the buffalo trail, three miles.

"The house moved sedately along on its four wagons with the appropriate number of oxen to the accompaniment of 'Whoa, Haw, Gee!' and the sharp snap of whips. I remember how high it loomed against the sky, an unusual and moving thing to me in more than one way, as it went down along the flat across Uncle Ben's place. The house was set on a knoll thirty rods east of the trail and one hundred north of the south line.

*Illustration by Dunn for a story about the oyster pirates
of the Chesapeake, in American Magazine*

"There I lived until I was seventeen years old, and the buffalo trail was plowed under. When the glimmering along the horizon got too much for me, I set out to find the shining palaces which must exist beyond it somewhere.

"I was seventeen and went to Brookings. 'Old North' was sombre against a sober first day of November sky. An old surrey stood astride the roof, its dilapidated fringes stirring in the wind.

"Dr. Brown saw me the next day; he seemed a severe and scholarly man. I had my doubts about a college education. The grade school District Number One, Esmond Township, did not equip for that. At any rate, all I was truly interested in was the Art course. So to keep me from mischief, they gave me English, Algebra and Physics and I failed them all. I took the Art, and there met that little lady, Ada B. Caldwell, who opened vistas for me. For the first time I had found a serious, loving, and intelligent interest in what I was vaguely searching for. She seemed to dig out talent where none had been, and she prayed for genius. She was tolerant and the soul of goodness. With my eyes on the horizon, she taught me where to put my feet.

"Oh, I have lived in a beautiful world and have known the warmth of much human kindness. The native sweetness of people clutches at my very heart.

"I studied at the Art Institute of Chicago. I say *studied*, advisedly, for little should be said about that. I should perhaps better say that I availed myself of the splendid freedom given me in that institution to pursue the activities nearest my heart, making some progress, with the kindliest advice given me by understanding instructors. This was from November 21, 1902, to November, 1904, when I went to Wilmington, Delaware, and really studied under that grand old man, Howard Pyle, whose main purpose was to quicken our souls that we might render service to the majesty of simple things.

"I was with him for two years, when one day after looking at my work, he sighed deeply, and, in the voice of a tired and disappointed old man, suggested that I get a studio somewhere and see if I could get some work to do; and I did both.

"I cannot claim that it was due to my wisdom that I picked the best time since the Civil War to enter upon the activity I did, for at the time it was just beginning to be realized by advertisers that the weekly and monthly periodicals offered a splendid field; and a great wave of advertising swept the country, on a flood of new magazines, and to supply these, illustrators were in great demand. The long-haired, flowing-tie artist disappeared, and in his place was a business man making $10,000 or more per year. While my own income never got very far into the five-figure class, I never believed that I was really worth what I received.

"Of course these things can't last; they didn't anyway, and now many of those same illustrators, with their wives, look with hungry eyes into the delicatessen window. *Sic transit gloria mundi!*

"I have been called many things, among them an artist, an illustrator for the leading periodical publications, a painter of mural decorations, am a member of various art societies, such as the Salmagundi Club of New York, Society of Illustrators, Artists Guild, Associate Member of the National Academy, art instructor at the Art Students League and Grand Central School of Art in New York.

"I was one of eight official artists commissioned Captains of Engineers' corps with the A.E.F. in 1918; the work done there is now in the Smithsonian Institution at Washington, D. C.

"My work during the past forty years has been of such character that I have made a good living, and it has given me some authority in the field of art. My credit is good, my judgment fair, and I use glasses only for reading.

"I find that I prefer painting pictures of early South Dakota life to any other kind, which would seem to point to the fact that my search of other horizons has led me around to my first."   *Harvey Dunn*

Many important events in Harvey Dunn's life find no mention in his letter. He does not speak, for example, of his civic activities in Tenafly. I am careful to avoid the term "political" because Dunn is no politician. But through a conscience which urged him to contribute his services to his community he found himself running for mayor about ten years ago.

"I was mortally afraid I might be elected," declared Dunn, "and I didn't know what to do about it. As it turned out I needn't have worried. I found I had eight friends in town who came forward handsomely and voted for the rival candidate. My gratitude to them was unbounded." (However, Dunn has been active in civic affairs; among other things, serving as president of the Board of Education.)

But let us get back to those early years when Harvey Dunn, lured from the farm by the "glimmering along the horizon," set out for Chicago to begin his formal art study. His account of his first encounter with art and civilization is much more than a good story; it expresses those qualities of clear vision and directness which are so characteristic.

"When I arrived in Chicago," said Dunn, "I was wild as the cattle back home—in the same way and for the same reason—I hadn't been penned up. And I was unfamiliar with the sight of man. All I knew about art was that I wanted to be an artist. Well, I got down there in Chicago and found my way into the Art Institute. Wandering through the halls I came to Room 90. It was a great, dark, gloomy room. Under a single electric light was a professor with eye glasses attached to a conspicuous black cord. I asked a fellow in the hall what was going on in there. 'Oh,' he said, 'that is a composition class.' 'What is composition?' I asked. 'Why that's learning how to put things together to make a picture,' he explained patiently. I couldn't see much sense in that. Seemed to me if you knew what you wanted to put in the picture all you had to do was to put it in. But I concluded there must be more to this art business than meets the eye. So I went in.

"The instructor was teaching composition. Three five-inch circles had been drawn on a piece of paper and he was suggesting how to improve the composition by varying the relative positions of those circles. Those who brought in good arrangements of the circles in outline would be advanced to the privilege of making shaded circles, from black to white, in their compositions.

"That night, in my room, I filled several sheets of paper with circles drawn with the aid of a coffee can. Every one looked the same, and I gave up.

"But I couldn't give up the idea of being an artist; it was too deep in me. I wanted to make pictures. And that night I tried to make a picture. A covered wagon—one of a wagon train—bogged down in the mire of the muddy trail, a melancholy and lonesome night, a man on horseback in the foreground. Dusk of a rainy day. Mist dripped from a low-hanging sky, the kind of mist that chills to the bone and saturates your clothing, covering it with myriads of little silver balls.

"Well, I made the picture as best I could and the next morning rolled it up and took it to school. I avoided Room 90; decided to try the senior composition class. Fred Richardson was the instructor there. My drawing was tacked up with the others and Richardson pointed to it at once. He approved of it, called

attention to its compositional virtues: masses, balances, oppositions, lines, etc. I listened, but I didn't know what he was talking about—and still don't."

This story gives more than a hint of what Harvey Dunn means when he says, "Art schools teach the complexities; I teach the simplicities."

I don't know whether Harvey Dunn has what he would admit is a teaching philosophy. But a few of his sayings culled from student criticisms are revealing:

"When the foundation is laid, that's when I step out. I don't want to direct any man's destiny.

"I repeat and repeat. Yet there's little to say. Little to know in order to make pictures. But that little seems very hidden from those who need it.

"Pictures cannot be helped by following my suggestions here, changing them according to my criticism. Criticism is made from one perception, and when you change your picture accordingly, you probably haven't the same perception. You wonder if the instructor means this, or that. You're wrong in changing it.

"I have nothing to do with you and with your way of looking at things. You must paint according to your perceptions.

"The only purpose in my being here is to get you to think pictorially. I try to find an entrance into your minds, try to find some channel of freedom for you.

"All of which puts in other words what Frank Jewett Mather has said: 'I have taught enough myself to know that one actually teaches only a poor student, at best one merely clarifies, releases and enhances a personal predisposition—really gives him no new ideas, but saves him some time in finding his own.'"

What Dunn has to say about ideas and letting them take full control of the process of picture making will always be remembered by his students:

"You'll never 'think up' an idea. We confuse ideas and thoughts. An idea is not something you 'cook up.' It comes to you when your consciousness is open and receptive. It presents itself. Say to yourself, 'Here's an idea, what is it going to do with *me?*—not what am I going to do with *it?*' Let the idea direct your energies. Whatever you put in your picture, take out; an idea won't run in double harness with human opinion.

"A picture, I find, that I'm afraid to tackle and put off doing till I must, because it seems difficult, is often the kind that dances right along. I believe it's because, approached like that, in humble attitude, it leads the way. I'd be careful, awfully careful. I am willing to follow it because I recognize I can't drive it.

"Picture making is just like a song. You don't sing it your own damned way, you try to follow the song.

"If your first layout is good but you begin to ruin it after two or three hours, lay it aside and start another picture. Then when you go back to the first you can see just what you need to finish it; and you can go at it with cold intelligence rather than the heat of the beginning—and you won't burn it up. It will be as though you were looking at another's work. It's the minute you take possession of the idea that the idea departs—and it always will, to the end of time.

"When a fellow's thoroughly whipped—and you've got to be whipped before you finish a picture—when he's thoroughly discouraged, then he's willing to *do it the picture's way.*"

Carl Erickson

THERE IS NO REASON, of course, why the suave delineator of chic femininity, whose drawings for twenty years have given poignance to America's smartest fashion magazine, should not have been born in Joliet, Illinois.

But it would not be expected. Such graphic sophistication one might insist must emanate from an artist Parisian born and Parisian bred.

Erickson, as a matter of fact, has lived most of his professional life in France—from 1920, in the early years of his career, until 1940. With his wife and daughter he left France several weeks after its occupation by Hitler's legions; taking with him no more of his goods and chattels than could be jammed into a few suitcases. However, he had his fortune in his hands; he needed nothing but a brush and a little color to reestablish himself back home.

Here he was right on Vogue's doorstep ready to continue his monthly contributions which have appeared in that magazine without interruption since 1923. He was also within arm's length of national advertisers who at once began to compete for his elegant drawings, as French merchants had done previously.

It was Victor Hugo, I believe, who was asked if the writing of epic poetry were not tremendously difficult. His classic reply, "Easy or impossible!", may appropriately be applied to such drawings as come from Erickson's inspired brush. They give the impression of having sprung to life without suffering the usual labor pains. But his performance looks too easy; its nonchalance is deceptive. It is *not* accomplished without a struggle. Erickson, indeed, is a hard-working man, a very serious artist who is usually practicing when not actually performing. For every piece of work reproduced in the magazines he has made dozens of studies. In spare moments he is usually busy drawing or painting from the model—he never draws without a model—and his sketchbook goes with him to the restaurant and the theatre. Although few are aware of it, he has done a lot of painting in oil, principally portraits.

All of which is no denial of Victor Hugo's epigram. Erickson's particular genius is pretty much a gift of the gods, even though he has met the gods considerably more than half way.

Erickson's art is primarily an art of line. Color may be added, as more often than not it is; but the net result is a colored line drawing. His greatness as a draftsman is best demonstrated, I think, in spontaneous drawings which he is under no compulsion to adapt to the ulterior purposes of publishers or advertisers. The silk-hatted cabby for example. In such drawings, particularly, his line, unrestrained by commercial exactions, is spirited, vibrating and tremendously expressive. A group of superb portraits in charcoal line ought to be mentioned in this connection for they demonstrate a facet of the artist's talent that is not well-known to the public; his published work being largely appropriated by the world

A brush drawing by Erickson — a preliminary study in black and white wash for a Vogue illustration that appeared in color. The original is 12 x 15 inches. Reproduced by permission of Vogue.

This charcoal drawing (from model) typifies
Erickson's genius in portraying feminine elegance.
The original drawing is 16 x 20 inches.

*The drawing on the page opposite
was made from a New York cabby
who is still to be seen in and about
Central Park. It is reproduced at
exact size of the original.*

of fashion wherein his rare appreciation of feminine charm is matched by his great ability to give it graphic reality.

Erickson is an impulsive worker. Standing at his board, which is tilted at a slight angle, he attacks the paper with a free arm thrust that reminds one of a fencer wielding his foil. The drawing isn't always good. Indeed the studio floor may be littered with innumerable trials before one is finally certified by that well-known signature, "Eric." There is no such thing as "fixing-up" an Erickson drawing: if it is not right as it first springs directly from his hand, it must be discarded and a fresh attempt made. The artist would no more think of going back to correct an error than would a musician during a concert performance.

Erickson's line drawings are usually rendered in Wolff pencil, charcoal or chinese ink. This latter comes in cakes or sticks which have to be ground in water in a small mortar designed for the purpose. It will yield a jet black or produce any tone of gray, depending upon the saturation of the mixture. Erickson finds it very responsive for black and white work and likes the way it behaves when color is applied over it. His color is pure watercolor or gouache depending upon the special need. He uses brushes of various kinds: bristle, sable and oriental brushes in bamboo handles. His bristle brushes are reserved principally for gouache.

Erickson's formal art training was brief. Two years in the Chicago Academy of Fine Arts gave him his start as a commercial artist. For a few years he did advertising illustrations in Chicago, his work being important enough to become known abroad. When he went to France he found a ready market for the products of his brush, illustrating French publications and doing drawings for advertising agencies. He was soon discovered by Vogue and, in 1923, his long association with Conde Nast publications began. His career has been a happy one in which his great talent has been recognized by almost constant demand.

*Here the artist is grinding a stick of oriental
ink which is his favorite medium for wash.
He combines it with his color mediums too.*

John Gannam

John Gannam chooses a comfortable chair, in his well-appointed living room, for the reading of a manuscript. As he reads he makes rough sketches, on his tracing pad, of picture possibilities in the story.

John Gannam's first art hero was an Indianapolis blacksmith. This swarthy "primitive" dipped brushes into cans of ordinary house paint and, stroke by stroke on the surface of a wood panel, created the image of a clipper ship under full sail. In the spell of this miracle the ten-year-old lad went home and tried to reproduce the smithy's masterpiece. The seed had been planted.

Frederick Remington was the instigator of his next artistic sensation. A small group of Remington illustrations exhibited in the window of a bookshop became John's art gallery. He hurried to the window every day after school as long as the pictures remained there. After supper he attempted to copy from memory the scenes that particularly fascinated him.

When John was fourteen his father died. The boy, forced to become breadwinner, left school and went to work at such tasks as could be found for willing but unskilled hands. There was little time or thought for drawing, though, as Gannam puts it, he was always "nursing the urge." An urge that occasionally got him into trouble, as it did at Chicago's famous Blackstone Hotel where he was employed for a few months. One day he discovered the menus. They were printed upon such fine paper! A surface as inviting for one's pencil as could be imagined. So it was that original Gannams managed occasionally to bob up in the dining room, a circumstance that did not brighten John's already tarnished reputation with the management.

After his debacle at the Blackstone, he spent four years at such varied occupations as running errands, operating elevators and working in machine shops, until at eighteen he found himself on a path that he vaguely felt he was destined to follow: he was working in an engraving shop. Here, he was only a messenger boy but he was in the presence of art, and by hanging around nights he could learn much about lettering, drawing and the way artists work.

This engraving shop job was more a matter of chance than intention, for until then John's artistic yearnings were quite inarticulate; they had not crystallized into any purpose. Even now, he sensed direction rather than plan. At any rate he was on his way. After a year or so in this shop and a few months in an illustration studio, still in the capacity of messenger, he secured employment in a fashion studio. By this time he was beginning to envision some sort of art career, although he could not even hope for a formal art education.

To be sure, he had once been in art school. While working at the Blackstone Hotel he had enrolled for a part-time course at the Chicago Academy of Fine Arts. This was of short duration. There was not enough energy left for study after his long working hours; and at the end of two weeks he was obliged to quit, never again to darken the door of any art school.

But now he took his education into his own hands. He pursued it fanatically. He charted his own course and carried it out with the meager means at his command. His was not a program likely to be applauded by art school directors, but its ultimate success would seem to demonstrate that school *curriculum* is far less important than student *purpose*.

John knew he had to learn how to draw the figure. Lacking art school models he discovered one in an antique shop: a bronze nude that had been given a heavy coat of thick green paint, a patina that added nothing to its virtue as a figure model. But he thought this would serve. And serve it did: he declares he made literally thousands of drawings of that dingy nude, the only model he had until years later when he hired living models for the execution of commissioned work. Photographs from the fashion studio files also served as models; and, as for examples of art work, he was surrounded by the drawings of illustrators employed at the studio. These he analyzed and copied whenever he got

130

A few of the many watercolor sketches made by Gannam merely as studies of a theme that interested him; not for an illustration or even a finished picture. The largest of these originals is about 12 x 18 inches. They demonstrate an almost fanatical pursuit of an idea, once it has obsessed him.

the chance. Soon he acquired sufficient skill to be trusted with rendering the hands and feet of fashion drawings.

After leaving this job Gannam set himself up as a free lance, executing commissions for $10 or $12, with a weekly take of around $30. That was spectacular success! But before long he was getting $60 a week at Grauman's. He continued to devote every spare hour of his time to drawing, emulating the work of top-flight artists with whom he rubbed elbows in this big Chicago studio. He recalls that he became able to make quite impressive samples, but that when he attempted commissioned work his skill seemed to desert him.

In 1926 he packed up his beautiful samples and took them to Detroit to the studios of Gray, Garfield & Ladriere, where a friend had advised him to demand $200 a week. "You know," said Gannam, recalling this incident, "that was one of the hardest things I ever tried to do. It's not easy to say '$200' when you're not used to it. But I managed to do it. The chilly silence that ensued confirmed my fears. I could hardly keep from gathering up my samples and attempting escape before the arrival of the police. But things were not as bad as they appeared. I was offered $135 to start, with the promise of the higher figure a bit later.

"Having got the job," continued Gannam, "my next anxiety was to hold it. But a miracle happened. Yes, it really was amazing the way my facility blossomed out in this Detroit workshop. Every drawing I touched came out beautifully. All my desperate struggles appeared suddenly to have come to an end."

Gannam spent four years in Detroit. All his work was in black and white, principally in drybrush. But on his own time he kept practicing in color, experimenting with various mediums and techniques. When he came to New York in 1930 he was prepared for anything, and found a ready market awaiting him in the advertising agencies.

But he had his eye on the magazines too, and as soon as he could prepare sample illustrations he called on that much beloved art director of Woman's Home Companion, Henry Quinan. Since then Gannam has illustrated for all the magazines and his pictures are usually reproduced in color. At present he is seen in Good Housekeeping, Cosmopolitan and Ladies' Home Journal. He continues to devote a portion of his time to advertising.

Two years ago he spent six spring and summer months in Canaan, Connecticut, his only real vacation in the past five years. He brought back 100 pounds of watercolors and pastels—not exhibition pieces, not a single picture has found its way into a frame. Unmatted, they are jammed into cabinets or thrown into a studio closet. They constitute an amazing record of intensive nature study. · A few, very few, are meticulously rendered landscapes; most of them are rapid sketches of effects: a girl in yellow sweater against the leaden sky of an approaching storm; a naked boy standing in a sunlit pool; meadows, hills and roads, seen under all conditions of light and atmosphere; waters of the Housatonic River tumbling over its stony bed—there must be fifty of these. Seeking the source of color not explained by reflections of sky and foliage, John waded out in the river, in hip boots, to ascertain the

color of the hidden rocks. One day he worked from misty dawn till dark doing innumerable color studies of his white house. He followed the sun around, sketching the structure from every direction and in the varying aspects of light throughout the day.

Light—that's what fascinates Gannam; light, color, values. He talks about values more than anything else, declaring that "in watercolor, values practically do the trick."

Gannam seldom paints on location. This may be due in part to timidity; he says he would have to pack up his sketching traps and flee if someone should happen to come along. But the more significant reason is that painting from memory is, for him, more rewarding. "How," he asks, "can a painter's brush keep up with nature's fleeting effects? I get the impression, try to fix it in my mind, then go home and record it. Word descriptions," he says, "have, for me, a tremendous power for fixing a visual impression. I've found that written notes, jotted down in the small notebook I always carry, are more valuable than an attempt to paint an effect that would be different five minutes after the first brush stroke." If a companion is along, John likes to describe the effect for him, otherwise he may talk to himself about it. He believes that observation is more searching when it is acting for the memory than when used for immediate transcription.

He often returns to his subject again and again, checking his sketches against further observation. It is not unusual for him to paint an elusive effect many times until he feels he has captured it. He is always after broad, if subtle, effects rather than detail: tries to reduce things to their simplest possible expression.

I have dwelt at some length upon Gannam's "vacation" because what he did in those six months demonstrates the way he keeps his finger on nature's pulse, and gives more than a hint of his approach to illustration problems. It helps to account for the vitality of his work. John is not satisfied with standardized statements, repeating them again and again, no matter how pleasing these might be. He tries to invigorate his work with the kind of surprises that nature uses to clothe the most ordinary objects with unexpected beauty.

That kind of study is, of course, not confined to the days of a rare vacation. Back in town, research continues. The only difference is in subject matter. City streets and their activity take the place of hills and meadows. Columbus Circle in a dense fog; buildings looming against a moonlit sky; a spectacular fire—sunlight cutting through dense clouds of smoke, and the red splash of fire engines: such are the objects of his study. Sometimes a certain effect of light or color becomes an obsession that is nursed for long periods, until finally understood and mastered. Gannam worried four years about the rendering of a brilliantly illuminated theatre marquee on a rainy night. Finally, after much trial and error, he mastered the problem, then brushed it aside to make room for yet another obsession.

In present-day illustration the artist is usually handed a definite layout for his drawing, along with the manuscript. "It is our usual practice," says the art director

The color illustration on the page opposite appeared in Good Housekeeping magazine

John Gannam, in his studio, surveys a comprehensive sketch for an illustration in Good Housekeeping. Strips of film from his Super Ikonta B camera hang on the door jamb. The lay figure patiently awaits the next pose. Empty coffee cups bear witness to the artist's insistence upon a clean cup for each fresh drink — of which there may be half a dozen at one sitting.

of one of our biggest mass magazines, "not to have illustrators make their own layouts. From experience we have learned that when they do we get either too much variety (in the design of the magazine as a whole) or too little. It is always our practice, however, to permit changes where illustrators have ideas for improvements. Often, when he begins to pose his models, an illustrator will get a much better layout conception than ours."

The illustrator, it would seem, gets a lot more fun out of the assignment—therefore puts more into it—when he is permitted to serve as creator rather than filler-in of someone else's conception. Looked at as a cold business proposition, an illustrator has much to gain from this modern procedure of magazine makeup: he is handed his assignment half done, and need not worry about suiting art director and editor when he follows their blueprint for his picture. Gannam, however, is one who insists upon *creating* his illustrations, and the art directors for whom he works have the intelligence to want him to do so.

Thus, at the outset, we find John engrossed in his manuscripts, a pad and pencil handy for notations of illustrative possibilities. Then comes the graphic

struggle with countless pencil and brush sketches. First ideas are as likely as later ones to be the best, but he won't be satisfied until he has worked all around the problem. He says he spends far more time in preparatory study and gets more fun out of it than in the execution of the finished painting.

When he has a satisfactory rough, and it has been approved by the publication, he summons models, poses and photographs them in the action of his composition. When it comes to the final painting, he is likely to dress his lay figure in the costumes worn by the models.

His pictures invariably are executed in transparent watercolor with whatever opaque painting may be necessary for the delineation of detail. Although he has painted in oil, he greatly prefers watercolor and believes he has barely tapped its possibilities.

Gannam employs the camera in his illustration work, as do all but a few of the older men who grimly resist this *sine qua non* of modern illustration—a reminder that the education of the modern illustrator has been complicated by the addition of this new tool to his bag of tricks. "It took me almost as long to acquire camera skill as to master my brush," says Gannam.

One of a series of illustrations by John Gannam for Pacific Mills

The camera has indeed created a new set of working conditions. It has revolutionized the modeling profession; few models, at least the best of them, will consent to pose hour on hour while an artist paints at his easel. And their prices would make such a performance impractical. Grade A models demand as high as $25 an hour; Triple X come even higher; the average, around $10. On the credit side of this situation is the availability of the finest types of both men and women attracted by a very pleasant and lucrative profession.

If the camera has had a generally baneful consequence upon illustration—many say so—John Gannam's accomplishment suggests that the fault lies more with artists than with their new tool which, like all tools, should be evaluated by its performance in the hands of a creator. Gannam doesn't let the camera do his *thinking* for him. If he discarded it entirely we would observe no change, either for better or for worse, in his illustrations.

Gannam is in no sense analytical; he works intuitively —and pays the price, for, he says, he "is always in a stew." He objects, however, to being called "temperamental," in view of the popular connotations "cantankerous," "petulant," with particular reference to the traditional cussedness of screen and opera stars. But Webster defines temperament as, "The characteristic of an individual which is revealed in his proneness to certain feelings, moods and desires, and which may depend upon the glandular and chemical characteristics of his constitution." My investigations have not gone far enough to authorize me to comment upon either glandular or chemical factors but Johnny, as he is known to his intimates, certainly is "prone to certain feelings, moods and desires." He has to whip himself up to his creative best—says his urge comes in waves—and then when the spell is on him he is upset by even the slightest interruption. He dare not venture from his studio, fearing that the creative mood might be side-tracked, perhaps through the chance meeting of an acquaintance who would start him thinking about politics or the war. This fear has actually led him to dodge friends on the street. "And," he confides, "a five o'clock date will spoil the entire day for me. I keep thinking about it, am uneasy in mind. It's a sort of threat hanging over me. To interrupt my work for a whole day would be absolutely fatal. I'd have to begin all over again." He says there are times when he scarcely leaves his studio for two weeks. During such periods he has meals cooked and delivered by the maid service in the building. Although he is conscious of no organic disorder, he predicts that his death will come through heart failure when the telephone rings on a closing date.

135

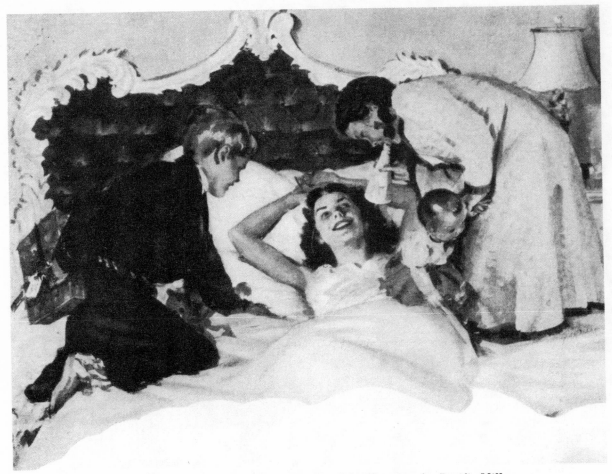

One of a series of illustrations by John Gannam for Pacific Mills

Gannam's studio apartment is on 67th Street, just off Central Park West, in a section that probably houses more artists than any other area of comparable extent in New York. Callers are ushered into his large, beautifully furnished living room which often serves as a setting for his illustrations.

The studio, a smaller room, faces the north. It is a pretty messy place when an illustration is a-borning. Sketches, sprinkled with cigarette butts and ashes, litter the floor and paint-cabinets; soiled coffee cups mingle with paints and brushes. (Gannam is fastidious when it comes to coffee. If he consumes six cups of the beverage during an afternoon—he brews his own on a small gas stove— there will be that many cups to wash in the evening.) A sizeable foyer, between living room and studio, is large enough comfortably to accommodate cameras, lights and lay figure. Off the foyer are a well-equipped dark room, a bedroom and bathroom. In the corner of his bedroom stands an expensive "Exercycle," acquired three years ago in a burst of physical culture enthusiasm. He got on it just once and, to use his own words, "There the damn thing sits rusting its insides out." The only exercise he takes is an occasional walk in Central Park.

Gannam is a bit on the heavy side, for his height; his weight is 160 pounds and he is 5 ft. 6 in. tall. He has a swarthy complexion and ever so little dark brown hair. He is a great favorite of the boys, and he invariably adds to the merriment of any company.

Painting by John Gannam for Air Transport Association

Glenn Grohe

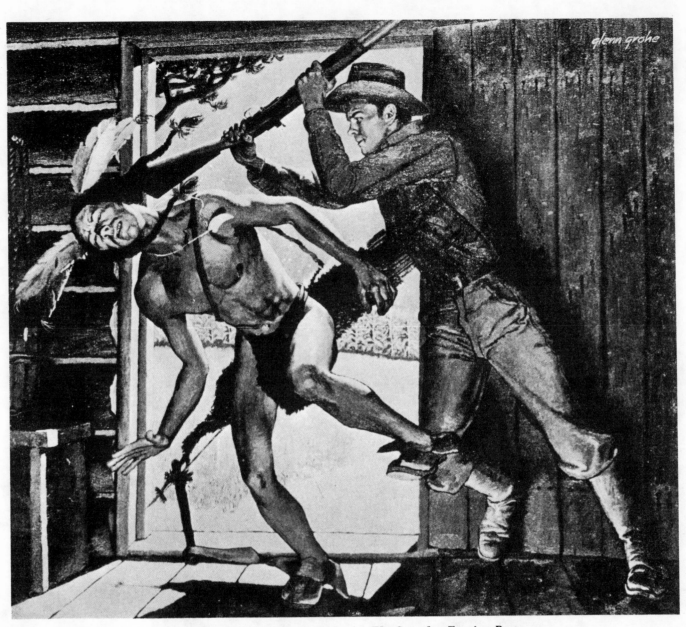

An illustration by Glenn Grohe for The Saturday Evening Post

Reproduced by special permission of The Saturday Evening Post, copyright by The Curtis Publishing Company

glenn grohe

GLENN GROHE is one of our younger artists who, I am willing to predict, is marked for great success in the field of illustration and—if he chooses to enter it—in the field of fine arts.

This can be said with confidence because in what he has done thus far there is conspicuous evidence of creative spirit, a strong sense of design and unusual feeling for color. He exhibits, also, a rather remarkable adaptability to the varied demands that are customarily made upon the resourcefulness of an illustrator for advertisements. One need only glance at the few examples shown herewith to be conscious of this versatility.

My hope is that art directors, both editorial and advertising, will increasingly recognize his special worth in commissions that give free rein to his imagination and creative power. I am thinking of such assignments as that splendid painting *Sieving the Baby*, which he did for the Travelers Insurance Company (reproduced on a following page).* Even without color, this painting is so masterly in conception and design that I have chosen to feature it with Grohe's preliminary studies for the picture and my own analysis of its composition.

---

* *This painting appeared in color in the magazines in 1940. It may be seen in the National Geographic Magazine for July 1940, in the front advertising section.*

Spring and Autumn, reproduced in color, is in the same direction. Though not as successful in design as *Sieving the Baby*, it demonstrates the artist's awareness of qualities that make a picture considerably more than a casual illustration. Its color is enchanting; the composition, though somewhat awkward in linear organization, is dynamic and is conceived with realization of form and space values. One notes the effective subordination of the automobile which, though placed in the immediate foreground, does not intrude upon the illustrative intent of the subject. This, by the way, is treated in a refreshingly wholesome spirit. Perspective and scale are handled so artfully that we feel the reality of the background vista as though it were near, without ever losing the awareness that it is far. Grohe has given to each element the space and size that its expressive quality requires, rather than that dictated by photographic representation. The decorative rendering of the foliage deserves praise, as does the simplification of form in the tree and the figures.

Grohe was consultant in the Graphics Division of O.E.M., did posters for O.W.I., and drawings for the Goodyear Tire and Rubber Company, Dow Chemical Company, Brown and Bigelow, and Sylvania Electric

CHRISTMAS CARD DESIGN BY GROHE

The original design measures 17 x 22 inches. The deer are in two shades of brown; the tree and other accessories are in blue grays with small area repeats of yellow and red.

A detail of the pebble-surfaced scratchboard drawing shown above, reproduced here at exact size of the original.

One of a series of cartoons in color for Brown and Bigelow. The color reproductions were 9 x 12 inches, the originals somewhat larger.

One of a series of full-page advertisements in color for the Dow Chemical Company, executed in tempera

SPRING AND AUTUMN

Tempera painting, 12 x 14

by Glenn Grohe

Products, to mention a few of the accounts that have profited by his talent.

Grohe has worked principally in tempera—he uses prepared gouache colors, but he likes to paint in oil for certain types of handling. His color work is customarily preceded by numerous pencil studies in which the structural aspect of the picture is determined. These are sometimes followed by color sketches in pastel. Although his principal asset is an intuitive sense of design, he fortifies this with careful analytical study of the drawing's organization. Thus he approaches all his problems with a designer's planning, no matter what type of rendering may be required in the final painting.

Glenn Grohe was born in Chicago in 1912, and received his rather brief art training there in the American Academy and at the Art Institute. He began his professional career in the Swann Studio, and came to New York in 1937 where, until two years ago, he worked with the Cooper Studios as a free-lance. In 1938 he married Louise Morris, of Seattle, whom he met on a boat on Long Island Sound. Mrs. Grohe is also an artist; and she paints in whatever time is left over after she has given Paul and Hilde the attention two lively youngsters have a way of expecting. The Grohes live in Westport, Connecticut, an hour's ride by train from New York.

THE SKETCHES SHOWN ABOVE are a few of several studies that preceded the actual painting of "Sieving the Baby." The one at upper left was the first graphic statement of the problem: it does little more than give approximate placing of the four figures essential to the episode. Sketch 2 traced over sketch 1 demonstrates the static aspect of this arrangement. It was followed by sketch 3 which indicates Grohe's search for expressive action and dynamic design. In sketch 4 he has developed his composition through abstract elements which, it will be seen, approximate the organization of the painting. Other pencil studies and color experiments in pastel preceded the final tempera painting. Mr. Grohe had nothing to do with the diagrams on the facing page. These were made by the author without even consulting the artist, and without knowing whether or not this kind of analytical approach enters into this artist's creative procedure. That, of course, does not matter. We see what we see in the completed work; whatever the means employed, it is a fait accompli.

The whole composition is, of course, built around the figure of the woman holding the baby. The artist's first thought was to present this figure dramatically engaged in swaying sieve and baby from side to side. This is noted in figure 1, page opposite, the body poised for an instant at the end of a right to left movement.

In 2 we have picked up lines that accentuate this left to right movement. Figure 3 illustrates the oppositions that are essential to the stability of the design. The tensions created by opposing elements is demonstrated further in 4, where axis lines of the figures have been boldly indicated. It is interesting to note the role the tilted jug plays in this orchestration of oppositions.

144

SIEVING THE BABY

Painted in tempera for Travelers Insurance Co.
by Glenn Grohe

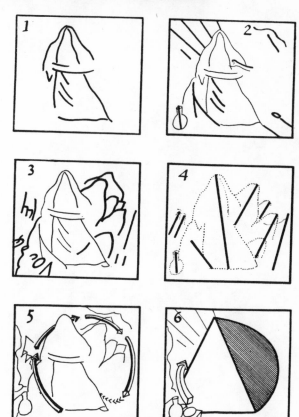

In figure 5, the arrows indicate the way we travel in and through the composition, in a direction that gets a powerful thrust from the outstretched arm of the kneeling woman and carries back and around the entire group, coming forward again to the mortar and flowing into the figure.

As soon as we begin our study of this composition we are conscious of its compactness. Figure 6 represents a geometric solid within which the entire group roughly is disposed. It is an expression of the cohesion of this well-integrated figure arrangement. The perspective of this picture is interesting from several points of view. Generally speaking, the horizontal lines seek a common vanishing point near the center of the picture, but there are distortions of circular objects that are controlled by design needs. The long diameters of the still life objects at the left point upward into the picture, the diameter of the mortar likewise points upward opposing those on the left. The stepping-back of the overlapping triangular heads carries out the perspective effect at the right. There is a strong feeling of depth at the left of the group. We are led into this depth through the narrow space between the kneeling figure and the smoke of the candle at the left border as indicated by the arrow in figure 6. The way this space seems to recede into dark distance, quite beyond the plane of the lighted rear wall, imparts a feeling of mystery that greatly enhances the illustrative quality of the picture.

The two drawings of the stand with jar and pans call attention to the purposeful distortion of these objects in order to make them "active" in the design as indicated in figures 2 and 4.

145

George Giusti

GIUSTI

Oɴ ᴀ ᴡᴀʟʟ in the Giusti dining room is an illustration designed to demonstrate for son Robert what happens to little boys who fail to appreciate the importance of eating lustily what is set before them. Their fate is dramatized in a half dozen of papa Giusti's drawings of a five-year-old boy who, disdaining the diet provided by wise parents, gradually shrinks in size until, in the final tragedy, he is reduced to a mere column of vapor. Here we have *prima facie* evidence of George Giusti's inherent genius for graphic salesmanship. Robert now eats his spinach, a selling job that seemingly gives his father as much personal satisfaction as do his successes in wider reaches of pictorial persuasion where he has won his fame as a top-flight advertising illustrator.

George Giusti was born in Italy in 1908, of Swiss parents who had settled in Milan. Here he received his early schooling and later entered the Royal Academy as an art student. His four-year course was comparable to that of certain American liberal arts colleges which offer majors in art. History, literature and the sciences shared the program with drawing and painting. The art training was of that classical-academic order which implies the most painstaking study of the figure and exact rendering of the form and color of objects and nature. Weeks were spent upon a single figure drawing which, once begun, was not permitted to be discarded for a fresh start. The influence of this "perfectionism" is apparent in Giusti's drawings which have exactitude and classical dignity.

Giusti's purpose when he began his art study was to become a painter, and all his efforts were in that direction. But at the conclusion of his course he was offered a position with a Milanese advertising agency. Contrary to his expectations he found this work sufficiently to his liking to make advertising art and illustration his career. After three years in Milan he went to another agency in Switzerland. Following another three years spent with this Lugano firm he moved to Zurich, where he opened his own studio and got himself a wife. In 1938 the Giustis came to America.

After a brief period of orientation, Giusti found a brisk market for his art in America. Some of his first work was for the Golden Gate Exposition in California and for the Swiss Pavilion at the New York World's Fair.

One is not surprised to learn that it was Giusti's boyhood ambition to be an engineer. Things mechanical continue to fascinate him, whether it is the anatomical structure of a human eye or the engine of an airplane. Such things he renders with perfect precision and an unusual feeling of reality within a pattern that is far from naturalistic. For example, in the *Fortune* cover which we reproduce, the cog wheel and tractor tread are delineated with technical exactitude but in a manner that combines two views in a single drawing. The wheel is a true circle, but the tractor treads are rendered as though seen at three-quarters view, although, it will be noted, with absence of linear perspective in the horizontal tread lines. More often than not Giusti violates photographic perspective in order to achieve more-than-photographic reality. Reality is a *desideratum* in most advertising drawings, but the artist who thinks of reality in terms of photographic naturalism loses the edge that a skillful artist has on the camera. The artist who subordinates design to exactitude is no more than a glorified retoucher.

Originality of conception and design are, of course, the basis of Giusti's success; even though they would not be enough without that quality of precise craftsmanship of which we have been speaking. His designs are always arresting in idea conception as well as in pattern arrangement. Like all commercial artists he is obliged, much of the time, to work within specified limits; but often his own conception is accepted in place of the original one suggested by client or agency.

Giusti prefers to make his drawings rather small. Usually they are but slightly larger than the reproductions. A broadly painted oil or watercolor can stand almost any amount of reduction, but any substantial reduction of delicate, hairline rendering robs the work of its charm. A little reduction is desirable however; it tends to keep the work sharp and brilliant.

Giusti works almost exclusively in tempera. He uses the airbrush, but with considerable reserve. He is careful not to lose the distinction of his own incisive brush line. Usually he carries his designs as far as possible with the sable brush, then applies the airbrush where

needed for soft gradations and very smooth tones. He uses colored inks in his airbrush, spraying them over the tempera. This, he says, gives greater brilliance and a transparent quality. Since the chemical basis of the inks is not compatible with water he warns that the underpainting in tempera should be thin to avoid cracking.

Although calm and deliberate in temperament, Giusti is a very rapid worker. He thinks his design out quite completely before beginning to paint. Usually not more than two or three rough pencil sketches precede his color comprehensive. This comprehensive is rendered with almost as much finish as his final painting. He carries it further than really necessary to submit to the client, but finds it profitable to do so because through his experience in making the comprehensive he becomes thoroughly familiar with the design. This contributes to greater directness and facility in the final rendition.

ONE OF MANY OF GIUSTI'S FORTUNE COVERS

*Note the skillful manner in which front view and perspective view are
combined to give the design more-than-photographic reality*

The silhouetted figures on page 148 are from the "Studio" Christmas Annual

*Trial sketches for cover
designs*

GIUSTI

Illustration for Mademoiselle

Page of a calendar designed for Isaac Goldman,
printer. The calendar is 8 x 12 inches. The original drawing slightly larger. The lion is reproduced at exact size of the drawing.

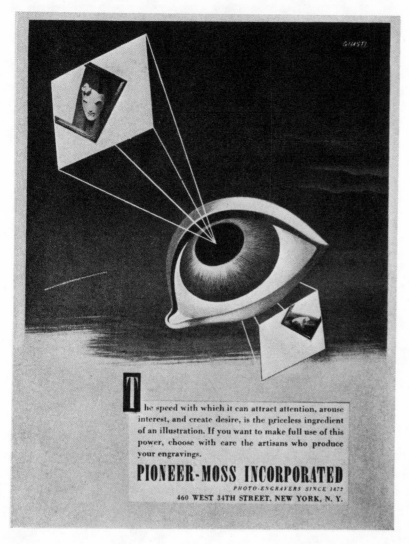

The speed with which it can attract attention, arouse interest, and create desire, is the priceless ingredient of an illustration. If you want to make full use of this power, choose with care the artisans who produce your engravings.

PIONEER-MOSS INCORPORATED

PHOTO-ENGRAVERS SINCE 1872

460 WEST 34TH STREET, NEW YORK, N. Y.

G I U S T I

Magazine advertisement for Pioneer-Moss, Incorporated. The original is in color, though it was reproduced in black and white.

Drawing for a newspaper advertisement. The client was the Philadelphia Evening Bulletin.

Giusti's policy is to show but one sketch. He points to the likelihood of a client selecting the least promising design when confronted with a choice.

Now and then Giusti combines photography with his brush and he does this with his own camera. But the camera is quite incidental in his work.

I was not surprised to find George Giusti orderly and well-organized in his work. His person and his studio are as meticulously neat as his work. He is an extremely personable young man, frank, soft-spoken, thoughtful and friendly. From the old world he has brought to America the fine qualities of culture and courtesy.

Drawing Figures is the title of Mr. Giusti's book published by Studio Publications in 1945.

Stuart Hay

An illustration by Stuart Hay for a Weare Holbrook story in This Week

Reproduced at exact size of original wash drawing

Stuart Hay

Artist of the laughing brush

OCCASIONALLY a great comedian appears before the foot-lights or on the screen, he strikes a pose and distorts his face; the audience roars. The next instant he wears another face; his body sags in exaggerated action and the crowd laughs again. The actor says not a word. There is no funny incident, no innuendo. None is needed; the characterization is sufficient. We have here a kind of hearty caricature, an exposition of man's natural absurdity.

Such is the humor that flows from the heart and brush of Stuart Hay. Even when the story is dull we can laugh with him. There are few comic illustrators who are independent of subject matter. Many stand or fall on the merits of the episode. Hay's preeminence in the field is of course based upon an unusual insight into human nature and a mirthful attitude toward the foibles of his fellow men. He must always be searching the faces of his friends and acquaintances for a hint of some new drollery which will appear in the persons of "Mr. Milfret" or "Dr. Pennyfeather."

But that unquenchable love of the ridiculous would not get far without the power of expression which is founded upon a profound knowledge of the figure and an uncanny facility for characterization. Hay is a well-trained draftsman. He has mastered his craft. He knows how to draw. Beneath those swift brush strokes there is a consciousness of bone and muscle in correct action. And the clothing on Hay's figures has an unfailing way of always being expressive and right.

Then there is line: perhaps the acid test of an artist. A great artist can say with a single line what lesser men can express only by laborious rendering of light, shade and color. Note how Hay can sweep a line along the contour of a back or a leg, a line that is conscious of structure, action and perspective; a swiftly drawn line of course, one that does not have to think what it is doing.

As to the washes of shadow and color suggestion, any artist knows that these cannot be as accidental as they might seem to a layman. Carelessly applied as they appear, they are rendered with an effective indication of form and light and shade.

Hay makes his drawings about twice the size of the reproductions. He points out the danger of losing subtleties of the original drawing when there is too great a reduction. He works on a rather light-weight illustration board. Sometimes the black shadows and lines are brushed in with waterproof india ink, particularly when gray washes are to be applied later.

Hay studied at the Cleveland School of Art, the Art Student's League, the National Academy of Design, and with Robert Henri. While in Cleveland he studied in a summer class under Henry Keller. The incident of the dead horse illustrates the seriousness of Hay and his fellow students. This horse, discovered lying in the street, was hauled by them to an abandoned quarry where it was left until nothing but the skeleton remained. The quarry then became a studio for the study of animal anatomy. Many drawings made from that skeleton help to explain Hay's understanding of the horse.

Hay's training also included evening courses in architecture at the Beaux Arts Institute and at Columbia University. Oddly enough he first went into architecture as a career, working as a designer for six years. This seems like a strange interlude for a man of Hay's particular type of genius but the artist declares that this experience was by no means a waste of time. Architectural training gives one a sense of structure which has many a practical application in drawing. Hay says that his experience in architectural offices also taught him how to work, expelling the notion so common among art students that one should work only when the spirit moves.

Hay's architectural venture was naturally short-lived. Inevitably he drifted into illustration—no, not drifted, because he had to fight his way as do most artists. With portfolio under his arm he tramped the streets of New York, haunting the offices of art editors for some time before he sold his first drawing. That first sale, Mr. Hay amusingly recalls, was a matter of accident. He appeared one morning in the editorial offices of the Butterick Publishing Company. Johnson, the art editor, was short one page in the make-up of the *Delineator* and had nothing at hand to fill that space. He asked Hay if he happened to have a drawing of proper proportion for the page. From his portfolio Hay pulled a drawing, "Don Quixote and Sancho Panza." It fitted the space exactly and the drawing was purchased. The young artist's cheerful acceptance of such a situation made a pleasant impression upon Johnson, who told of a poet who had been asked a few days previously if he

Text continued on page 158

The head sketches on this and opposite page are based on the doorman at Mr. Hay's apartment house in New York

The cow that had a taste for art. Drawing for a Weare Holbrook story in This Week.

A PAGE FROM STUART HAY'S SKETCHBOOK

In making his illustrations Hay does not use models directly, although he is constantly draw-ing from models and filling sketchbooks with studies for later use. Of course he possesses keen observation and has a remarkable memory which retains impressions of types he has seen. There is no "morgue" in Hay's studio. He does not believe in using photographic scrap.

A glance at his sketchbooks gives a hint as to his method of study, and shows how he develops types. After drawing the model in a variety of positions and attitudes, he experiments with vari-ations of the features, exaggerating certain characteristics, exploring the various possibilities of that particular type.

*Exact size detail
from a wash drawing*

*Below —
Excavation watchers are inclined
to grow restless while waiting
for a W.P.A. worker*

*Illustration by Stuart Hay for a
Weare Holbrook story in This Week*

Continued from page 155
had a verse that would fit a hole two by three inches. The poet had walked out in disgust. Not so Hay; he was glad to have made a sale at last and to have an actual reproduction to bolster his future sales efforts.

From then on his work rapidly became popular and his drawings began to appear in *Country Gentleman, American Magazine, The Rotarian, Pictorial Review, New York Herald-Tribune Magazine* (now *This Week*) and many other publications.

Mr. Hay's hobbies are carpentry and stone working, making all sorts of things that have to be done for his summer home in Connecticut. He is especially fond of working with wood and declares that next to his art he would choose to be a carpenter, provided he could be his own boss and construct anything that particularly interested him. Hay suggests that all artists ought to have a hobby which demands physical exertion and work with the hands, since they are sitting or standing still so much of the time at their art work.

In studying Stuart Hay's drawings, we are impressed by the knowledge that lies behind a few easy-looking brush strokes. The superficial student may hope to begin at the point where such men as Hay have finally arrived after years of more or less academic study; but he should be reminded that a career, as well as a house, must be built upon a foundation. The best school of cartooning or caricature is not necessarily one that advertises as such, but the one that offers the soundest training for any artist, whatever his ultimate goal.

DRAWINGS BY STUART HAY

Made for This Week

A detail at exact size

159

Peter Helck

Peter Helck and his son Jerry in the 1906 120-h.p. Locomobile which won the famous Vanderbilt Cup. This is one of several historic automobiles in Helck's collection.

I BEGIN the Peter Helck chapter with his Caterpillar Tractor painting, on page opposite, for several reasons.

First, it is, in my opinion, one of his finest illustrations to date; second, it points up the tendency of art buyers to think of Helck when a picture is required that must rate better than average esthetically; third, it reveals the essentially creative attitude of an artist who enjoys distinction both as painter and illustrator.

It is not easy, even with a man of Helck's talent, to achieve a high position in the "fine arts" world. A successful illustrator is always in such great demand that, unless his creative urge is tremendous, he is forever at the beck and call of art directors to the neglect of his soul's esthetic welfare. Not so, Helck! He has managed to find a good deal of time for painting easel pictures that have been widely exhibited in the big national shows here and abroad. He has held one-man shows of his oils and watercolors. His pictures have won prizes and have found their way into collections.

Peter Helck was born in New York City in 1893. His first experience was gained in art departments of New York department stores, art services, publishing houses, lithographic plants and film companies. Later he opened a free-lance studio, doing much work for film companies, and gradually easing into national magazine advertising. He studied in 1920 with Frank Brangwyn in England and did much work for British motor advertising; then he went to Spain, dividing his time between study, painting and advertising work for Madrid agencies. Afterward he made a sketching trip through southern Spain, northern Africa, Sicily, Italy and

France, returning to work in New York in 1922. After another motor and painting trip in Spain and Majorca, he went to London where he opened a studio for study and commercial work for both English and American clients. While in England he spent considerable time motoring and painting throughout the British Isles. By 1927 Helck was in New York again, doing advertising drawings for important industrial firms and illustrating stories for the magazines. Incidentally, he is a freelance in the true sense, having no ties with artists' agents or representatives. He prefers to deal directly with clients.

In reviewing Helck's work as an illustrator I am struck by its remarkable development year by year. It continues to grow in strength and grace. An article on him that I wrote seven years ago is obsolete now because the present Helck is standing on the shoulders of the man who, even then, was well up front in his profession.

Helck's particular strength is in industrial and agricultural themes. Railroads, automobiles, tractors, trucks and farm activities he paints with authenticity and with a dramatic power which expresses the romantic appeal these things have for him. He is passionately fond of locomotives; they are frequent subjects of his canvases. His love of automobiles has even led to a historical collection which is housed in a large barn on his farm in Boston Corners, New York. Here, the visitor can see a 1904 Chain-drive Mercedes; the 1906 120 h.p. Locomobile which won the Vanderbilt Cup Race in 1908; a Renault Town Car of 1907; a 1910 Cole Race-

Text continued on page 167

THIS IS MY BIRTHRIGHT

Tempera painting by Peter Helck for the Caterpillar Tractor Co.

This picture won The Art Directors Club Award for Distinctive Merit in 1945

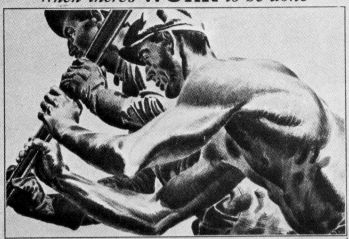

This series of illustrations, relative to the Delco-Remy advertisement, serves to show how the artist's ideas must be modified frequently to suit a change in plan by the Art Department of the advertising agency. The original idea was a more complete representation of the specific task that was being performed by the two workmen. In the two studies above, Helck relates them to a kind of structure that would be familiar to engineers. In order to secure necessary space for additional text copy, the design was cut down as seen in the reproduction of the printed page. The artist's research in preparation for a correct illustration of under-river tunnel construction was wasted. This is by no means an exceptional occurrence. Sometimes it is due to clients' revised specifications; at other times the agency's Art Director may be responsible for the change. At any rate it is a condition any experienced illustrator must be ready to meet. Mr. Helck made two dozen or more preliminary studies for this Delco-Remy job. The pencil sketch, opposite, is about one-half the size of one of these preliminary studies.

"HI YA, SOLDIER!"

Illustration by Peter Helck for a Pacific Mills Advertisement

ROBERTSON COMES THROUGH

Painting by Peter Helck (for Esquire) of the 1908 Vanderbilt Cup Race

about; a 1913 Locomobile Touring; a Mercedes-Knight Sports Tourer of 1920 and a 1921 Brewster Town Car.

Helck's Boston Corners home is a farm, one hundred miles from New York City, located in a fine agricultural section that supplies settings for many of his illustrations. Here he does most of his work though he also maintains a New York studio. His models are the men and women who belong to the land. Chief among them is a neighbor, "Ernie" Roberts, who runs his farm and serves as both model and general utility man. Handy with tools and having an aptitude for locating correct properties he has rigged up blacksmith shops, chemical laboratories and locomotive cabs in the studio. He also serves as critic of Helck's rural subjects; by his help he has saved Peter from the sort of errors expected of a city-trained artist living in the country.

Peter Helck believes that the function of an illustration is to illustrate. That applies not only to the action of the story but to every detail of every accessory in the picture. Whether it be a period costume or a bolt-head on a locomotive, it's correct if you see it in a Helck drawing. As this artist says, "cultivate a policy of knowing thoroughly as much as possible about the subject you are called upon to illustrate. Your audience contains experts in everything you will ever put into pictorial form. Even the casual reader seems ever ready to take pen in hand to prove his powers of observation, and the lack of same in the illustrator."

But Helck is not actuated by the fear that some one will catch him faking. Sincerity and thoroughness are the basis of the man's character; his attitude toward life. With Helck, all things must be right and he will go to surprising pains to be sure they are right. While authenticity has nothing to do with art, it is a major requirement, or accepted as such by the artist who truly illustrates.

When you look at a Helck drawing of a train, for example, you know that it has three dimensions, that it is made of steel, and that it is soundly constructed. When he draws a typical urban crowd, he puts in the different kinds of people you would expect to see in such a crowd. And the people in that crowd are soundly constructed, too. And each one is doing something that seems perfectly natural for him to be doing. Helck has a fine sense of color and of values. He makes use of a play of light and shadow on his subjects that not only helps give them the necessary solidity but adds a satisfying third dimensional design.

The series of Delco-Remy drawings, although done several years ago, will give more than a hint of Helck's thoroughness in the development of every job. Although, as I have said, the character of his work has greatly changed, his present procedure is the same as formerly and his preliminary study is no less exacting.

167

He is one of relatively few contemporary artists who do not use the camera.

Practically all of Helck's present work is executed and reproduced in color. His illustrations are painted in tempera on illustration board. For his easel pictures he likes to work on a Gesso ground, for which he gives the following recipe:

Gypsum Gesso Ground for wood panels, pressed wood, pulp board —

1. Size—glue water, 2½ oz. glue to 28 oz. of water; use rabbit-skin glue.

Prepare rabbit-skin glue—break up sheets into small bits. Place 2½ oz. in 28 oz. water for 12 hours—then warm.

2. One measure of glue water, equal measure of zinc white, an equal measure of gypsum.

First steps in sizing: Apply size thinly on both sides of board. Allow to dry well, then mix glue water as stated above with the white and gypsum. Apply first coat thinly, not wet, stippling it. Allow to dry thoroughly before applying successive coats. Apply all coats warm, not hot. Allow all coats to dry thoroughly. Apply coats at right angles to each other. Six to eight coats on both sides are sufficient. Seal edges too. Both sides are done so that there shall be no warping. Then spray Formalin solution 4% which sets and preserves it. Smooth brushes should be used for application of ground, and sandpaper for any degree of smoothness desired.

Peter Helck is a quiet, slender man, modest and soft-spoken. His unfailing courtesy and helpful interest in his fellow artists has made him a great favorite. He goes out of his way to encourage young artists. He is one of those substantial men who command the respect of their contemporaries and give distinction to the profession.

In response to a request for discussion of examples of his work here reproduced, Helck made the following comments upon "This Is My Birthright."

"I'll never forget the day Mr. Dick Rose of N. W. Ayer phoned regarding my doing this picture for Caterpillar. 'Can you do a painting for us—a gorgeous landscape, a work of art? If Inness were living today we would want him to do this assignment.'

"After this obvious wish for something a bit beyond the usual advertising page, I was greatly shocked to receive later an approved layout from the client—because it showed the space for the 'masterpiece' most violently trespassed upon by the insertion of an unwieldy type-panel. I thought of Inness, envied him in fact.

"A wire to Mr. Rose reminding him of the inspirational phone conversation and stating my perplexity was quickly and amiably answered with: 'Forget the layout. Make us a fine painting. Will design the page around it.'

"This ad was scheduled for September insertion; and according to an old tradition in the advertising profession, this seasonal fact called for a September picture. It was May—spring plowing and sparse spring foliage beset the eye in our valley. However, I spent two days drawing a field and supplemented this study with paintings I had made in these, and other hills in early autumn.

"The picture appears to have been well received, generally. Even more satisfying to the artist is the fact that both N. W. Ayer and Caterpillar were most gracious in their removal of the afore-mentioned obstacles which threatened the success of the venture."

"Robertson Comes Through" was the first of several commissions from Esquire picturing history-making automobile races and featuring such boyhood heroes as "Daredevil Joe" Tracy, Willie K. Vanderbilt, Barney Oldfield and Ralph de Palma. "One day," says Helck, "Mr. Bernard Geis of Esquire phoned to inquire if I would be interested in doing two or three sporting paintings for their gatefold series on the History of American Sport. For subjects he suggested 'Bobby Jones holin'-out at the British Open.' 'Babe Ruth slamming one out of the grounds at a World Series,' or perhaps 'a split-second finish at Kentucky Derby.' None of these appealed strongly, so—taking a shot in the dark I inquired if he had considered 'Automobile Racing' as subject matter. He had not, but did so instantly.

"I asked if he had ever heard of the Vanderbilt Cup. He had, and believed, rightfully, that it was a Bridge Tournament or Sailing Yacht Trophy. My seniority in years was apparent; so I told him about those grand, old sporting events run over the open roads of Nassau County, L. I., in the early 1900's. I insisted that they had all the pictorial requisites for an exciting, sporting painting—color, drama, human interest—boasted that I had seen them and still held the thrill.

"I referred to the race of 1908—the first in which the United States triumphed—as an epic moment in the development of the American automobile. And that, finally, I was the personal owner of this old Cup Winner, and its spectacular driver of 36 years back was my good friend. Mr. Geis appeared momentarily dazed by my enthusiasm but recovered quickly to ask, 'When can you get started?'

"The doing of this picture was sheer fun, notwithstanding the work involved. Equally nice was the response from a surprisingly large number of people throughout the land, who hold sentimental attachments for the days of the early car, which, perhaps, had much to do with Mr. Geis giving me the go-ahead on other race subjects."

In "Hi Ya, Soldier!" Helck is very much at home in telling an appealing human story. "Shortly after Pearl Harbor, in the little New England town of Great Barrington," he recalls, "I was doing some sketching of the Christmas shoppers, illuminated store windows and general night effects. Under a floodlight at a main crossing was a towering traffic cop. I stood watching him, admiring his swashbuckling grace as he gestured and indicated with expressive hands the flow and direction of traffic. Particularly worth noting was his affable greeting to a serviceman, who slowed down to exchange the season's good wishes.

"When Mr. Kurt Jostyn, art director of Williams and Saylor, asked me to do the Pacific Mills Christmas page, I suggested this situation and that evening mailed him a small pencil sketch, together with some graphic description as to color and tone. Due to his understanding, and that of Mr. Williams, this fragmentary sketch was approved by the client without the usual procedure of showing a preliminary in color. This picture, like the

TANKED TREASURE TEMPERA PAINTING BY PETER HELCK

two preceding ones (Caterpillar and Vanderbilt Cup), was done with gouache and tempera on good illustration board. Innumerable tracing studies preceded the application of color. Details—such as the muddy road in the Vanderbilt and the traffic-marked snow in the Pacific—were modeled in plastilene to assist in the drawing. I employ this latter practice *only* when the real thing cannot actually be seen."

In this outline of Peter Helck's career and his methods of study and work there are many lessons for the young illustrator. There is one that is worth pointing out in particular—and it will be noted here and there throughout this book, in the work of other practitioners. I refer to richness of background and to passionate interests that eventually find expression in a

man's work. Specifically, in Helck's case, there is his love of automobiles, and railroads; of all things that go on wheels. He not only has loved these things all his life, he has *experienced* them. Thus he has had something very special to *contribute* to editors and art directors; his function has been far more creative than that of the artist who, without his personal passions and experiences, must merely wait to be told what to do.

A man's work is bound to be limited to the extent of his own contribution to it. If he is creative and zestful in his living, as well as in his art, he will have something very personal to give to the world. He will be something far beyond the delineator of other people's ideas— an ideal that might well be given more attention by the schools which try to prepare young people for the profession.

Earl Oliver Hurst

EARL OLIVER HURST

at work in his studio.

His assistant is seen in

the far corner mount-

ing drawings.

THERE IS HUMOR in nearly every human situation. Even in the midst of tragedy people do funny things, ridiculous things. The humorist is one who is able to laugh at life even in its most solemn moments. Witness the jokes that come out of battlefields and bombings. Humor in such grim circumstances is so deeply overlaid with tragedy that it takes a measure of genius to expose it to view. Indeed much of the humor in ordinary events—too subtle to be seen by the multitudes—awaits discovery and dramatization by a Will Rogers or an Earl Oliver Hurst.

Hurst's humor is of that character. It springs from a deep understanding of human nature and a feeling of sympathy—albeit mirthful—for those who find themselves victims of predicaments. More than that, it results from the artist's propensity to identify himself with the actors in the comedy. This is not surprising in one who has Hurst's capacity for viewing his own misfortunes objectively. Some of his biggest laughs have been at his own expense.

A Turkey Dinner

There was, for example, that Thanksgiving dinner, back in the days when Hurst was still struggling on the lower rungs of the ladder. Thanksgiving day dawned without a turkey in the Hurst larder. This was serious, but not too serious. Hurst asked his wife to prepare a turkey dressing, adding that he would get the turkey. When the feast was spread and the candles lighted, the Hursts bowed their heads over a gorgeous synthetic turkey—artfully fabricated of craft paper—nesting on the platter of luscious turkey dressing. The Hursts laugh now at the memory of that event; they laughed just as heartily at the time. It was a good joke, even if it was on them. Incidentally they still have that paper turkey.

The "Chagrin" Period

This happened in what might be called Hurst's "chagrin" period. The Hursts at that time were living in the little town of Chagrin Falls, Ohio, whence the artist had retreated from Cleveland, in an experiment which turned out dismally enough to make his residence in this oddly-named place particularly appropriate.

In Cleveland he had been doing a great variety of art work. From the art department of the *Cleveland Plain Dealer* he had gone to a newspaper syndicate where, as assistant editor, he did comics, political cartoons, fashions; wrote editorials and managed a newspaper mat service. A year later he was art director in a direct-mail house. Here he was handed every sort of job from spots to elaborate house organs. With his one hundred dollars a week he wasn't doing so badly for a youngster, but he discovered that covers he was designing for booklets were being pirated by others for use on national magazines. Why, he asked, should he not be doing the "big time stuff" himself. He couldn't see how, by remaining in his present situation, he would ever get such a chance. If, he reasoned, he should break away from this treadmill and have time to experiment, he could, in perhaps a year, develop enough skill to put himself in the running. Full of confidence in this plan he withdrew from circulation and rented the Chagrin Falls home ($25 per month) whence he took his young wife, Edna, and one-year-old Joan.

The events of the fateful months that followed require the pages of a book for the telling. Expectations of early success were not realized. Life became one financial crisis after another. But the Hursts kept laugh-

Continued on page 176

On page opposite —
Advertising Drawing for Jantzen Bathing Suits

172

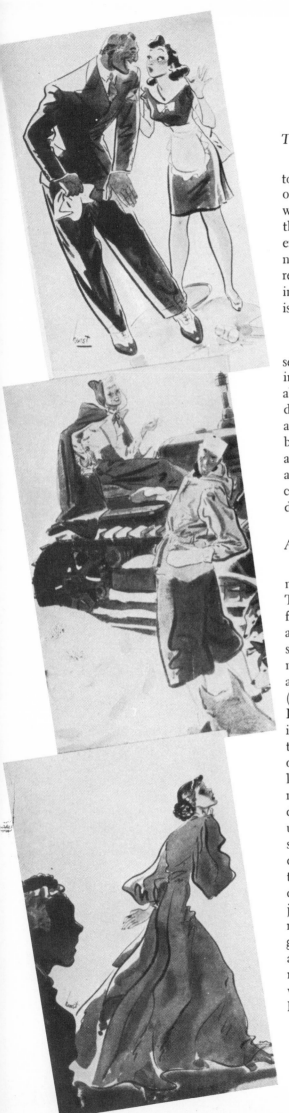

Earl Oliver Hurst discusses

The Illustrator as Stage Director

In creating fiction types it is just as easy for the illustrator as it is for the director of a play to miscast his actors. And good casting is just as vital on the pages of a magazine as on the stage. This story was about a prize fighter and a little waitress. He was a little style-conscious and she was a little plump. As I recall the story he was a homey type, and to break training was to burst out with an extra piece of pie a la mode. I believe I succeeded in depicting a chap who had never heard of a Brahms concerto and who would expect Picasso to be an Italian restaurant; he certainly does know DiMaggio's batting average and can tell you in what round Firpo knocked Dempsey through the ropes. The little waitress, isn't she just the kind of gal who would fall for him?

The casting problem here is in marked contrast to the foregoing. The girl is self-sufficient, nonchalant, smart. She is used to luxury. In the story she is heading her father's freighter tractor business in the North and is confident of her ability to direct it. The young man—definitely a tenderfoot—has flown up to dissuade her from the enterprise. By his sporty overdress, plus his apprehensive attitude, he is shown to be out of place; his mittens—note—have never been worn before. This is a vignette with a cropped edge, using almost three complete sides as natural edges. The man's figure helps to soften the abrupt crop of the picture, and its action, together with the dogs behind him, keeps the interest within the composition. The tracks in the snow, though logical enough, are a deliberate device to pull the white of the paper into the solidity of the picture.

A Problem of Line

I think this illustration is an excellent example of the function of line movement in a drawing. "She gave him her very best theatrical exit," was the caption. The problem of soft translucent drapery clinging to a figure at one time and falling away again was the job to be done principally by line. A photograph with a speed camera can catch a thing of this kind, and one would think that any such shot would be the answer to the problem. I frequently do use a camera to make a study of a certain part of an action. I say part of an action, because there are certain degrees of an action which if portrayed as the camera gets it (factually) do not convey the impression of action that the mind registers. I think the simplest example of this is that of a horse taking a hurdle. There is a split second when the four feet come together, and if stopped at that point the action would give the impression of the animal balancing himself on all fours on the hurdle. The action that registers itself as a horse taking a hurdle is that long arc of motion with front and rear legs fully extended. And so it becomes a matter again of recording impressions. As I recall this job in the making, I first drew my impression of this haughty young thing traipsing across the page, chin up, and definitely overacting. Then I called in a model, read a portion of the script to her, and had her act it out. She flounced across the studio, probably a dozen times, while I studied her action and the action of the drapery. I then took two or three shots with a miniature camera. Bear in mind that I had already done a sketch of my first impression, without models. In the completion of the job I found that most of the photography was slow and clumsy compared with my impression. However, there were notes of conviction that these snaps did give me that made it worthwhile. Incidentally, I have no set way of going about an illustration. There are times when I feel the need of a great deal of research material, and times when I use none; times when I use models, and occasions when I use none. And the same is true of photographic work. But in all cases I first put down on the board, even if not very convincingly, my first impression

174

some of his illustrations

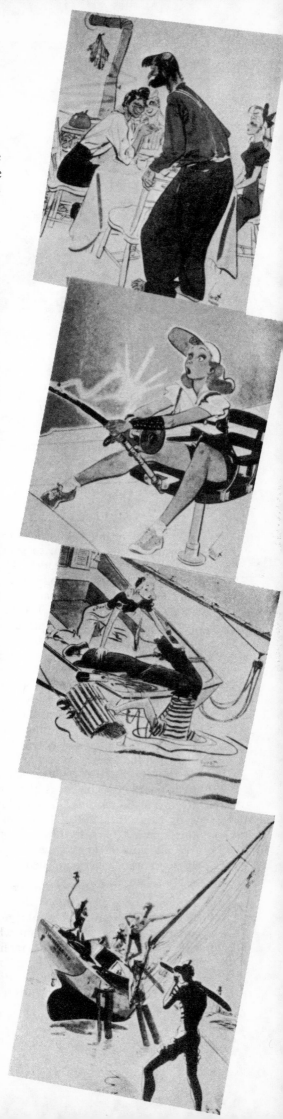

and the arrangement of the entire composition. In this way I believe it possible for the designer or artist that is in one to control the situation. It is so easy to be controlled by a photograph, with all of its detailed interesting information, which may not have one particle of good design in it.

From the Storehouse of Memory

Like most illustrators I store up impressions, and earmark them for some future use. The rear view of Boris Karloff in "Arsenic and Old Lace" was one of those never-to-be-forgotten impressions. The folds in those pants that seemed almost to hang at half-mast, their ludicrous elephantine appearance so completely fascinated me that I just couldn't wait to try them out on someone. When this hill-billy pappy came along, Karloff's pants were waiting for him. An interesting problem in this illustration was to convey the impression that the little girl at the right was definitely "out." To convey this I turned pappy's back to her, and further isolated her by the contrast of her stiff expression with the evident amusement of the other two. Problems of this kind give the illustrator more concern than matters of draftsmanship, physical composition and technical handling.

When the Gag's the Thing

In illustrations wherein the gag or idea is foremost, the artist must approach the drawing in a special way. The usual picture-making problems are present of course but all elements must be arranged for an emphatic focus on the idea. There must be a dramatic concentration of interest at the point where the gag heads up. In the Collier's cover—a typical dumb Dora with the fishing pole—that point is the snap of the broken line; outside of the not-too-exciting body action of pulling, that is the only action. This actually becomes the high spot or gag in the picture. It's the kind of thing that has to be felt. I don't think I could have built it up if I had studied it for weeks. But having experienced just that sensation I began to feel this line snapping and the first thing I knew it happened.

In this episode of the fouled lobster pot the focal point is the submerged head and shoulders of our hero. The composition had to be built around this; the lines of the figures, the boat and the ripples in the water all designed to that end.

Pointing-up a Situation

Shoring her up so she won't fill with the incoming tide. I hadn't experienced this when this job was done, but did soon after. A flat calm, gnats and helpless guests, the skipper is ever the goat.

The figure in the foreground is interesting partly because the picture had to have foreground interest, and yet not take too much away from the center of interest—the boat. To keep this foreground figure strong, but not too interesting, I threw him mostly in shadow and, by contrast, the boat interest became more brilliant. In this case the lines of rigging and the rake of the mast all become part of a design in line; the hard straight lines are softened by the soft bending flexible lines of the figures. Going back to the foreground figure, he is highly stylized and actually out of drawing from a standpoint of realism. However, I feel that it is part of the artist's job to exaggerate or minimize to bring about a desired impression. Undoubtedly this fellow is too long geared, but the line movement is given greater vitality by his lanky figure. This entire situation might have been treated realistically and every inch of the space covered, but I believe the potent elements of design are brought out better through elimination. The blank white space for sky brings in the white paper as part of the picture.

175

Continued from page 172
ing and performing miracles of resourcefulness. Edna learned how to entertain the unexpected dinner guest on her last quarter and yesterday's left-overs. Earl taught her how to renew her meager wardrobe by dyeing each of her two summer dresses a different color every few weeks. The clock, pried from the instrument board of their old Cadillac, was hocked to buy gas for tomorrow's driving. Through it all there was merriment and sublime faith in the future.

Yet the experiment failed. At this point a relative doing well in business offered Hurst, at a very attractive figure, an opportunity to go into partnership with him. He turned the offer down so suddenly that the well-meaning relative was offended; Earl never questioned that the future would bring success in his chosen field of art. At the end of his financial rope, Earl returned to Cleveland and began to pick things up where he had left them. In his anxiety to pay off his debts he took on more work than he could execute in his best manner. It was in this situation that he was given an assignment by Chester Siebold, art director of General Electric Company. Pressed for time as usual, he began work one morning and, working steadily all day and night, delivered the drawing the next morning. Siebold scowled as he examined the work, then asked how much it was to cost him. "I gulped a few times," said Hurst, in describing the scene, "and told him the price was eighty-five dollars. Siebold hit the ceiling. 'Why,' he said, 'I can get better drawings than that in Chicago for fifteen dollars any time.' Then I hit the ceiling, and we nearly came to blows. I told him I'd never make another drawing for him; I was through. Ragged out by work and loss of sleep, I was in a state of complete indifference as to what happened.

A Dinner Engagement

"Siebold stood by while I shot my bolt; then astonished me by asking if I would go out to dinner with him that evening. I asked him why on earth such an invitation. 'Well, Hurst,' he replied, 'only because I like you and want to talk things over with you,'—adding—'after your temperature has dropped to normal.'

"That dinner engagement was a turning point in my career. Siebold began by affirming confidence in my ability. He told me I was capable of better things, but warned that I'd have to change both my attitude and working habits if I ever expected to be a real illustrator. He asked me if I thought the job I'd just delivered to him was my best work. Of course I had to admit it was not, but I defended myself by reminding him that I had a family to support and had to turn out as many jobs as possible.

The Siebold Plan

"'Here is what I want you to do, Hurst,' he said, 'I want you to promise me that in the future you will make not one drawing for each assignment, but three or four, then deliver the best one of the lot.' I was aghast at such a proposal, which, if accepted, would reduce my income by at least two thirds. But Siebold kept right at me, rushed me like a salesman trying to sell a bill of goods. Finally I weakened, and agreed to try out his cockeyed idea just as soon as I could save up enough money for reasonable security while doing it. Apparently not quite convinced of my sincerity he insisted we shake hands on the pact.

"For the next six months things went on as formerly. Then one day I called Siebold on the telephone. 'Chet,' I said, 'today I go off the deep end with that crazy idea of yours that we shook hands on some months ago.' I had determined to give his proposal at least a trial. I made five finished drawings of my first assignment under this plan. Not until then had I realized the soundness of Siebold's advice—and the slimness of my income under this arrangement. As I examined those five drawings, standing against my studio wall, I was really shocked to think that according to former procedure I would have delivered the first one, truly a fumbling performance compared with the subsequent drawings. From then on I followed Siebold's plan religiously. In a few months I had justified its author's faith in me and the great wisdom of his advice—I was soon doing far more important work than had ever come to me preceding my move to New York."

Still a Good Plan

To this day Hurst has honored the pact made with a handclasp over that dinner table years ago. He doesn't make three or four trials as formerly, but there are at least two drawings for every job. Sometimes he will completely finish both of them; at other times he will carry only one beyond the line rendering; after all, in a Hurst drawing, it is the quality of the line that counts. Line is the dominant element in his work, a factor which might not be at once obvious to one who is first struck by his effective massing of vivacious color. Examine any of his illustrations critically and you will realize that while his color is essential to effective dramatization of the idea, it is really supplementary to a remarkably expressive line. Study Hurst's line carefully. You will see how it fluctuates, now full and lush as it accents some dominant action, now delicate as it defines a subtle bit of expression; but always sensitive, directed by complete knowledge and technical mastery.

SURPRISE IN ARMOUR   DRAWING BY EARL OLIVER HURST

The original, 20 x 28 inches, appeared in color in Collier's, October 18, 1941

You will never find a deliberately drawn line in a Hurst illustration: only a swift moving brush will produce that sense of aliveness which is the essential characteristic of his work.

Hurst in Action

Our photograph shows Hurst in characteristic action as he starts an illustration. He fills sheet after sheet of tracing paper with vigorous pencil drawings. The first, torn from the pad, falls to the floor; another soon follows. After an hour or two the studio becomes littered with these experiments—all in line—to express the idea he is trying to put over. Not until his conception matures does Hurst take up his brush and begin his final drawings on heavy watercolor paper. The painting of the final picture doesn't take long.

Hurst's manner of working varies. While he will often resort to the preparatory experiments already described, at other times his drawing is so completely visualized that he takes up his brush at the outset without having made a single pencil study on tissue. Much of his best work has been produced in this spontaneous manner. In whatever way he proceeds on his drawing board, the bulk of his creative effort has already been accomplished before he touches brush or pencil. His kind of "idea" illustration—"gag" is really too superficial a term for it—implies keen perception constantly on the alert. Most, though not all, of the ideas for his cover drawings are his own. Sometimes the art editor produces one. In either event the idea is discussed with the art editor before it gets on paper. Then comes a rough sketch which, if acceptable, is followed by a finished drawing. Hurst's sketches are very rough but he suggests that an artist whose work is not known to the art editor would do better to submit a finished drawing.

It's a Business

Illustrating for magazines and for advertising is a business as well as an art. You will find the successful illustrator capably organized to meet the exacting demands of art directors and editors who in turn are under the pressures of modern industry. Assignments have a way of coming in bunches, with utter disregard for the artist's convenience. A ten-day deadline for a story is automatically reduced when the ringing of the telephone heralds the arrival of another. Then there are those unscheduled stories which can't be put off indefinitely. Hurst says he works best under such pressure, but without efficient organization he could not satisfy his clients. A capable assistant, Hurst usually has an apprentice around, does many things to save his employer's time. Research is one of his important tasks. He is contact man between artist and art director. He acts as secretary and bookkeeper; he mats and delivers drawings. Hurst's second assistant, also in the photograph, must not be overlooked. Shag, his Scotty, takes up his post when his master begins work, and is ever alert to retrieve erasers and pencils which fall from the drawing board.

Inks and Models

Hurst renders his drawings with waterproof inks: black for the line work, and colored inks for the washes. As has already been stated, he very nearly completes his line drawing before applying color. Where the color washes flow over the black ink lines they soften them. When pure black lines are wanted, perhaps in the foreground, Hurst leaves those lines until the last, drawing them on top of the washes. He never attempts to go over a line to strengthen it; in doing that, he declares, he would lose what he most prizes—spontaneity. He likes colored inks because, he declares, one tone can be applied over another without losing the freshness of the wash, and one can work back into them without their getting messy.

Speaking of models and photographs, Hurst explains that direct use of either of these aids is of little use in his type of work. They are even likely to get in the way of his original conception. "In casting characters for a story," he says, "I never expect to find types in a model. Types for any given situation have to be created from memory and imagination. The only model I used for *Surprise in Armour* was Al, my assistant, who posed for both the colonel and the rookies. In every illustration I first put down on paper, in pencil, my impression of the entire situation, no matter how poorly conceived or how far from fact it really is. I keep that before me from first to last because this first impression is usually the one I want to carry through to the finished drawing which is finally checked against the model or photograph for accuracy."

Art Training

Hurst received his art training over a long period of years while he was a breadwinner. He studied in the evening classes of the Albright Art School in Buffalo; then in France at the University of Beaune—this at the conclusion of front-line service in the A. E. F. in the first World War; and, while he was working nights, off and on, on the *Cleveland Plain Dealer*, in the day classes of the Cleveland School of Art. For seven years after his marriage he continued spare time study. He believes that art school training is certainly desirable in spite of the success of many artists who have been denied its benefits. "But," he adds, "success as an illustrator depends more upon what you are at the outset than upon any kind of art training."

In this story of an illustrator's career considerable emphasis has been placed upon the growing pains of his formative years. These struggles, while by no means forgotten, can now—in the day of success—be recalled with amusement, not to say satisfaction. When Hurst endorses an advertiser's check for $1000, payment for a single drawing, he must think of the days when $25 was his usual "take" for a similar—if less masterful—piece of work. For Hurst is one of our highest paid illustrators. Today he has reached a pinnacle that, I am sure, he never quite envisioned in those days of the "Chagrin" period.

Walter Klett

Woman in Padre Hat   Oil painting 20 x 24

KLETT

Glamour

is his business and his art

CHIC WOMEN, smart women, glamorous women—they are Walter Klett's stock in trade. He paints them for the magazines and, when the press of publishers' commissions is not too great, he paints them on canvases that accumulate in his studio, awaiting the right moment for a one-man show in a New York gallery.

Some of the latter are portraits, but they are portraits of types rather than individuals. For Klett does not consider himself a portrait painter in the usual sense: his interest in his sitter is impersonal though by no means cold. We might say that it is seduced by woman as a species. The woman, however, must be a noble specimen; Klett cannot understand the preference so many painters seem to have for run-of-the-mill wenches as picture motifs. He refuses to believe that a drab, prosy woman is the *sine qua non* of a good figure painting. He thinks Velazquez, Goya, Van Dyke, Rubens, Titian, Botticelli, Perugino and Reynolds, among the many old masters who loved beautiful women as picture subjects, bear him out in this. Although wholly in the stream of modernism, Klett is a worshiper of the Renaissance painters who created such glowing canvases of distinguished sitters.

Klett, in his fine arts phase, does not confine his interest wholly to women. A score of colorful abstractions decorate the walls of his studio apartment. Based upon musical compositions they are some of the finest non-objective paintings I have seen. These, it appears, serve as a kind of spiritual catharsis for an artist who goes in for periodic check-ups on his esthetic health.

Klett's ambitions as a painter are, naturally enough, reflected in his attitude toward the art that is his livelihood. There are illustrators who are ever willing to follow the current trend, ready to supply the trade with just what it demands and no questions asked. Klett, though by no means unbending in his relations with clients, persists in the notion that the more *art* there is in the art of illustration the better for everybody and the more fun for the artist. "Ninety per cent of illustration is not art," he says, "but most of it *could* be if the buyer were willing and the artist able."

To which, one day, *Collier's* art editor William Chessman replied, "All right, this buyer is willing. Go ahead and illustrate your next story however you like and let's see how it comes out."

Klett's illustration for "The Mirror" by Gladys

Schmitt is the sort of thing Chessman got when he thus gave the artist his head. "My idea," says Klett, "is to express the mood of the story rather than to show a particular scene from it. And even though it has unity with the story, the painting still should be able to stand alone, as art enjoyable for its own sake. It is my desire to incorporate into an illustration as much of the esthetic quality of modern painting as the public will accept."

Contemporary practice in magazine make-up is something of an obstacle to the realization of that ideal. By and large, illustration today is conceived as interior decoration. The modern magazine usually is designed by the art director as an ensemble, with much regard for novelty in layout and balance of interest in planning single pages, spreads, vignettes, and color sensations. More often than not the shape of a vignette on the page is deemed as important as what goes into it. When the picture is placed at the heading of the story, as the feature illustration so often is, the title frequently

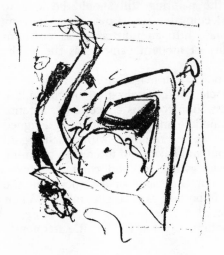

Klett designs
page layout and illustration for Collier's

Here are a few of Walter Klett's several trial layouts for the first page of the Dina Cashman story reproduced below. His problem was to incorporate a column of type in the picture designed to occupy an entire page. The roughs were done in pencil and watercolor on 19 x 25 inch sheets of tracing paper.

Illustration for "The Mirror"
a story by Gladys Schmitt in
Collier's

The original painting in oil
was 20 x 24. It was repro-
duced in color in Collier's.

The lead pencil study was
made from the model at ap-
proximately two-thirds size of
the painting. This is Klett's
usual procedure for close-ups.

Dancer   Oil painting 20 x 30

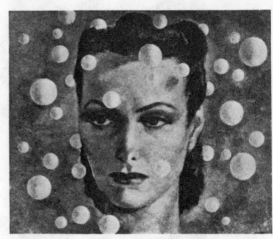

Head with Spheres   Oil painting 13 x 16

Illustration for a Good Housekeeping Story

breaks into it and in some instances a whole column of text, as in the first page of the Dina Cashman story illustrated on a preceding page. When the artist is given an unbroken rectangle, as was Klett in "The Mirror" and in the *Good Housekeeping* story, he is relatively free to go his own untrammeled way. Some art directors are glad to leave page layout to the artist, believing that layout and picture composition are inseparable, and that the artist is best fitted to do this one-man job. Whether or not his procedure is followed, the editor-in-chief is dictator and a word from him might, often does, upset plans, even after the design for the illustration has been agreed upon by art director and artist and the picture has actually been painted.

Klett, like practically all contemporary illustrators, makes some use of the camera but he usually draws directly from the model for close-ups, such as his illustration for "The Mirror." These are done with graphite pencil on 19 x 25 inch sheets. For large-scale paintings he works in oil on masonite board. Other commissions are executed on illustration board with watercolor. Usually he makes a number of rough layouts, designing his picture and the page arrangement at the same time, as demonstrated herewith.

Klett was born in St. Louis and began his art education there in the St. Louis School of Fine Arts. After a few months of formal study he took his education into his own hands and left school. Soon he was designing window backgrounds for women's apparel shops, doing fashion drawings and advertising illustrations.

In 1925 he married and moved to Chicago where he worked for three years before coming to New York. Now in constant demand—principally for fiction illustration—he works almost exclusively in color.

At the time of our interview, Klett was planning a month's vacation in Florida, his first in two years. After weeks of trying, he finally had secured train reservations. Then came an editor's plea that he postpone his trip long enough to make a picture for the first installment of a new serial. Success, the tyrant!

Klett's studio on 52nd Street is large and beautifully appointed. It expresses the perfect taste and the love of good living which characterize this artist. Klett's passions, outside his painting, are music, the theatre and the dance.

Walter Klett's drawing reproduced on the page opposite was m
several years ago when he was fond of working on a dampe
piece of paper which produced foggy lines and edges. The rep
duction, but slightly reduced from the original, was done o
heavy cream sheet of paper. Fashions change in illustrative te
niques as in clothes; the particular charm of this rendering
given way to other characteristics in Klett's present manner
working.

Robert Lawson

The Illustrations of
ROBERT LAWSON

The spot is from "The Treasure of the Isle of Mist" by W. W. Tarn, Putnam, 1934. Slightly reduced from original drawing.

The illustration is from "The Golden Horseshoe" by Elizabeth Coatsworth, Macmillan, 1935. The technique in both of these drawings is typical of the transitional stage in Lawson's method of work from his early fine pen line to his present brush and tempera style as seen in the drawings on the opposite page and in "Ferdinand." This illustration is reproduced at exact size of the original drawing, though it was intended for a slight reduction in the book.

Illustration in brush and black tempera from "Swords and Statues" by Clarence Stratton, Winston Company, 1937.

IF YOU should be so fortunate as to be a guest at Robert Lawson's home on Rabbit Hill in Westport, Connecticut, you would discover, among other things, a ten-foot bookshelf of volumes illustrated by the artist and his wife, Marie Lawson. Fingering through those volumes you would be impressed by the delicious sense of humor, the technical versatility, and the thoroughly competent craftsmanship of both artists. There you would see illustration at its best, carrying on the high traditions represented by such pioneers as Howard Pyle.

Although Lawson has concentrated on books for the past few years, his experience as an artist has been varied. Perhaps we should begin at the beginning when he was an ambitious youngster just out of the New York School of Fine and Applied Art, where he studied for three years under Howard Giles and Rae Sloan Bredin. His first drawings were done for *Harper's Weekly* and it was in the battle with that first commission that he discovered how *not* to make an illustration. "I proceeded," he explained, "as we had been taught in art school—finding suitable models for the characters and posing them in the proper action. I had a desperate struggle with those illustrations; the models seemed to hamper, rather than help. I vowed that I would give up illustration if I had to rely upon models—and from that day to this I've not had a model in my studio."

In addition to illustrations for *Harper's Weekly*, *Delineator*, and *Vogue*, Lawson, during those early years, did considerable work in advertising art. He also designed scenery and costumes for the Washington Square Players, wrote, costumed and directed a large pageant, did book plates and tried some portraits.

His career was interrupted by World War I in which he served with the Camouflage Section of the A.E.F. Back home again he took up his pen and brush, doing a variety of work, except for a period when he and his wife did nothing but Christmas cards.

That, by the way, is an interesting story. The Lawsons had acquired a lovely old colonial house in Westport, Connecticut. There came an opportunity to make designs for Christmas cards—continuous employment and good pay. The Lawsons resolved that each should turn out one card every day until the house was paid for. For three years they held to this schedule until the

mortgage shrunk to the vanishing point. Lawson declares that those years were splendid training for the more important work that was to follow.

No doubt many readers have in their reference files some of those beautiful colored drawings Lawson did for the Johns-Manville Company advertising asbestos roofing materials. They established a new *high* for advertising art; nothing better has ever been done. At one time the famous Lawson gnomes were pressed into valuable service for Jacob Ruppert's beer. In these drawings the artist was given free rein in humorous fantasy that resulted in many unique advertisements.

Those amusing little folk, elfs, dwarfs and pixies, have always been seen in Lawson's company whenever the properties permitted. In his etchings—that is still another chapter—they gambol over many a lovely bitten

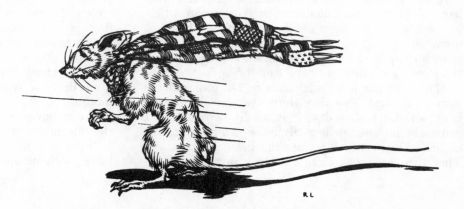

Illustration for
BEN AND ME
Written and illustrated by
Robert Lawson
Little Brown, 1939

on it, you know. Why down in the Bluegrass Country—"

"Yes, I know," said the Fox hastily. "What did you do with them?"

"Oh, just took them on a little romp down the Valley, through a few briar patches, ended them up on that electric fence of Jim Coley's. Stupid brutes, though. Hardly could call it sport, very low class. Now down in the Bluegrass Country the hounds were real thoroughbreds. Why, I can remember—"

"Yes, I know," said the Fox, melting into the bushes. "Thanks just the same though—"

[19]

plate, and in decorative drawings they mingle ingeniously with flowers, insects and other ornamental elements. So persistently over the years has Lawson loved these whimsical creatures, they seem to have become a sort of graphic language for the expression of the artist's otherwise inexpressible sense of the mystery and beauty of worlds seen and unseen.

In selecting examples of Lawson's work for reproduction we have tried to represent the various techniques that he has used in different periods of his career. His earliest pen work is characterized by fineness of line—he tells us that he even diluted the ink for greater delicacy. The difficulty of reproducing such drawings led him to a slightly bolder treatment which in turn gave way to the vigorous brush technique that we see in the *Ferdinand* drawings. Lawson has from the first done beautiful lettering that frequently is an important factor in the decorative drawings for which he is so famous.

In answer to our request for a discussion of the problems of illustration, Lawson referred us to an article he once wrote for the *Publishers' Weekly*. This is so illuminating that we can do no better than to quote from his words in that publication—which we do with the gracious permission of the Editor:

"The first, the inevitable query is 'Do you read the book first?' Just how they think one can illustrate a book without first reading it is wholly beyond me. I will make no attempt to analyze the mental processes, or lack of them, which prompt this invariable question. They then proceed to cite numerous instances, in de-

fense of the question, which have proved to their satisfaction that the illustrator had never read the story, or had read most carelessly. A careful analysis of these instances has convinced me that, in about ninety-five cases out of a hundred, it is the reader who has done the careless reading; in four cases there is a question as to the mistake, and in the remaining one case the illustrator's error is unimportant and trivial.

"I would like to say most emphatically that the illustrator does read the manuscript—many times before, and all during the process, so that by the time the illustrations are finished the manuscript is usually a ratty, dogeared mass of paper; and long passages of the text have been unconsciously committed to memory. I might also add that I have occasionally found mistakes and inconsistencies in the text, unnoticed by both author and editor. Naturally, I point these out with great glee. Just to convince yourself of the careful study of the text which is necessary, try this little game some dull winter evening. Take an unillustrated book—pick out an incident which you would like to illustrate, and then make a list of all the different things which will have to go into that one drawing and where you found them. Notice how far afield you must go and how carefully you must search the text to find what you need, and also how much you must add to make it a completed illustration. You will be surprised.

"In point of frequency the next question is—'How do you go about it? How do you select the incidents you wish to illustrate, and, having chosen an incident, how do you know what things to put into the drawing to make its meaning clear?'

"This is a more difficult question and can only be answered in part. In the first place it brings up the whole question of just what is meant by illustration—is it merely to do in pictures what the author has already done in words, or to go on and carry out in a pictorial and decorative form the spirit and atmosphere the author can really only suggest? The infinite detail which it is possible to put in a drawing to enhance the scene, would, all too often, if written, hopelessly retard the action and drama of the narrative. To my mind this is the true function of the illustrator. He must steep himself in the atmosphere of the book, and then transfer that feeling to his drawings. I do not mean this in any vague or Bunthorne-like way, but, deliberately, consciously, he must plan his arrangement, handling, technique and color to reproduce the spirit of the written words; so that even if the drawings are merely decorations, without any of the characters, settings or accessories of the story they would still convey the particular temper of the book.

"How this is done cannot be explained any more than an actress can explain how she creates a character from the few words the playwright has put in her mouth.

"I can, however, explain the mechanics of going about the illustration of a book.

"First, the illustrator reads the manuscript once or twice, without any thought of definite illustrations—

From "Ferdinand," Story by Munro Leaf; drawings by Robert Lawson. Viking Press, 1936. The appeal of Ferdinand apparently is irresistible. Well over a quarter of a million copies have been sold in this country, it has been published in eleven foreign languages, and it is still (1945) a very steady seller.

simply to see what it's all about and to gather the general atmosphere. Then he usually goes through it again, and picks out those incidents which simply *demand* to be illustrated, because of their dramatic or atmospheric qualities. Then he goes through it again, and, according to the number of drawings allowed by the publisher, either subtracts some or adds more to help carry out the action and spirit of the text.

"The next step, usually, is to make a dummy the exact shape and size of the book, and to plan, roughly, the drawings themselves in their proper sizes and places.

"Then, with the drawings in this tangible form, he goes through this dummy again, adding here, eliminating there, until the drawings would, taken by themselves and without text, give a very clear idea of the feeling and progress of the story. Then all that remains is to plan more carefully and, finally, to do the individual drawings themselves.

"The last and most difficult questions are—'How do you know what to put in the drawings? What made you think of this arrangement or that point of view? Of this costume or that funny face?'

"These last, of course, any illustrator can answer only from his own point of view, and, even then, not very clearly.

"For my own part I can say that only twice in something over twenty years has a definite idea for a drawing come out of thin air by the process called, I believe, inspiration. Instead, it has come by sitting down with paper and a pencil and actually thinking about the subject; by scratching and rubbing out and starting again. Eventually some combination of scratches and smudges,

Decoration in "brushed" Wolff pencil by Robert Lawson. Slightly reduced in size from the original. The highlights are touched with opaque white. Courtesy New York Herald-Tribune Magazine.

of irritation or desperation will stir a memory of something once seen, which will suggest an arrangement or a point of view, and from then on it is simply a problem of building this up and elaborating upon it until the desired result is attained. I should say, approached—it is never attained.

"The life of any illustrator, I am sure, is an endless process of observing and stowing away in some curious rag-bag part of his mind all the thousands of ill-assorted facts and impressions that he will sometime be called upon to use. All his waking hours he passes in what is usually considered a rather vacant daze—observing strange faces; how different sorts of shoes wrinkle; clothes, people, lights and shadows; how a plumber carries his tools and what sort of horses pull milk wagons.

"The landscape painter places himself before a landscape and paints it; the portrait painter paints a stout lady who places herself before him to be painted.

"But the poor illustrator may, at any moment, be called upon to dive into his memory and produce—correctly and recognizably drawn—a coast guard cutter or a razor blade, an Egyptian princess, a Chinese junk,

Illustration for "They were Strong and Good"
Written and illustrated by Robert Lawson
Viking Press, 1940

Awarded the Caldecott Medal in 1941

are wrong. Some one will, of course, and write an unpleasant letter.

"Many telephone calls I have made or answered at strange hours of the day and night. 'How many stripes are there on a Lieutenant Commander's sleeves? What year was Dick Turpin born? Have you a picture of a 1909 Ford? Have you any sea gulls?'

"Beside the question of accurate details there are often questions of the meaning of things. One editor, whom I am very fond of otherwise, has a habit of always sending me poems and articles to illustrate which are so involved in subject that none of the editorial staff can agree on their exact meaning. I am not only supposed to understand them, but to make a drawing which will make them more clear to the readers. It is not really very difficult because no drawing could make them more obscure, so almost anything will make them clearer.

"I almost rebelled, however, when he sent me an article entitled 'Life After Death,' and then warned me over the telephone to be sure to observe the usual editorial taboos—'Don't make the figures in the drawing look dead (that's gruesome).'

" 'But they are dead,' I protested, foreseeing trouble of the most subtle nature.

" 'Yes, of course,' came the reply, 'they are dead, but you must make them so people will realize they are dead, and yet alive—it's "Life After Death," you see.'

"I did see, but it was quite a problem.

"It is, perhaps, this variety of problems, and the never ending succession of new and different things to be done that make the profession of illustration so fascinating. The illustrator becomes immersed in a new book, a story or a commercial job and is practically away somewhere for two days, or a night, a week or a month or more. He comes up for air, looks about a while, and then is gone again, into some new delirium of work. Months and years slip by, and he suddenly notices that the George Washington Bridge has been completed, that Radio City has been built, and that fashions have changed.

"He makes a mental note of them for future reference, and is off again on a new and different adventure in the world of his own. Perhaps creating visions of the cities and people of the future; or recreating glorious deeds and golden times that are past. Hand in hand with the author he treads the far high fields of the imagination or penetrates the breath-taking realms of science or industry. Whether he is reliving the dark days of the Revolution, campaigning with Marlborough, selling beer or cigarettes to New Yorkers, or viewing with Melville or Stevenson new lands and strange seas, he is, for a while, living that life and seeing those scenes.

"That is why so many illustrators seem uninterested

a Christmas tree with all its candles, a circus parade or a little girl eating spinach.

"In addition to the memory rag-bag, he must also have at hand, or know where to locate quickly, a tremendous amount of data; costume, architecture, furnishings, anatomy of man, bird, beast and reptile; marine architecture, and a hundred other things, either in book form, or in clippings filed away and classified. And no matter how much of this he may have, some author or editor will demand details which just cannot be located.

"It is all very well for an author to mention a Roman centurion in gleaming armor driving by in a chariot, and for an editor to demand it in an illustration; but at twelve o'clock of a Sunday night with the drawing due Monday morning things are difficult for the illustrator if he cannot locate all the details. Just what was the correct costume of a centurion of the Tenth Legion in 85 B.C.? How many spokes were there in a Roman chariot wheel? What sort of harness did the horses wear and how many horses were there? Lacking any definite information there are then only two courses open to the illustrator—one is to use lots of dust clouds and movement to hide all details of which he is uncertain, the other is to go ahead and, as well as he knows how, with elaboration and thoroughness, make his mistakes so convincingly that no one will know that they

Illustration by Robert Lawson from "Adam of the Road," by Elizabeth Janet Gray, Viking Press, 1942

in minor politics and 'world movements,' and advertising patter, and why they often forget to tie their shoe laces."

Lawson has been writing his own stories in recent years—since this chapter was written. And, judging by the acclaim his books have received, his fame as an author vies with his success as an illustrator. His *They were Strong and Good* (Viking Press, 1940) was awarded the Caldecott Medal by the American Library Association as "the most distinguished picture book of 1940." *Rabbit Hill* (also Viking) was the Junior Literary Guild Selection for September, 1944. It entered its third printing, 29,000, that year. *Ben and Me* (Little Brown, 1939) recounts the adventure of a mouse who, nesting in Benjamin Franklin's fur cap, shared some of the Philadelphia printer's adventures. *I Discover Columbus* and *Watchwords of Liberty* (both Little Brown books) were published in 1941 and 1942 respectively. In 1944 Lawson produced his first adult book, *Country Colic*, for Little Brown.

Ervine Metzl

85

ERVINE METZL
PEINTURE
Antique et
MODERNE
20
PARK AVE.
NEW YORK city

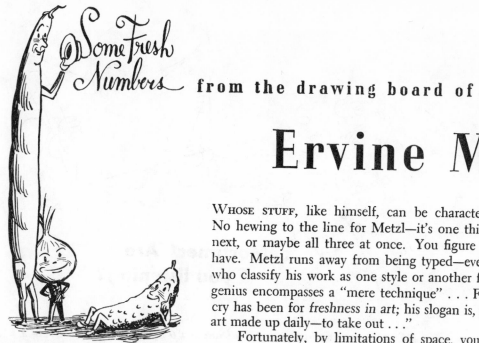

Some Fresh Numbers

from the drawing board of

Ervine Metzl

Crowquill pen drawing, advertising the Fresh Foods of a large chain of restaurants.

WHOSE STUFF, like himself, can be characterized by the term "fresh." No hewing to the line for Metzl—it's one thing one day and another the next, or maybe all three at once. You figure it out—the art buyers never have. Metzl runs away from being typed—even as a Metzl! Art directors who classify his work as one style or another fail to realize that the man's genius encompasses a "mere technique" . . . For over twenty-five years his cry has been for *freshness in art*; his slogan is, and always has been, "Fresh art made up daily—to take out . . ."

Fortunately, by limitations of space, you are spared a blow-by-blow description of *how* Metzl works. Suffice it to say that Metzl, who is notor-

Pictorial announcements can be informative, amusing and original. This was used as a direct mailing piece.

This map — one of 10 painted in full color for the Seabees of the U. S. Navy, and printed in offset lithography — was done in watercolor and colored inks with an underpainting in line and tone of black, thus producing the basic foundation for the drawing.

From a drawing in pen and ink using a #0 Speed Ball pen to create a same thickness line. Used as an advertisement for The Saturday Evening Post.

A full-page advertisement for a woman's magazine. Drawn in ink and transparent watercolors. The type and hand-lettered headings were done separately, and superimposed.

198

iously lazy, attacks every problem from that slant. Because he hates to work (and consequently works harder than most), his choice of medium among his varied techniques is simple—whichever is easiest to handle, fast and short. Though his work looks spontaneous—and is—much labor and planning, rough sketches and tissue overlays go into the performance. Aside from the spontaneous inspiration which seems to be his mainstay, he will swipe anything he can—from photos and clippings to an Al Parker or an Al Dorne! Since he has no conscience whatever, he feels completely self-righteous in achieving his end by these unscrupulous means.

Now for a word about Metzl himself. He is a strange contradiction, a paradox: at once shy and unassuming, self-effacing and modest. He is rather handsome—in an ugly sort of way. He hasn't a temperamental bone in his body, and is extremely calm under circumstances which are calm. He hates most advertising art. His firm conviction is that the average commercial advertising art picture is to the eye exactly what commercial radio with its plug-uglies is to the ear. He admits to an intensification of that conviction on innumerable occasions when he has beheld his own contributions to advertising art. He dearly loves children and dogs, is kind and gentle to old ladies and extremely attentive to young ones. He studied (if one can call it study) at the Art Institute in Chicago for a total of three months, more or less.

A page originally printed in rotogravure for the New York Times Magazine Section. Done entirely in line and ink washes, using rather free pen line and wash to create a "done-on-the-spot" effect.

This drawing was a mixture of charcoal, pen and ink, and pastel. Reproduced in two colors, yellow and black, creating the effect of stage lighting. It was printed in the Woman's Home Companion.

He has run the gamut from selling newspapers and rustling dishes in one-arm joints to holding the venerable position of teacher of Graphic Arts at Columbia University in New York City. He is, in short, to quote some of his friends—and who else but a friend would say it?—a genius. I know this to be true, for I have been with him constantly since his inception one balmy, starry, moonlit night in the month of May, in the year of our Lord, eighteen hundred and . . .

But why should I go telling folks how old I am?

E. M.

And that, dear reader, is Ervine Metzl. Much of what he has said is true, but in painting his self-portrait

he has enveloped his likeness in an atmosphere that, while expressing the efferverscent Metzl, certainly obscures some salient qualities and falsifies others. If you should drop into Metzl's studio on Park Avenue, you would see a part of what I mean. It is not a "typical" artist's studio. The walls are lined with bookcases filled with rare volumes. Above them hang a few pictures: Degas, Gustav Klimt, Renoir, a lithograph or two. A cast of Michelangelo's *Moses* presides over all. It is the library of a scholar, a man of taste. There is nothing

This cartoon, in pen line and black watercolor washes with an all-over wash of green ink, produces an underseascape. It was printed in two colors in The Saturday Evening Post.

The political cartoon, at the right, is a charcoal tone and line drawing for Fortune Magazine. It was printed in two colors, the second color, in a tint of red covering only the curtains, framing the picture.

in sight that suggests commercial art or relates to the day's work. Yet all the masters assembled in that room are Metzl's daily companions.

What this all suggests, of course, is that the sources of Metzl's inspiration are in the great things of all time rather than the evanescent models of the hectic present. It implies that he has provided his career with a sound anchorage that is proof against vicissitudes of fashions.

The pictures printed here give more than a hint of Metzl's versatility, yet they do not include some of the finest things he has done in the past. Among those are some very distinguished posters he did while working in Chicago. I wish these might have been shown here.

The picture, below (an advertisement for Pacific Mills), is one of a series combining drawing and photography. The photograph of the child was made in the studio of Tony Venti and printed on a large-size, sensitized mat paper. All of the props and background were removed on the plate, thus leaving the child and sheet floating in an area of white. The stars, sky and clouds were then painted — over the photographic print — in charcoal, gray washes and colored ink, with the planets done in chalk. Printed in two colors, black and a night blue.

Wallace Morgan

VETERAN ILLUSTRATOR

WALLACE MORGAN began his career as a newspaper artist in 1898. At the time of this writing (1945) he is still going strong. His first job was on the old *New York Telegram*; later, as a member of James Gordon Bennett's staff, his work appeared in the *Herald*. That was before the perfected halftone process substituted photography for the illustrator's pen. There was, to be sure, the specially printed halftone section of the Sunday edition, but for run-of-the-mill train wrecks, coronations, explosions, strikes, murders, and trials the artist was indispensable. His ink drawings could be quickly reproduced by the line process.

Recalling these exciting days, Morgan said, "We used to go out with the reporters, just as the camera men do today. It was a terrible rush, but excellent training. We had to set down the story in simple, direct fashion right on the spot, in crowded streets, inaccessible places, and on moving vehicles. Our assignments took us into fashionable society and into tough places also. But it was swell training for an artist. I can't think of any better way to learn about life and character, or to develop one's faculty for recognizing the dramatic moment in any situation."

In 1905 Morgan was given a special Sunday newspaper feature, a page for the Sunday *Herald*, called "Fluffy Ruffles." It was a combination of verses by Carolyn Wells and Morgan's drawings.

This was the first series of its kind. There were plenty of comic pages and occasional girl pages but this was the first continued cartoon story. Fluffy Ruffles was a smart little girl of her times. She always dressed in the swankiest clothes and was ever getting herself into amusing and sentimental situations. Hats, shoes, and dances were named for her. She was the inspiration of a book and a musical comedy.

This syndicated feature, which ran for almost three years, brought the artist into prominence and attracted the attention of magazine editors. Morgan's first magazine illustration appeared in *Collier's* and he worked for that publication for several years.

Some of his most interesting work on *Collier's* was done in collaboration with Julian Street. Street did the writing, Morgan the drawing. Traveling about the country together, on a three-months' tour, they produced the serial "Abroad at Home." "American Adventure," another serial in *Collier's*, was the result of a five-months' tour of the South. These illustrated "travellogs," delightfully humorous, and gently satirical, recorded the unvarnished impressions of discerning, though casual, tourists—impressions that did not always please the subjects.

Other series by Street and Morgan appeared in *Everybody's Magazine*: one on Foreign Theatres, another on Night Clubs—then called "Cabarets"; and "Welcome to our City."

"Mais non, non, non — comprenez-vous?"
Drawing by Wallace Morgan

If such features were written today they undoubtedly would be illustrated by photographs, and readers would never know of their loss. They would think they were getting realism; but often the photograph gives far less of life than the pencil of a gifted illustrator.

With the rank of Captain in the Engineers Corps, Morgan served as Official Artist with the American Expeditionary Forces in the first World War. The training of his newspaper days served him well in this capacity. During a year in France he was present at every major operation of the American Army.

Morgan, with other official artists, was billeted in the town of Neufchâteau in Lorraine. Quarters were also provided there for use as a studio where the artists developed drawings and paintings from sketches made at the front lines. The artists were given no definite directions but were allowed freedom of movement, subject to certain necessary restrictions. They shared the hazards of the boys in the trenches, except "going over the top."

Morgan carried small sketchbooks, about 5 x 6 inches, in which he made hurried notes with his pencil. Few of these sketches are more than shorthand scribbles, many of them as unintelligible to the layman as stenographic notes; but to the artist they served as valuable aids to memory, records of impressions, later to become the basis of finished drawings.

Since the war, Morgan's illustrations have appeared in many of the better magazines and in the newspapers. His favorite medium is charcoal, though he frequently uses ink, wash and color. He prefers the brush to the pen for his line drawings.

Printemps — Cartoon in The New Yorker Magazine (1941). Original is 12 x 18 inches.

Courtesy The New Yorker

Illustration by Wallace Morgan for a story in Harper's Bazaar. The original is about 11 x 18 inches

He never uses models. Apparently those years of newspaper sketching from life laid a deep foundation for his knowledge of the figure and of human character. Add to that his uncanny ability to etch clearly upon the sensitized film of his memory what he sees—and the thing is explained.

In making an illustration Morgan assumes that his first drawing will be his final drawing. He does not develop his picture in preliminary small sketches. If it doesn't progress to suit him he discards it and makes a fresh start. He works quite large, usually on a 20 x 30 illustration board.

* * *

We are fortunate today to have with us some of the men who began their work in the latter days of the so-called "Golden Age" of illustration. It is profitable to ask and receive their estimate of conditions under which they produced. Those days, to be sure, are gone forever, but it is worthwhile looking back upon them, not in the spirit of nostalgic memory, but with the hope of finding some inspiration and perhaps some instruction that may contribute to the improvement of the illustrators' art in these so different times.

Wallace Morgan is one of the veterans who have bridged the gap that separates past and present. His magnificent drawings are still appearing in current publications. His comments that follow—we asked for them —are candid and critical of contemporary work. I think they have a message for those who are trying today to carry on the great tradition of American illustration:

"The so-called 'Golden Age' of American illustration," says Mr. Morgan, "was a great age, but not a golden one. Illustrators didn't make much money then. But it was a great age, because in those days illustration was really thought of as a fine art and not as a commercial proposition. There were, of course, men who were not great; there was indeed a great deal of mediocrity and a great deal of stupid stuff—dull, bad stuff— but there were a few really talented men, and it is by their work that we remember that age. Those men were thoroughly trained in art, and, with the exception of Howard Pyle, I believe almost all of them studied not only here, but in Paris, Munich, and in the great galleries of Italy and Spain. So they were filled with the history and tradition of art. They had seen people and places and things that gave them a knowledge of the world that appeared in their work, giving it a distinction far above technical excellence which, of course, was high.

"Another happy thing—no, a great thing, in those days—was that there was very little editorial dictation. The magazine sent the story to the man thought best suited for the particular story, and gave him carte blanche. There was only one restriction, and that was more of a warning than a restriction—not to give away the story. Later on, they were so afraid this might happen, that a special copy of the manuscript, in which the main point of the story was left out, would be given to the artist; really an excellent idea. But there was something about working in those days, and expressing yourself without being told just what to do and how to do it, that made the drawings of those talented men really worthwhile, and gave a quality you see very little of today."

Asked for specific criticism of contemporary illustra-

Full-size detail of a charcoal drawing for the picture on page 206

Courtesy Harper's Bazaar

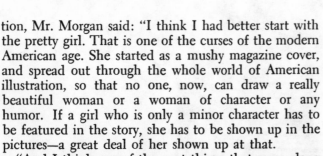

tion, Mr. Morgan said: "I think I had better start with the pretty girl. That is one of the curses of the modern American age. She started as a mushy magazine cover, and spread out through the whole world of American illustration, so that no one, now, can draw a really beautiful woman or a woman of character or any humor. If a girl who is only a minor character has to be featured in the story, she has to be shown up in the pictures—a great deal of her shown up at that.

"And I think one of the next things that came along was the layout. Now, the layout has made the magazine very much more exciting to look at. But it has made it necessary for men to force their compositions into all

Above: Reproduction of one of Wallace Morgan's charcoal drawings, now in the government archives in the Smithsonian Institution at Washington.

Below: A page (exact size) from Morgan's war sketchbook.

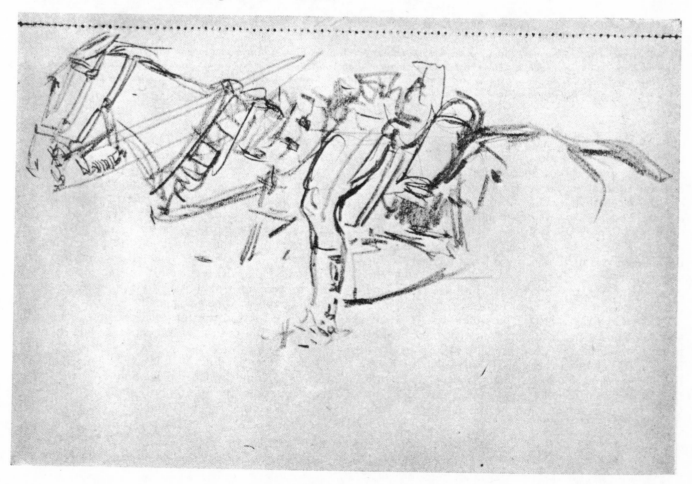

209

This unfinished charcoal study, for an advertisement for Macy's, gives a hint as to Morgan's method of work. The original is 11 x 15 inches. The artist begins at once upon what he hopes will be his final drawing, without preliminary trial. If it doesn't go to suit him, and he decides to make drastic changes in composition, he takes a fresh sheet of illustration board and starts again.

sorts of strange shapes and sizes, and thereby hampered the full expression of ideas, and made it almost impossible to fill some of these spaces with a picture that was really an illustration. So the emphasis came to be more on the decorative quality than on the illustrative quality. And that, of course, brought about more editorial dictation. The result was that the part of the story that was to be illustrated was given to you, and the shape it was to appear in was given to you, and the medium it was to appear in was given to you, and everybody began to work for the business office, and the editorial office, instead of expressing themselves.

"Then came the camera. The camera is a very valuable thing and a necessary thing, and has been used by many distinguished artists as a guide to help in drawing something otherwise almost impossible to draw. But men became more and more its slaves, and, with the development of color photography, even more so. Color photography came to be the model to mimic

and ape. Most illustrations came to have more photographic quality and less expression.

"The photograph of course is static and results in a lack of action, lack of humor, and lack of character and expression. Everything is static. Photographs of horse racing, for example, sometimes look very exciting, but, as a matter of fact, the thing that makes them look exciting is the attitude of the jockey, not the movement of the horse. It is that crouching, eager position of the jockey that makes those race pictures look so exciting; if it weren't for the jockey, the horse wouldn't appear to be going at all."

Wallace Morgan was for seven years president of the Society of Illustrators, of which he is now honorary president.

Books recently illustrated by Mr. Morgan include: *So Far So Good* by Charles Hanson Towne, Messner; and a Book of the Month title, the Fireside Book of Christmas Stories, Bobbs-Merrill.

Oberhardt

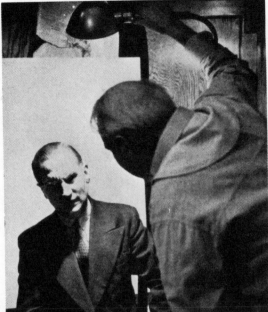

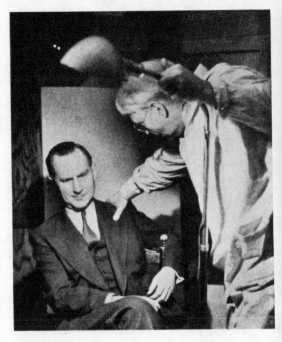

Oberhardt says:

HEADS are my preoccupation, therefore to me the world is full of heads: heads I would gladly pay to draw and heads I would gladly pay not to draw. The only thing I do not like about drawing heads is that I can't always tell the truth about my sitters; they must be portrayed in a favorable light. The artist holds his sitters just as you hold your friends: you hold them by not always telling them the truth and nothing but the truth. The artist must always mix his medium with the milk of human kindness.

My sitters are always celebrities of the business, literary or political world. To show them in a favorable light and yet to tell the truth is one of the most fascinating problems of portraiture. I enjoy more liberty in my interpretation and conception of the sitter than most portraitists because the sitter does not foot the bill, my commission coming from the publisher or advertising agency.

The first thing is to put the sitter at his ease in my studio so that I can study his features before actually starting the portrait. My time on a head is usually limited to one or two hours; I am required to work speedily, not out of choice but of necessity.

Conversation is used to keep my sitter alive; lights, to display his most favorable aspects—because getting a likeness at the expense of a sitter's physical defects is poor portraiture.

There are two approaches. The one I choose depends on the sitter:

1. If he is picturesque, I design the head as a unit and work simultaneously on the drawing in relationship to all parts.

2. If he has an expressive eye or mouth, I concentrate on these features and subordinate the rest.

In my present sitter's case we have an expressive face without any exaggerated features. It will be necessary to concentrate on getting the spirit that animates his kindly face. The eyes are deep-set and, being in shadow, play an unimportant part, pictorially.

An artist frequently has to forego a pictorial lighting effect based on shadows, because this accentuates defects such as wrinkles, bags under the eyes, double chins, etc. Lighting can be complimentary and also uncomplimentary. Mr. H. has no lines. Therefore I can show a strong lighting effect, instead of eliminating his lines by direct front illumination.

In this pose, which calls for animated expression, the problem is to keep the sitter in a kindly mood. If, however, the sitter does not naturally have this quality, it is accomplished by breaking down his reserve and establishing a friendly relationship. When he responds, the problem is an easy one. If he is self-conscious, the artist is in difficulties. Making a successful portrait is always a cooperative job. You generally succeed by getting your sitter to talk about his hobby, which is not difficult if he wants to cooperate. If he has a poker face, he is hard to draw, because poker faces never change no matter what goes on inside.

Once the sitter reveals himself, it is necessary to work fast; keep him in the right psychological mood, and be sure to have all features synchronize. If the eyes are smiling, the nose serious, and the mouth pouting at the same time, the portrait is certainly *not* synchronized.

Work only when the sitter hits the right expression. This, of course, cuts your time down considerably but it is better than having a finished drawing without co-ordinated features. All the elements call for spontaneous registration and sometimes make the expressive face difficult to draw unless each feature is done separately as you go along.

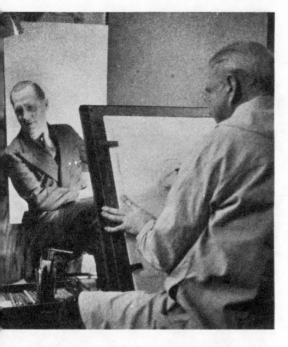

The pictures on these and two following pages show a master draftsman at work and demonstrate his procedure in constructing one of his famous heads.

All heads have basic forms. Our sitter's head is of the long, oval type. You will find that his features are all governed by this form as a whole. There is no harsh discord anywhere in the rhythm; the oval is repeated throughout. This is the problem of design which every portraitist must solve. Laboring for hours on a head will not compensate for lack of knowledge. We unravel what we know, quickly; therefore speed is logical with most of us. So "go to"—without fear—for better or for worse!

Referring again to the problem of expression and lighting—if the sitter is of the lively type, a bright and strong light is appropriate. On the other hand, when a sitter is of the dignified type, a preponderance of dark, subtle tone with a soft, concentrated source of light is in order.

Let me explain further this terminology:

No. 1—Bright, strong illumination means eliminating middle tones and concentration of interest. A single source of light, provided it is not too strong a contrast, produces restful atmosphere. This lighting, in conjunction with a quiet linear movement, is expressive of poise and symbolizes maturity.

No. 2.—A cross-lighting, with rapidly alternating space division, helps to accentuate the quality of restlessness, which, in turn, is expressive of the activities of youth. This is the psychology of line.

These theories are based on observation and have nothing to do with rules. To prove this, observe youth as well as age and you will realize the difference in the rhythm of their movements and their choice of colors. Further, you will also recognize that when age simulates youth it is incongruous—and is, perhaps, the result of a complex. If youth displays the conservative characteristics of age, again a physical or mental reason can be attributed. Since all these characteristics have a counterpart in line and tone, they are invaluable to the

In this series of photographs we see Oberhardt arranging the lighting upon his subject and making the first strokes of the drawing shown on the following pages.

"Obie" is easy to sit for. His personality spins out such pleasant hours that you forget any appointments you may have, or decide they aren't nearly so important — for here is a keen, friendly philosophy of art, closely knit to a philosophy of life.

213

portraitists if applied intelligently. However, if these observations are applied as rules, you are pointing to formula and mannerism. If you use them as a stimulation for further research, you will develop an individual approach.

Tone in a drawing affects the observer psychologically by its contrasts and, also, by its modulations. As for rules, they can never be followed, for you can never use the same approach twice. I frequently have to draw my sketches in business offices where I find lighting conditions unfavorable. These are the moments when method becomes taboo. You can't be like the man who depends upon his memory for his humor and his imagination for his facts. The first few strokes in a sketch always determine the success of a drawing. If they are not convincingly placed—the artist must start over again. A drawing cannot be salvaged by fussing with detail: it only wastes precious time and tires one out. Every stroke must count and become an organic part of the sum total—that, and nothing else, is productive of speed under pressure.

Since all parts are related, you can work comprehensively if you work in relationship to the effect as a whole; or start with a detail, complete it, and add each new unit relative to the whole.

Strokes must be placed to stay. Remember, a sketch is the shorthand of art and not the *sleight-of-hand* of art.

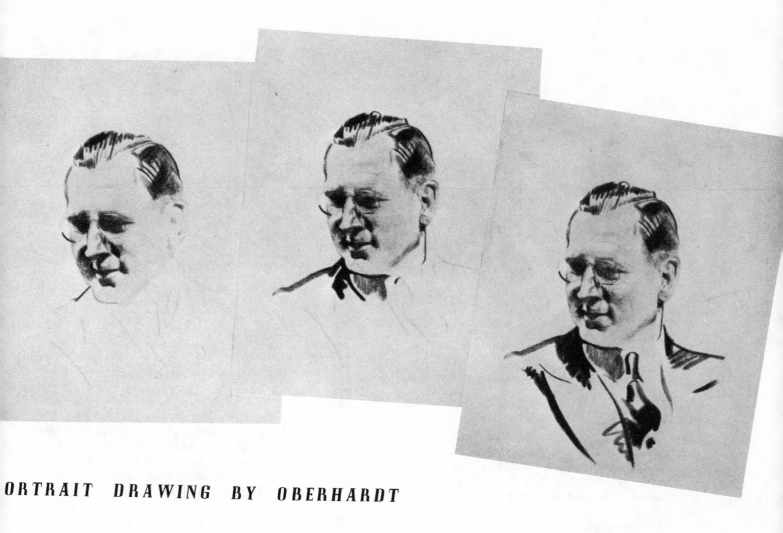

ORTRAIT DRAWING BY OBERHARDT

Avoid haste, and don't take pride in hectic activity. Practice speed only when absolutely necessary—an artist is not a magician. Technique evolves gradually. It is the blossoming forth of years of intelligent study, not surface imitation of accepted mannerisms or formulas. Do not waste time on cleverness which might develop into mere facility. Correct draftsmanship alone has little to do with a likeness, although, without it, there is no art value. What you must strive for is expression in a face: that elusive something we call *personality*. Just a diagram of the face is uninteresting. All you must really strive for is interpretation of personality through form. Do not copy form. A child often gets the spirit that animates a face without knowledge of drawing. A face of a deceased friend has still the same form, but no longer bears a likeness to himself because the personality that animates form no longer functions.

How can form be recognized? Form can be recognized by mental comparison with geometrical shapes— for instance, the angle, the circle, the oval, the square, the oblong, etc. All heads are encased in one of these forms, as a whole or in part. There is no outline in nature, but only interlocking shapes and planes, the animated interplay of which constitutes expression. Harmoniously correlated forms make for beauty; inharmonious forms make for character; a mixture of both stamps it with individuality. And last but not least—the people whose faces are ancestral indexes. We have all seen the

Portrait of Frank Weitenkampf

Portrait of C. D. Williams

man whose family claims he has Aunt Marie's blue eyes, grandfather's nose, Uncle Remus' chin, etc. Although the features have family relationship, they do not harmonize, as is often the case in families. This conglomeration of features does not always mix well, and we have an interesting but homely face—and, sometimes, the caricature of the family.

I'm often asked about my method used for distributing the blacks in my backgrounds. I follow only my feeling of harmony, and aim to distribute them accordingly. I accentuate, modify, concentrate, or subordinate as the problem demands. If the head balances perfectly by itself, no blacks are needed in the background. If, however, the head is minus this quality, I use the background to complete my pattern plan. No part of a drawing should have strokes or masses that are irrelevant to the design.

No two heads call for the same treatment. In the drawing where an eye plays the important part, a likeness of its expression, alone, can determine its success. Contrary to general belief, an eye has no expression. The expression is determined by the contraction of the lids and brows and the play of so-called "crow's feet." The eye itself need not be drawn but merely suggested. Sometimes a highlight correctly formed and placed on its surface reveals both shape and expression. A highlight is not a white speck, as generally believed, but is always related to the organic form of which it is a part.

The contours of shadows have, likewise, very definite, form-revealing shapes. When highlight and shadow forms are correctly delineated, the middle tones automatically organize themselves in a drawing.

Young artists are frequently nervous when drawing celebrities. That frequently keeps them from producing their best work. If they will bear in mind that the sitter is as self-conscious and nervous as they are, they will then become correspondingly cool and composed.

I was affected by it at first, and once complained about it to my friend Hudson Maxim, the noted inventor. Mr. Maxim, who was an outspoken philosopher, always expressed himself with vigor and humor. His advice cured me of all further inhibitions. It was: "Don't let celebrities awe you. The more you get to know them, the more you will find the halo generally hangs over one ear."

Not all celebrities look their part, as the following anecdote will show.

I was commissioned by *Collier's* to do a portrait of Mr. X, a noted writer, and was patiently awaiting his arrival at the appointed hour. But Mr. X did not appear. After allowing a few hours to pass, I dismissed the matter, only to find myself answering a knock at the door by—what I regarded—a very unprepossessing looking man. Believing him to be a hopeless type as a model, for whom there would never be a chance for employment, I patronizingly offered to register his name. I asked him to wait—closing the door—while I got my book. On returning, I let him put his name down on my hopeless list. Lo and behold, it was my tardy sitter—the celebrity!   *End of Oberhardt's Writing*

Matlack Price, in an article in *American Artist*, said some things about Oberhardt that are worth quoting here. The paragraphs that follow are random excerpts from his text.

A spirited, cursive "O" signed to a drawing, or an equally briskly written "Oberhardt" always meant two things to me. They were the hall-mark on drawings of sterling quality, and they meant, too, a personality—keen, kindly, philosophical—and militant always for true standards of fine workmanship. And I am sure there are many others in the far-flung field of advertising who have felt the same about both the man and his work.

If you know Oberhardt, indeed, you cannot separate

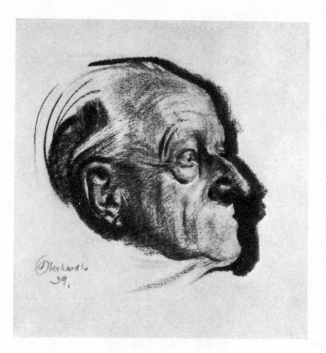

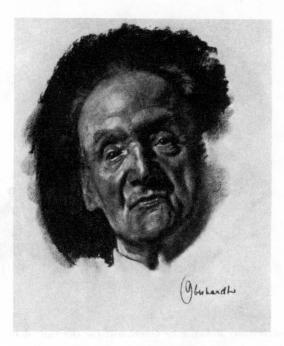

Portrait of Louis Ruyl

Portrait of H. S. Nichols

the two—they are so perfectly consistent. Here is a man of convictions but no prejudices, as befits the true artist; a man who will make no compromises with sound drawing and sound craftsmanship. I can't imagine Oberhardt saying or thinking that any drawing he ever delivered was "good enough." Either it was as good as he could make it, with everything he had—or it wouldn't ever leave his studio.

There are not, today, too many artists with enough principle or conscience. Excuse them, if you will, by mumbling something about the pressure of modern conditions, the low standards of some Art Directors, the lack of appreciation of clients. Oberhardt's work makes no excuses and needs none—and there's far too little of that sort of thing in the field of illustration today.

Perhaps all this sounds a bit grim, and as though our artist might be a preaching old grouch, achieving in his attitude only a balance of appreciation for his own work and disparagement of all other work. Nothing could be further from the fact, for like all the men who count (all I've ever known, anyhow), Oberhardt is so modest, so quiet, about all he does that you have to remember that it's only pygmies who shout and scold.

His personality spins out such pleasant hours that you forget any appointments you might have, or decide they aren't nearly so important—for here is a keen, friendly philosophy of art, closely knit to a philosophy of life. You settle not only all the more vexatious art problems, but most of the more vexatious problems of the World as well.

How, after all, could any artist become recognized as one of the foremost portraitists of men if he were not a philosopher, if he were not endowed with insight, understanding, sympathy and a very human sense of humor.

Joseph Pennell and Charles Dana Gibson have characterized Oberhardt's portraiture as "a masterful likeness which brings out the soul and presents the inner man."

Portraiture in charcoal makes the strongest appeal to Oberhardt although he is at home in other mediums and various themes, illustrating for books and magazines. Of late, most of his work has been in the advertising field. Oberhardt has made drawings for many national accounts—too numerous to be itemized here.

Oberhardt, unlike many illustrators, stands firmly against photographic aids to art, at the same time that he properly recognizes the legitimacy of photography as an art in its own right—an important distinction.

Oberhardt traveled the old-fashioned, long, hard-working road to art—but he isn't smug about it. He just thinks the best way to learn to draw is to learn to draw—no matter how long it takes. I reminded him that all the youngsters today want to get right out and make a living at it. They can hardly wait three years. Sometimes I've asked them if they cared whether it were an honest living they were planning to make of art—or be phony artists. Oberhardt thought (as you can readily enough guess) that he'd prefer an honest bricklayer to a phony artist.

I was looking at an article I did on Oberhardt in an advertising magazine in 1923. It emphasized the important contribution he had made to advertising in putting *real character*—not rubber-stamp faces—into his drawings. Not only was he always as exacting as a casting director in selecting types—he exacted from his own hand a true *delineation* of the type.

Both advertising people and artists, who have observed Oberhardt's work, have found (often to their naïve disappointment) that there is no "trick" in it. His training, for one thing, was much more thorough than that

217

Advertising drawing by Oberhardt for the United Fruit Company

One of several drawings for an A & P newspaper advertising campaign. Oberhardt's supremacy in character delineation, combined with technical virtuosity, have made his drawings in great demand by advertisers.

A roster of the personages who have sat for Oberhardt includes many among the great and the near great. Among them are Thomas A. Edison—a splendid head; three presidents—Taft, Harding and Hoover; Luther D. Burbank; Henry Cabot Lodge; Col. Edward M. House; "Joe" Cannon; Major Gen. James G. Harboard; Walter Lippmann; and two well-known Reverends—Drs. Fosdick and Cadman. Sergei Rachmaninoff was one of his famous subjects, as were Irving Berlin, William Green, Joseph Pennell, Henry J. Kaiser, Charles Dana Gibson, Clarence Budington Kelland, Charles Schwab and Walter B. Chrysler.

Some of Oberhardt's proudest work has been the five hundred or so portraits of men in the Armed Forces, drawn from life in the hospitals, as a morale-building contribution toward the war effort—a great service sponsored principally by The Society of Illustrators and the New Rochelle Art Association. These portraits have been donated to the men and mailed to wives, parents or sweethearts.

The distinction of election, as associate, to the National Academy of Design was a timely recognition of Oberhardt's place in the World of Art.

which the student in school today, or out of school, for that matter, regards as necessary. Four years in the National Academy of Design in New York and three years in Munich gave him a solid foundation. Especially solid, I imagine, the three years in Munich, where artists (before more recent "expressionist" lapses) took their art pretty seriously—years on the "antique" before you were even allowed in a life class.

On Page opposite:
Portraits by Oberhardt of Men in the Armed Forces of Four Nations.

The central figure is an American sailor; top center, a Scotch infantryman; top right, a Royal marine; center right, a Chinese merchantman; lower right, a British sailor.

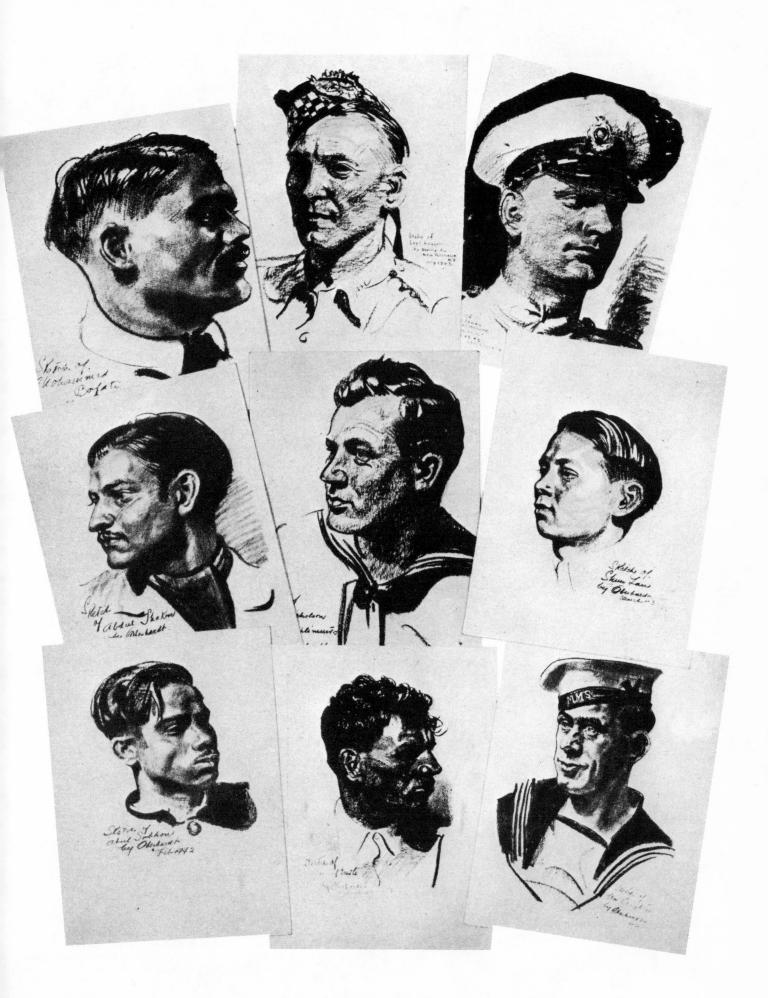

Henry C. Pitz

An illustration by Henry C. Pitz
for "There Was A Horse" by Phyllis Fenner, Alfred Knopf

Sidelights on Book Illustration

By HENRY C. PITZ

MANY COMPETENT ARTISTS who can paint good pictures imagine that illustrating books would be child's play for them. As a matter of fact the market is glutted with picture makers. Yes, even good picture makers. The successful book illustrator is much more than a good picture maker. First of all he loves books and book making in all its aspects; he lives in a world of books. Usually he is an avid reader of books. Through this intimacy with books he has acquired a kind of sixth sense through which he instinctively knows just how to illustrate any particular book.

I was raised among pictures and history books and I learned to love both. By the time I had reached high school I was torn between two desires: to make pictures and to teach and do research in history. Both have been largely combined in my illustration, for a good half of what I do is in the nature of historical or "costume" pictures. I read history for enjoyment and find that the scraps of knowledge I pick up are of direct help to many of the manuscripts I illustrate.

Actually my reading has left only a light deposit of facts but I think it has enabled me to enter into the spirit of some previous ages and imaginatively to identify myself with certain epochs. I am not very much interested in the kind of picture that merely records the literal facts of history. I like to see pictures in which all the figures are human beings very like ourselves; in which they wear their clothes (no matter how strange they may seem to us) as naturally as we wear ours. I like historical pictures that live and breathe and are not merely archaeological documents.

One of the joys of an illustrator's life, as I have found it, is that I have had the good fortune of being able to illustrate many of the books I loved as a boy—*Beowulf, Ivanhoe, Westward Ho, Voyages of Columbus,* to name a few. Then think of the liberal education in book illustration! No one can comply with the varying demands of an illustrator's career without broadening his interests in all things and getting to know all types of people. Illustration is indeed a great adventure.

I won't go into art training here. To have a thorough knowledge of the figure and much facility in drawing is a fundamental necessity—that goes without saying. It seems important to me that both knowledge and facility should be so great that models are unnecessary when the illustration is being made. I seldom do my illustrations from models. But at other times I am constantly drawing from models to sharpen my knowledge and to increase my facility. And I prefer to draw people at their accustomed tasks rather than to draw the statue poses of a professional model. Particularly in historical pictures I find that almost every model seems stiff and ill at ease in a period costume. The result is likely to be artificial.

How to get started? That is about the first question I am asked. First let me caution against the expectation of commission on the initial round of the publishers, who are not sitting in their offices just waiting for you and your samples. One day some time ago I was in the office of Joseph H. Chapin, for many years art director of Charles Scribner's Sons. He was talking about the "good old days" when there were not over a dozen men whom he could call upon. He didn't even have a record of their names, he knew them all inti-

It is said that Henry C. Pitz (born in Philadelphia in 1895) has illustrated more children's books than any contemporary artist. He teaches illustration also — is supervisor of illustration courses at the Museum School of Industrial Arts. His students not only study book illustration, they illustrate books, which is quite a different matter. Pitz' accomplishments are by no means confined to illustration; his paintings and prints have won numerous prizes in national exhibitions. Editor.

mately. But times have changed. Mr. Chapin stepped to his filing cabinet, pulled out three drawers filled with cards, hundreds of them, each card bearing the name of someone who had called upon Mr. Chapin at least once.

Sounds terrifying! But let's take a little terror out of those files. Remember that probably a large proportion of the applicants got disheartened after the first call. Therefore if you do no more than call a second time with fresh samples, you will have done something more than a goodly number of those potential rivals of yours. And if you have the persistence to keep going back even ten times you will have won your way into the ranks of the small minority from which all successful illustrators are chosen. For stamina and determination are almost as important as talent.

Very few have something really original, personal and different to offer. If you are one of these your chance will come, though you must not be discouraged if you have to wait months for it. In the meantime you will keep the publisher reminded of you by showing more examples of your work from time to time. Don't feel that you have to take everything you have ever done the first time—a half-dozen well selected things will be better than fifty irrelevant pictures. From your original drawings have photostats made which, reduced to page size, can be sent through the mail and are small enough for the art director's filing cabinet.

HENRY C PITZ

Illustration by Pitz for "Swords in the Dawn" by Beaty. Longmans, Green

Many beginners do their first work for the Sunday School magazines. These are weekly sheets distributed each Sunday by the Protestant denominations. Each denomination gets out several editions for different age groups. Many of these papers are very well edited and printed. They pay from fifteen to twenty-five dollars per drawing.

For your first book you may be paid $150, $200, or $250. Experienced illustrators get up to $600, sometimes more. The publisher will probably expect you to design the jacket, though not necessarily. If your work does not lend itself to jacket design, some other artist will be brought in for that.

The more you know about book designing, layout, paper and typography, the better. Although your advice upon these matters is not likely to be sought at first—all the big publishers have designers and production men—the publisher will be more appreciative of your understanding of his manufacturing problems. Sooner or later he may ask you actually to design a book. I have designed many books, making complete dummies and specifying all that went into their manufacture.

It would seem unnecessary to say that considerable technical knowledge of photo mechanical processes is important. Yet few beginners are sufficiently informed about engraving and lithography. They do not fully realize how vital it is to know how to prepare drawings for the particular process to be used in reproducing their drawings and for the kind of paper upon which they are to be printed. This cannot be explained in a short article. It must be learned either in the schools which include that phase of illustration or in the school of experience itself. A book such as Greer's *Advertising and its Mechanical Production* (T. Y. Crowell) can be a big help.

No matter how good your work is, do not be surprised if instead of an out-and-out contract you are given a manuscript and are asked to make two or three sketches showing what you can do with the story. It is one thing to make up samples and quite another to take an assignment. The publisher cannot be blamed for assuring himself of your ability to carry through before he gives you a contract.

Even after you have done some work for him he may suggest that you submit pencil sketches for an entire

Illustration by Pitz
for "The Aran Man" in
The Saturday Evening Post

offerings on the counters. Talk to the librarian in charge of the children's room of the local library. Look at the children's magazines designed for various age groups.

Not that the illustrator will hope to adapt himself to all groups. On the other hand he will certainly become a specialist, finding himself best suited by his interests and technical qualities to boys or girls of particular age groups. I found myself specializing in books for boys, stories of combat, of naval battles and wars, concentrating on pictorial content rather than design, and using simple and bold colors.

As to color, most drawings are made for black and white reproduction only. Frequently one or two flat colors are added and often the frontispiece—sometimes all pictures—are in full color. How to make the best use of single flat color with black is an interesting problem, one that the student should experiment with. Such drawings should be among his samples. To most beginners the necessity of restricting oneself to two, three or four definite colors seems an unsurmountable hardship, but look at the work of the best illustrators of children's books and you will see that it can be done. But it will be impossible unless you can see your pictures in terms of definite bold design. In fact an illustrator without a well developed sense of design is under a great handicap in working for line reproduction.

series of illustrations. This really protects you as well as the publisher: it avoids the possibility of spending hours upon finished drawings which may not be acceptable.

When you are finally considered an experienced illustrator, the publisher will be delighted to leave the whole matter in your hands, knowing that your judgment is wholly to be relied upon. He may invite your suggestions upon paper, typography and other problems in design and manufacture.

The greatest opportunities in the book illustration field are in the realm of children's books. Comparatively few adult books invite the services of the artists, although there seems to be an increased interest in this field. To make drawings for children the artist must become acquainted with children, with children of three and with children of thirteen. Between these ages are age groups having varied interests in life and varied tastes in pictorial art. What will appeal to boys of eight and girls of ten? What children prefer realism, imagination, romance? The illustrator must know the answer to these questions. They are easily found by browsing in the bookshops, asking what books are selling best, how youngsters react to the various kinds of

In illustration, as in all else, there are styles and trends which the beginner will do well to study, but it would be well to exercise a certain amount of discrimination. There are certain fads which sweep the world of picture making from time to time which are necessarily ephemeral in nature. Perhaps for a would-be illustrator to ape a passing fad in order to cash in on the wave of the moment is merely being canny, but to expect a superficial trick to last a lifetime of picture making is to display lack of intelligent selection. The real and great illustrators are those whose works contain elements of eternal value. If the beginner is in search of something of that kind and something capable of infinite development, let him consider that a knowledge of and insight into the character of human beings are qualities that never go out of fashion in illustration, qualities that make for success in years ahead.

Although to the beginner the securing of his first commission may seem to be the only thing of moment, it may be well to ponder on the fact that he is preparing for a lifetime of picture making.

George Price

A **peep** into the private life of
a notorious funny man—and
complete instructions
on how to become a number one
graphic humorist

GEORGE PRICE does not—as many believe—spend leisure moments hanging, head down, from chandeliers.

In order to dangle from chandeliers there have to be, *ipso facto*, chandeliers from which to hang. There is not even one chandelier in the Price home at Tenafly, New Jersey. There are, however, a wife (charming) and three growing boys (hungry). The demands of these, and a whole lot of old paint that has to be scraped from nice pine panels of a pre-Revolutionary house, recently acquired, leave little time for dangling or the practice of levitation.

The superstition that George Price possesses occult powers was doubtless engendered by that series of drawings in the New Yorker, known as *The Saga of the Floating Man*. The notion was supported by a photograph of the artist reclining upon thin air midway between floor and ceiling of his garret studio.

We determined that in this chapter we would either confirm or deny the veracity of those reports of strange behavior by one of America's best loved graphic humorists. Even if we had to journey to Jersey to do it. Which we did.

As he draws, George Price sits at ease in a General Grant Period rocking chair. Eight-year-old Wilfrid seems amused at something — probably not papa's drawing.

What we found was an outwardly normal and kindly man, who evidently is a good husband, an indulgent father and a substantial provider. The only mark of psychopathic tendency—it has already been hinted at —is an insane preoccupation with paint scraping. This, if an isolated symptom like the eating of dirt or plaster, would be serious enough. But considered as an expression of genuine antiquarianism it need not cause undue alarm. It is likely to burn itself out at any rate: paint scraping, when motivated by fanaticism, can be practiced with pleasure for the nonce, but in ten years—our rough estimate of the extent of this project—its delights are likely to pall.

George Price's fanaticism can be readily understood when one stands upon the hearthstone of the original wing of his abode, built in 1745, and looks up into the great flue which begins overhead at nearly the ceiling level. Who but one with a sodden imagination could be immune to the spell of this historical place? Price himself was an out-and-out modernist until his feet touched this hearthstone. He had even paid an architect to design a strictly modern home for him. The pictures by French moderns—Roualt, Gauguin, Matisse, et al., which would have adorned that modern residence, seem just as much at home in the old colonial rooms where they now hang along with several

"He's been up three weeks now and there's nothing we can do about it."

228

"A simple 'yes' or 'no' will be sufficient, madame."

←1511-1525

Drawings by

GEORGE PRICE

Courtesy
The New Yorker

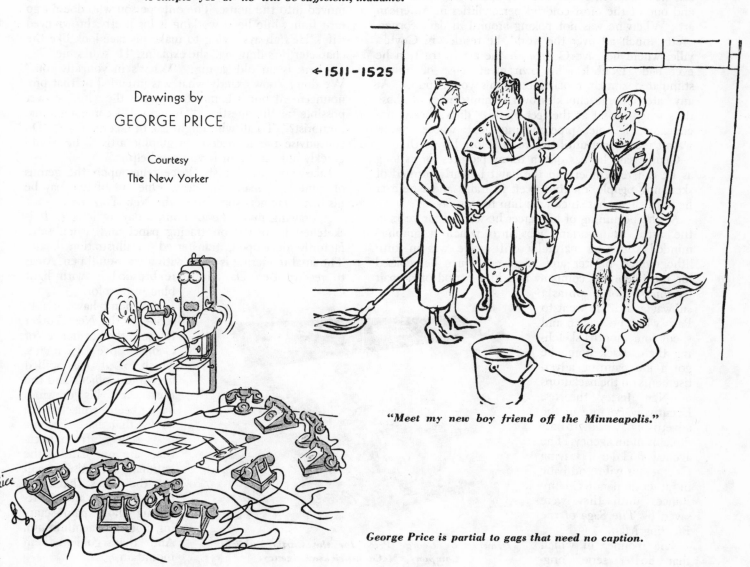

"Meet my new boy friend off the Minneapolis."

George Price is partial to gags that need no caption.

by Pop Hart, Prices's special hero in the art world.

If we seem to be approaching the point of our story by a circuitous route it is because, during our visit, the talk about Price's art had to follow the antiquarian hour. This, we hasten to explain, was not really his fault. We egged him on.

"I don't know as I belong in an art magazine anyway," said George, when we finally got around to his drawings. "I don't paint pictures, neither is my work projected from what is generally considered an 'art' viewpoint. A humorist's concern in composing his drawings is to bring out the full flavor of a whimsical idea or gag. This is by no means easy, to be sure, but whether or not it is art is another matter." And, we might add, we don't care anyway. What we want to know is how George Price got that way and how he produces those hilarious drawings that for many years have kept readers of the New Yorker, Collier's and the Post in good humor.

Of course he himself doesn't really know. Who, indeed, can explain what gets into a person to make him sensitive to the comedy or the tragedy of life as the case may be? All we can do is to examine the circumstances of a life and speculate concerning their influence upon the career.

George Price was born in Coytesville, New Jersey. His next door neighbor was Pop Hart, vagabond artist and one of the most colorful personalities in American art. When he was not poking around in dark corners pretty much all over the world, he resided in Coytesville, where he gave George all the art instruction he ever had. Doubtless his own great sense of humor stimulated similar proclivities in his young pupil. At any rate, George chuckles over reminiscences of those days when he sat at the feet of this "dirty, messy, uneducated, lovable, pipe-smoking gent whose genius wasn't recognized until two years before his death."

George says he has drawn funny pictures for as long as he can remember and the habit he early formed of sketching people, on the street, in trains and wherever he finds them, has stuck with him to this day.

At the beginning of his career he worked for years at the usual unimportant jobs into which a graphic-minded youngster naturally drifts. He was in turn lithographer, printer and engraver. Once he worked for the telephone company and in a period of despair he almost took a job as a subway guard. He went to Paris when he was 26 and spent four months sketching there. Back home he got a job painting advertisements on the backdrops of New Jersey theatres. Eventually he rose in the advertising world to art director of an agency. The agency f o l d e d, leaving George, his wife, and baby in rather desperate circumstances until they were saved by The Saga of the Floating Man.

The manner in which that floater series orig-

inated, by the way, gives as good an idea how to think up gags as can be recommended. George and his wife, Florence, were chatting one evening with friend Lou Kamp who was living with them at the time. Suddenly Lou said, "How about drawing a guy floating over the bed. His wife is saying to a visitor, 'He's been up three weeks now and there's nothing we can do about it.'"

They all laughed for a few minutes, then George said, "No, it's too crazy." "Well," said Lou, "draw it anyway. Maybe we'll get off this bean diet." George finally did make two drawings. The New Yorker took one. Others followed until the floating man, in the 22nd and final episode, was shot down by his wife who confided that, "He never knew what hit him."

That, in a nutshell, is the way to become a great humorist. At any rate it was the beginning of George Price's career in the New Yorker, which for many years has been the highway of his fame.

But a beginning, after all, is only a beginning. Just what it takes to be a steady producer of fun and nonsense is at least suggested by Jack Sher who wrote in Sunday Magazine: "I've watched George Price work in that garret studio while his son George, Jr., played the clarinet not two feet from his drawing table. At the same time Wilfrid, 6, was using one of his father's legs as a stop for an electric train. Downstairs the infant, Charles, was howling while new furniture was being moved into the house. The only person who doesn't go near him while he is working is his pretty, brown-eyed wife. 'He's always trying to make his face look like the character he's drawing,' she explains. 'He scares me!'"

There is an old saying: "What's in you ails you." We don't know exactly what was intended by that pronouncement but it comes to mind as the wisest answer possible for the question, "How can I become a graphic humorist?" To all who might ask of George Price, "Do you advise me to become a graphic artist?" he would quickly answer, "Not if you can help it."

Like most cartoonists, Price relies upon the genius of some "gag man" for ideas. One out of ten may be his own. He gets some from the New Yorker.

A drawing may take an hour, a day, or longer. It is sketched in pencil on tracing paper and, when satisfactorily developed, transferred to illustration board. The final rendering is done with a crow-quill pen. Areas to receive Ben Day tints are brushed in with light blue watercolor.

You don't have to subscribe to the New Yorker to see the evidence of George Price's g e n i u s. Much of it has spilled over into Collier's and the Post. And his drawings have been collected in books that have become best sellers. If publications are not careful the national advertisers will get the lion's share. Indeed they are already reducing those paint-scraping hours to a minimum. And "thar's gold in them mountains!"

Drawing by George Price for the Curtis Publishing Company. McCann-Erickson Agency.

Ray Prohaska

AN HOUR IN PROHASKA'S STUDIO

THE SIGNATURE OF RAY PROHASKA is a familiar one to readers of *Good Housekeeping, Redbook, Woman's Home Companion, Post, Cosmopolitan* and other publications where boy is forever meeting girl.

There is a reason for this, beyond the essential fact that Prohaska is one of the best craftsmen in the contemporary school of illustration. He is an expert in feminine charm. His girls are smart; they are fashionable; they are glamorous. They are "nice" girls too. They come from good families.

So I was not surprised to see copies of *Vogue* and *Harper's Bazaar* lying about in Prohaska's studio. I was surprised to see the artist actually making a hat to be worn by one of his *Redbook* girls. He could have bought that hat at Bonwit Teller's—for a price. Instead he looked at it, then took a taxi to 14th Street where he purchased a cheap hat form. Back in his studio with scissors, ribbons and a miscellany of milliner's findings, in a half hour he produced a reasonable facsimile, plus a touch of Prohaska chic.

Now and then Ray will even resort to dressmaking. Lying on a studio table was a rose-colored bodice with a dainty bow at the neckline. I picked it up. "That," said Ray, "is a bit I made for a girl in a *Whitman's Sampler* advertisement. Little more than her head and shoulders appeared in the painting. So the bodice and that bow had to characterize her as a girl of impeccable taste, a good dresser. It is a bow which, if you were up on such matters, you would recognize as very smart. You know," he continued, "women look at the clothes first—in illustrations as well as in real life."

Prohaska is not pigeonholed as a boy and girl illustrator. Editors will give him any kind of story. But I speak of his women first because they have so amply repaid him for the pains he has lavished upon them.

It is not my intention here to enter into a critical discussion of Ray Prohaska's work. I wish only to take the reader on a visit to his studio where we can observe just how he creates those illustrations that have brought him such enviable success.

The timing of our visit is fortunate. Prohaska is at work on a double-page spread to head the story of *Lily and the U.S.A.* by Vina Delmar. (This appeared in *Good Housekeeping.*) His procedure, which is typical of his present method, is pictured on the following pages.

First, of course, there is the manuscript. Even though the scene to be illustrated has already been selected by the editors and a layout for the picture made by the art editor, the manuscript has to be studied for character, action and details of setting. In contemporary practice, layouts are often made by the art director who is responsible for the design appearance of the magazine as a whole. He has to style every page with reference to every other page. Most illustrators appear satisfied with this procedure. Indeed many say they are thankful to have that much of their task performed when they are handed the manuscript. Plenty more remains to be done anyhow.

Prohaska begins his graphic work with innumerable pencil studies. In these he plays around with his composition. Many of them are abstractions.

After he has developed the composition to his satisfaction he begins to cast the characters and set the stage for the chosen scene. From the first reading of the manuscript the characters have been taking shape in his mind but he tries, if possible, to find models which conform reasonably well to preconceived types.

Prohaska goes to great lengths to secure just the

Text continued on page 237

Illustration by Prohaska for "The Message" by Mary Parrish in Good Housekeeping. Prohaska designed the hat, dress and gloves worn by the girl. The costume was made up by Marion Valle.

One of many studies (16 x 7 inches) on tracing paper: experiments with abstract compositional arrangements

THE CREATION OF
A PROHASKA ILLUSTRATION

The pictures on these pages record the essential steps in the illustration by Ray Prohaska of the Good Housekeeping Story "Lily Hunter and the U. S. A." by Vina Delmar. They reveal the artist's customary procedures.

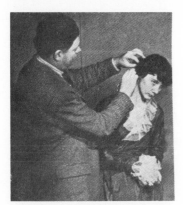

Prohaska arranges coiffure — he is an expert on feminine smartness

Prohaska found and photographed this sideboard in an antique shop

One of many photographs of the scene. Prohaska sometimes makes as many as 30 or 40 shots with his Contax or Rolleiflex Cameras.

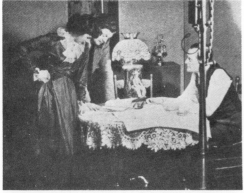

Before making camera shots the artist goes over manuscript with models to familiarize them with the action they are to dramatize

Lily Hunter and the USA

This is reproduced from the "Comprehensive" in color, which was submitted for the Art Director's approval before the final painting was begun. The design follows quite closely the layout prepared by Gene Davis, then art director of Good Housekeeping.

Reproduction of the color illustration. The original oil painting is 47 x 22 inches

THESE THREE HALFTONES *illustrate Pro-haska's technical method of painting.*

Above: Drawing in line with brown india ink on canvas that has been toned with burnt umber or burnt sienna.

Upper right: The essential light tones are painted in white and the darks laid in with monotone browns or greens. This is a tempera underpainting.

Lower right: The final painting is in oil colors, which are applied in transparent glazes and impasto color.

Illustration for "The Last Hour," a Good Housekeeping story.

For this illustration Prohaska made many photographs. Three of them are shown here.

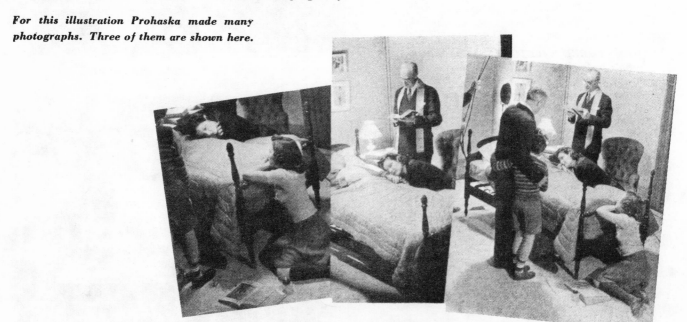

right properties for the setting. He stresses their importance in creating the proper atmosphere and giving conviction to the illustration. All the furniture and the accessories for this *Lily and the U.S.A.* story came from second-hand and antique shops in the neighborhood. The table, chairs, flower stand, lamp and table cover were brought right into the studio. A photograph of the sideboard, taken in the store, had to suffice. That is the only property missing in his studio set-up, as can be seen from the photograph on page 234.

The costume problem was readily solved by a visit, with the model, to a costumer, where a gown once worn by a belle in 1914 was found.

A photograph shows the artist instructing his models as he reads to them, from the manuscript, those passages which describe the action of the scene that is to be dramatized. The properties have been assembled. All is in readiness for the next step, which is photography.

The camera is a relatively recent addition to the tools and equipment of the illustrator. What it has done to or for his art is a controversial question with which we are not concerned at the moment. The fact is that practically every contemporary illustrator relies to a considerable extent upon photography. The traditional practice of having models pose for hours on end while a painting is in progress has just about disappeared, due to the fact that a good model may receive from $5 to $25 per hour for her services. Then, too, the good ones are hard to get. They are usually booked a day ahead for a specific hour. So today, models are brought to the studio and photographed. From the many exposures made (usually dozens of them) the artist derives what factual information he needs. Just how creative he is in his use of these photographs depends upon the artist's imagination, originality and technical training with pencil and brush.

Some illustrators rely upon professional photographers for their camera work. Others have acquired sufficient skill to manage their own photography. Some, indeed, are accused of being better photographers than artists. Years ago, when Prohaska was working on the West Coast, he got his first experience in photography through working with newspaper camera men. Now he does all his own camera and laboratory work. He has all the necessary equipment in his studio including a darkroom. He uses an f3.5 50 mil. Rolleiflex camera as well as Contax f.2 50 mil. He often makes forty or fifty exposures of his subject. Thus, he declares, he has that many chances of catching just the right gesture and expression of an individual, and the most significant emotional interplay between characters who transact the given scene again and again as the shutter of the camera clicks.

As the artist paints he has many of these prints before him. They serve as sources for a drawing which may not follow any one of them entirely, although it often does. It will be seen, however, that much of Prohaska's creative work has already been done before he picks up his brush to paint. He certainly goes much further in stage setting than many illustrators. Note, for example, how he dramatized the death-bed scene for *The Last Hour*, another *Good Housekeeping* story. For this illustration he made a most exhaustive search for models with the right character basis. He had the scene enacted over and over while he made innumerable photographs. His painting is the result of careful selection of the best parts of many of the photographs; plus the further use of the model for final check-up on the painting.

Prohaska's painting procedure is interesting. First he tones his single prime canvas with umber, sienna or terre verte. Upon this he transfers the lines from a pencil drawing which invariably precedes work on canvas. These lines are then strengthened with brown, waterproof india ink. Waterproof ink is used so that corrections made in the tempera painting (by washing parts off) will not obliterate the ink line foundation.

Upon completion of the ink outline drawing, Prohaska makes an underpainting in casein tempera. This is not a colorful painting. It serves principally to establish the values. The lights are laid in first in white; the darks and middle tones in browns and grays.

This underpainting is then varnished with *etherial varnish*, a mixture of damar and turpentine, and allowed to dry over night.

Before beginning the final painting, the canvas is moistened by scumbling over it with a 50-50 linseed turpentine medium. This makes it more receptive to oil paint. The final oil painting is done partly by the glazing of transparent oil color. Impasto color is also used generously throughout the painting. He follows the procedure of thick and thin painting throughout.

I have written at some length about Prohaska's use of the camera; this because his methods are fairly typical of the part played by photography in contemporary illustration, and there is great interest in this new influence upon the illustrator's art. While photography, as we have seen, is a much used tool in Prohaska's studio I must not give the impression that his art in any sense depends upon or derives from the camera which, after all, is of no use whatever in the hands of one who is not a thoroughgoing artist in the first place. Prohaska draws directly from models at nearly every stage of his work. And when it comes to color of course the camera must be laid aside altogether.

Perhaps I should have used more of my space to speak of what is likely to make the greatest impression upon the visitor to his studio. That is Prohaska's enthusiasm for drawing and painting. On his studio walls are framed drawings and paintings of models. Cabinet drawers and portfolios bulge with figure drawings. I wish we might have had the space to reproduce more of these drawings which are a delight to see. They are the expression of accomplished craftsmanship and of devotion to the great traditions of art.

Ray Prohaska was born in the town of Mulo on the bay of Kotor in Yugoslavia. His parents brought him to America when he was seven years old. His early years were spent on the Pacific Coast where he received his schooling and much of his early experience in the art world. After studying at the California School of Fine Arts he had a fling at almost every kind of art work—lettering, posters, theatre displays, political cartoons, still life and advertising drawings of all kinds. Until he came to New York in 1929 he had done no illustration work whatsoever. In San Francisco and later in Chicago he did advertising drawings for J. Walter Thompson Co., Botsford Constantine Co., N. W. Ayer & Sons, Grauman Studios—and numerous other advertising agencies.

Robert Riggs

ROBERT RIGGS

FROM WHATEVER ANGLE we approach Robert Riggs we encounter a career that is colorful, yes, extraordinary.

He lives in a museum—alone, and likes it—keeps snakes for pets, is fanatically interested in primitive things, and does all his creative work at night. Cézanne and Picasso were and are chief among his graphic heroes, yet his infatuation with them was the cause of his failure for fifteen years, when he was influenced by them instead of by Vermeer or Rembrandt, who, he came to realize, are his truer guides. He says, now, that he should have taken his prayer rug to the museum and bowed down before the modern masters, then gone home to be his realistic self. Riggs never uses models or photographs. He doesn't make preliminary studies. He begins his pictures by completely finishing the head of the central figure; until this is rendered to his entire satisfaction he will not touch the work elsewhere. He likes to make mistakes; says he relies upon them. In correcting mistakes he produces accidentals that stimulate his imagination and give direction to his creative powers. For the past twenty-five years he has been searching for the ideal medium. Now, he thinks he has found it—by accident.

But let me introduce you personally to the man whom I interviewed in his Philadelphia home.

Riggs lives on the second and third floors of a house in the Germantown district, about fifteen minutes by taxi from the North Philadelphia station. Tall, genial

and of ample girth, he greeted me at the head of the stairs. He was in shirt sleeves, his collar open at the neck, and he chewed upon a large cigar that is as characteristic a feature of his countenance as is the friendly smile which punctuates his conversation.

He led me to what I have called his museum: two rooms—they are his living rooms—filled with exhibits of North American and African relics. The rooms were as dark as night until lights were switched on, the black window shades having shut out the afternoon sun.

All the walls of these two rooms are thickly covered from floor to ceiling with his collection: ceremonial masks, fur trappings, tomahawks, quivers, wampum, charms, scalps and mummified fingers. African relics occupy the side of one room. The *pièce de résistance* of this exhibit is a large gourd decorated with human jawbones. Primitive drums and other standing objects around the room encroach upon the floor, which is further made hazardous for unfamiliar feet by a lion's skin rug that thrusts its ferocious head out into the traffic lane.

Nestling under a reading lamp among these barbarous treasures are the artist's overstuffed chair and radio phonograph. Here Riggs says he loves to recline, close his eyes and listen to exotic music from Africa, India and Siam, from his extensive library of victrola records.

A third room on the same floor serves as a reptile house. Its walls are lined with glass cages for the accommodation of a variety of snakes, alligators, iguanas and such like occupants. Skeletons and skins of deceased individuals supplement one's interest in the live specimens. Into the cages of the latter, Riggs will thrust a hand and bring forth his writhing pets who coil themselves about his neck and caress his cheek. He will even invite guests to share this pleasure, as he did me, by letting me hold a seven-foot indigo serpent in my timid arms, a treat never before vouchsafed me.

Sleeping quarters and studio are on the third floor which, like the second, was darkened by black shades that sunny day. On a wall of the studio an exhibit of Riggs' lithographs, uniformly framed, give one an opportunity to study the artist's various periods of expression

Robert Riggs and Felix Adler enjoy a chat behind a Ringling Brothers, Barnum & Bailey circus wagon.

This illustration of a Coney Island amusement scene was painted in color by Robert Riggs for Fortune Magazine

in a medium which brought him fame as a graphic artist. The table upon which he both draws and paints is beside one window, and his lithograph drawing table at the other, although the darkened windows supply no illumination upon his work.

We returned to the museum-like living rooms. Riggs seated me beneath the scalps and settled himself in a chair handy to the jawbones. At my prompting he unfolded the story of his career and made deductions, from his trials and errors, that should, I think, have considerable constructive value to those for whom the path of glory lies ahead.

That career really began when the artist was a boy of ten or eleven. There is nothing unusual in that; the creative urge is usually pretty active at that age. But the promise of genius is seldom so convincing as it was in this lad's passion for picture making. His mother preserved thousands of his drawings, a few of which Riggs and I examined during the interview. The ma-

jority of them illustrated the many-sided life of the circus, of which Riggs has always been a zealous habitué.

When Riggs was eighteen and a student at James Milliken University in Illinois—he was born in Decatur —he was making charcoal drawings from the model. He says of these portrait and figure studies that, as studies, he has never improved upon them.

Following his two years at Milliken he went to New York where for a year he was enrolled in the Art Students League.

The first World War interrupted his study; the next two years were spent in the Army. After the armistice he was one of many who remained in Paris for several months studying in French institutions.

Back home he got a job sketching in the Art Department of N. W. Ayer & Son, advertising agency. He has devoted most of his time to commercial art ever since, largely under the auspices of this agency.

But in those early years he managed to find consider-

Advertising Illustration by Robert Riggs for Reynolds Metal

able time for painting. And with money saved up from his commercial work he traveled about in Africa and the Orient, painting as he journeyed from place to place. He spent six months in Siam and an entire year in the tropics.

Riggs took me into his storeroom and pulled out a huge roll of canvases representing that period of ten or twelve years when, as has already been mentioned, he was trying to paint in the broad manner of the moderns. These canvases—all about 36 x 48 inches—record such a struggle with brush and paint as few artists experience. They are a record of frustration which, as Riggs declares, was the result of his failure to recognize the destined path he should have followed.

Riggs is a congenital realist. The central theme of his artistic life, he declares, is "people and light." While, of course, he realizes that organization of the abstract elements is the one essential in any work of art, he feels that the realistic element may or may not be included, and he chooses to include a great deal of it. His inherent genius for flesh-and-blood realistic illustration is largely responsible for his eminence in the world of art.

Is it not strange then that as a young man he was

impelled in just the opposite direction; that he was lured into the maelstrom of post-impressionism which, as the late Bryson Burroughs said, "aims at something like an abstract of realism, in which the subject is represented in its essential aspects . . . free from the accidental circumstances of any particular appearance"? Riggs, to whom the "accidental circumstances" are the essence of his convincing realism!

Is it not odd that Riggs who—although he did not recognize it at the time—had already found his forte in drawing (a dry medium) should abandon his crayon and begin covering yards of canvas with enormous brushes, attempting to do what was really not in his heart to do, what he actually did not want to do?

Not strange at all, he will tell you; it is all explained by the human tendency to worship that which is contrary to one's own nature. This, he says, is a common experience with artists, and, tragically enough, many never rediscover themselves as did Riggs when after years of floundering he laid aside his brushes and paint box and began drawing on stone with lithographic crayon.

It is quite natural that Riggs, in view of his own misdirected years, should urge artists to discover themselves

*The Coronation Scene, from the opera "Boris Godounov" by Modest Moussorgsky,
interpreted for the Capehart Collection by Robert Riggs. With a rich brush, the
artist has brought to life the turmoil within the usurper-Tsar's mind as he appears in
the courtyard of the Kremlin on the way to the cathedral to assume imperial rank.*

243

CLUB FIGHTER

A Lithograph by Robert Riggs

The detail shown below is reproduced at exact size of the original. Note the scraping technique.

at the start of their career; discover not only what they really want to do but ascertain just what medium will "uncork" their talents. His belief is that every artist is by nature either a *wet* or *dry worker*. If he is a wet worker he is at his best when painting in oil. A dry worker will excel in watercolor or tempera (both mediums dry quickly) or in crayon technique. Furthermore, he insists, some talents—like his own—are "uncorked" by drawing mediums rather than by brush mediums. His conviction that the wrong medium can absolutely frustrate an artist's career seems to him to be amply proved by his own experience.

"The right medium," he says, "is the one which impels the artist to plunge in fearlessly, experimenting as he works. He will do things he had not planned; accidentals will come to his aid, stimulate his imagina-

tion. His creative spirit will be released.

"In the wrong medium, that is, the unnatural one, the work is carefully thought out in advance and carried through according to conscious plan. Hence it may lack the spirit of spontaneous work, not having tapped the well of things *felt* more than *understood*, which express themselves through accidentals."

Riggs, as I have said, put away his paint brushes and took up the lithographic crayon. "When I have a piece of charcoal or crayon in my hand," he declares, "it assists, rather than opposes me. The point, rather than the brush, is what assists me."

With the point of a crayon Riggs could exploit his penchant for realistic fidelity to the limit. He has been accused of indulging it beyond the limit. Not content with suggestion, even in the shadowy areas of his pictures, he insists upon delineation of detail where others might do little more than vaguely hint. He has to explore and make vivid every aspect of the scene portrayed.

In his studio when I called upon him there was a nearly finished drawing upon a lithographic stone. Riggs let me examine it through a magnifying lens. I was amazed at the miniature-like character of his rendering. Yet the work of this artist is noted for the impact of its striking, bold masses as well as for its realism.

In taking up lithography Riggs had come upon a medium that would do his bidding. Yet even in this medium he had to learn to work backwards before he got what he wanted. By working backwards I mean working from black to white; instead of the customary method of building up dark tones on the light surface of the stone, Riggs coats its surface with tusche. In this black ground he scrapes his light tones. The method

"Center Ring" a lithograph by Robert Riggs

lends itself to the rendering of almost infinitesimal detail since the scraping tool can be as fine as a needle point, though a razor blade is the tool mostly used.

Scraping his drawing into the blackened surface of the stone is a technique that has given Riggs his greatest release and produced his best work. But the method also imposes a limitation that finally became serious as the artist pushed his technique further and further for more complete expression. By this method the stone is incapable of producing great delicacy in the lightest tones. To overcome this difficulty Riggs began to employ a second stone. This stone, charged with a light gray ink and printed over the print pulled in black ink, adds those subtleties lacking in the black impression. For still more subtle effects he is now experimenting with a third stone that prints yet another value of gray.

Riggs' powerful lithographs made him a prominent figure in the fine arts field. They also were noticed by the advertising agencies and magazine publications, so much so that his drawings and paintings are in constant demand. His illustrations are prominent year by year in the Art Directors Annual exhibitions. He is a frequent winner of Art Directors Club honors.

Only occasionally does Riggs draw his illustrations on stone; there is really little point in that since no more than one original is required for reproduction. Yet his illustrative technique is similar since he works on scratchboard by the same black to white scraping-out method. His originals are rather small, only slightly larger than the reproductions.

His color illustrations are produced with the brush, though, as he says, he has to *draw* rather than *paint* with his brushes. His medium is highly individual: the result of experiments to discover a medium that, 1. is dark, 2. dries quickly, and 3, is permanent. Being a dry worker, oil color was automatically ruled out. Tempera answered all requirements but the first; it was not dark enough. He found that dry pigment mixed with shellac satisfied the first two requirements but shellac was not permanent. He tried various varnishes and finally adopted mastic. This he dilutes with alcohol: one part mastic, one and one-half parts alcohol. He mixes his dry pigments with this medium on a cardboard palette that is discarded after the day's painting.

Color applied with this medium dries almost immediately, and succeeding colors can be overlaid without mingling with the first color. Riggs is enthusiastic about this technique. He believes that at long last he has a medium which enables him to achieve subtleties of lighting not otherwise obtained.

The work of Robert Riggs is now appearing as illustrations in the magazines. In these, as in his advertising drawings, dramatic composition and intense realism combine to give great power to his work.

Leslie Ragan

*One of more than 100 posters Leslie Ragan has
designed for The New York Central System*

*The original painting for this Moran Towing Company advertisement is
13½ x 8¼ inches. It is rendered in blue and black watercolor. The water
is in various shades and tints of blue, the sky is blue-gray; black pre-
dominates in the painting of the tugboat.*

PAINTER OF TRANSPORTATION AND INDUSTRY

THE THIRTY-FIVE-STORY New York Central Building straddles Park Avenue just north of Grand Central Station. Leslie Ragan's studio on the eighth floor is exactly on the axis line of this famed boulevard that stretches north as far as eye can see, and covers the tracks on which 565 trains arrive and depart daily. An appropriate perch for the man who, doubtless, has painted more pictures—mostly posters—for travel, transportation and industry than any other American artist. He has been at it for twenty-five years: almost his entire professional life, which began with study in the Cumming School of Art in Des Moines—Ragan was born in Iowa—and continued at the Art Institute of Chicago. After one and one-half years in the Air Force in World War I, he returned to Chicago, where he taught three years in the Chicago Academy of Fine Arts and began doing posters for the railroads and heavy industries.

His first work in New York was for General Outdoor Advertising, and for the now defunct magazine *Holiday*. He soon began designing posters for the New York Central System; has done in the neighborhood of 100 to date. These poster-paintings of scenic beauty encompassed by the reach of the Central's lines constitute a unique pictorial record of many of America's famous landmarks.

Ragan has also done a great volume of work for other railroads, among them the Norfolk and Western, one of whose posters is here reproduced. For the Budd Manufacturing Company he is doing a continuing series of posters illustrating streamlined trains built for various railroads. In pre-war days he did many posters for the steamship lines. At present he is executing commissions for the Moran Towing Company.

It is no accident that Leslie Ragan has become a specialist in trains, ships and industrial subjects—he has always loved these things and is passionately fond of travel. As an illustrator for transportation he gets plenty of that, for he insists upon seeing the subjects of his posters with his own eyes first. The camera can and does supplement his observation and sketches—he

counts upon it for detail. "Make your own notes on the spot," he advises. "Go down into the mine, wander about in the factory, climb over your engines, ride in them. Get the name of a man on the job who can be consulted when questions come up later. Learn all you can about the functions of details that you may want to simplify in your picture. Do not place too much reliance on photographs, they are sure to be greatly distorted. Don't guess and don't use other artists' drawings as reference. And don't expect similar industries to use identical methods or equipment."

Ragan paints his posters in watercolor on Upson Board. This is a pebbled-surface wallboard, procurable in most lumber yards. After cutting a panel to finish-size (28 x 42), it is wiped lightly with a cloth dipped in denatured alcohol to remove any grease. Then art gum is used to remove loose fibre. The Upson panel is placed upon the easel and the rough sketch projected upon it by means of a Balopticon. The image is traced lightly in soft, black pencil. When ready to begin painting, the board is placed upon a horizontal table so that colors may be flowed on without their running.

Ragan uses opaque watercolors. He limits his palette to white, aurora red, cadmium yellow light, cobalt blue, milori green and ivory black.

The first painting is made with very thin washes, using some white with each color. Second painting is thick and opaque, especially in the lighter tones. Third and last painting is in thin washes again. By this means transparencies, water-marks and other effects are obtained and the painting is again "loosened up." As a result, Ragan's posters look remarkably spontaneous.

If the painting is to be reproduced by means of photo-litho, a good engraver can retain all the quality of the original by side lighting. This will reproduce the pebbled surface as well as give a transparent effect to the color.

Ragan's preliminary sketches (roughs) are likewise done in watercolor on a rough-surface illustration board. These are, in effect, finished renderings and they are usually followed quite definitely in the final painting.

249

In this New York Central streamlined locomotive Ragan has subordinated wheels and other detail to the all-over simplification of the essential form of the envelope.

The West Point poster, done in 1934, is typical of a long series of travel posters depicting points of interest on the New York Central Lines.

WEST POINT
UNITED STATES MILITARY ACADEMY
HIGHLANDS OF THE HUDSON

NEW YORK CENTRAL LINES

The banana (travel) poster is dramatic in color as well as in design — green bananas against a blue sky, bronze-brown figure.

Leslie Ragan has done many posters for the Norfolk and Western, of which this is a brilliant example. He admits his preference for locomotives that, like this one, show all their fascinating anatomy, so suggestive of life and power.

One of a series of posters for Edward G. Budd Manufacturing Company, illustrating streamlined trains built by this company for various railroads. They are reproduced in color for magazine advertisements, as well as for posters.

251

Norman Rockwell
by Norman Kent

Norman Rockwell

The immortal whitewashing scene from "Tom Sawyer"

When in 1940, George Macy commissioned Norman Rockwell to illustrate "Tom Sawyer" for the Heritage Press, the artist promptly made an extended pilgrimage to Hannibal, Missouri, where he made sketches at the scene of the author's boyhood home town. Sixteen pictures in full color constitute illustration for the two-volume set of Mark Twain's beloved classics — "Tom Sawyer" and "Tom Sawyer and Huckleberry Finn" — regarded by most critics as the finest graphic interpretation among the many illustrated editions of these books.

The Artist Himself

THE PICTURE OPPOSITE these words is a self-portrait of an artist whose name and fame have been a-growing for thirty years. Today, millions of Americans know N o r m a n Rockwell for his paintings on the covers of the *Post*, for his graphic interpretations of The Four Freedoms, for his constant portrayal of THE COMMON MAN. In his art, they see themselves and their friends; they re-live their own foibles and embarrassing moments; they see America in a passing parade through the eyes of this penetrating and lovable artist.

Technique alone could not have brought him to this enviable estate. Many artists with more brilliant techniques have enjoyed a vogue for a span of years, only to be replaced in the affection of art directors and public by yet another style—new ways of looking at the same things.

From the beginning of *his* career, Norman Rockwell possessed an intuitive power that caused him to look on his fellow man with sympathy and affection. He first found in small boys—especially the run-of-the-mill, garden variety—a special delight. In some of them he sees *Peck's Bad Boy*—in others, *Tom Sawyer* and *Huck Finn*, but in many cases, it is the "ten year old" around the corner, or even your own Johnny. They do not look like professional models when they appear in *Post* covers. And, indeed, they are not. Rockwell uses his neighbors for models—the townsfolk in nearby Arlington, Vermont, and, on occasion, an unsuspecting and coerced stranger in whom he has found a character ideally suited to the job on the easel.

For next to his love for small boys (he has three of his own, and is himself one—though a fifty-one-year-old boy) Rockwell likes *old* people. He finds the same fascination in their weather-beaten faces as Rembrandt did. He portrays them with respect and real admiration. In his artistic care they are treated as though their years had made them tolerant and cheerful; in them he reveals no meanness or irritability, but if he sees a trace of sorrow there, it is a feeling understood by all and he paints this too, without apology.

Humor is not lacking in his art and in fact underlies all of it. One has only to be in the artist's presence for a half hour and hear him tell one amusing tale after another—many, recounting episodes in which he was the victim—to know that in his own personality, and in his ability to laugh at himself, lies the spiritual key to the treasure house that is his reservoir of ideas.

In a story by Louis H. Frohman, which appeared in the *International Studio* in 1923, Norman Rockwell made a statement that revealed an ideal he has held to ever since. He said: "People somehow get out of your work just about what you put into it, and if you are interested in the characters that you draw, and understand them and love them, why, the person who sees them is bound to feel the same way." To Rockwell's remarks Mr. Frohman added: "What a simple recipe this is, yet anyone seeing his work must feel its truth and realize that one of the ingredients mixed with Rockwell's paints is his genuine love for all his race."

Mind you, this was written twenty-two years ago. How many other artists have been able to seize the forelock of humanity with such a grip (as Rockwell did) and make it the basis of their whole outlook? Though their techniques and mediums vary, we find in this company men like Dickens, Cruikshank, Hals, Daumier, Tarkington, and Twain.

Let's examine the artist's career and expose other things that may help to explain the success of this illustrator.

Norman Rockwell was born in New York City in 1894 into a family of moderate circumstances. When he was ten, the family moved to Mamaroneck, much to the delight of young Rockwell, who preferred the small town to the city. At sixteen, Norman left high school and entered the Art Students League of New York. Instead of objections at home, he had his family's encouragement. His grandfather—William Hill—had been an English portrait painter of ability. It was a good tradition handed down and quickly absorbed.

His instructors at the League were two grand teachers—George Bridgman and Thomas Fogarty. The latter was a famous illustrator who recognized Norman's natural ability for illustrating and it was through him and due to his encouragement that he was able to gain commissions. Rockwell began doing illustration for juvenile publications—*Boy's Life, Youth's Companion* and *St. Nicholas*—and occasionally, a book for McBride and Nast.

When the artist reached twenty-one he was sharing Frederick Remington's old studio in New Rochelle with Clyde Forsythe, a cartoonist, where he continued to grind out a volume of work for a boy's magazine—drawing a monthly cover and illustrating two stories—all for the princely salary of fifty dollars a month.

"What you ought to be doing is getting stuff ready to show to the Saturday Evening Post," said his studio mate, Forsythe, "not fiddling around with your present work" (or words to that effect).

Rockwell was at first overwhelmed, even at the idea, but his natural ambition to progress caused him to get busy making a few sketches. These he submitted to Forsythe. They were the traditional, slicked-up, pretty girl variety. Forsythe hit the ceiling. "No, no, not that; be yourself, do the kid stuff you do naturally." Norman took the good advice and painted two pictures of boys and made a sketch for a third.

What happened when the young artist reached the august offices of the art editors of the *Post*, laden with his canvases in a specially built wooden case, is now history.

An assistant took the paintings in to his chief. While he was gone, Rockwell gazed nervously at the big-name paintings adorning the walls. Finally the assistant returned without Norman's finished covers, reporting calmly that the *Post* would buy both, and would the artist go ahead with the execution of the third. Would he? Oh, boy!

Rockwell recovered from the glorious shock rapidly. Went out of the Curtis Publishing building walking on air and promptly repaired to Atlantic City for a holiday!

His first cover appeared on the stands in May of 1916.

A detail of charcoal study for an illustration made the exact size of the final canvas (three by five feet). This is step number two in the artist's process.

This pencil sketch is one of many trial compositions made by the artist after he had chosen a dramatic incident from "A President's Wife" by Howard Fast, which appeared in the Ladies' Home Journal in August, 1939. Comparison with the final illustration on the opposite page reveals how consistently the artist has maintained and realized the basic structure of this, his first and most important creative step.

Since then he has painted many more than two hundred. "Editors," said Jack Alexander, a feature writer for the *Post*, "and associate editors have come and gone in that time, and the present ones are as enthusiastic over Rockwell as were their predecessors."

Scarcely had Rockwell got under way on his *Post* covers than the country entered war against Germany (1917). Although at first rejected when he attempted to enlist in the Navy, being under minimum weight, Norman went home, and, overnight, indulged in a startling diet. Bananas, doughnuts and warm water did the trick and on renewing his application the following day, the young artist was accepted! He was sent promptly to the Navy Yard at Charleston, South Carolina.

For a time his identity as an illustrator was undiscovered, until one day he made a drawing of a chief petty officer. From that day on, especially under the prideful eye of his Commandant, Rockwell, installed in the officer's quarters, spent his time painting portraits, and making sketches of visiting admirals and other high-ranking officers. He was even permitted to do some *Post* covers. These contained a strong patriotic

Continued on page 260

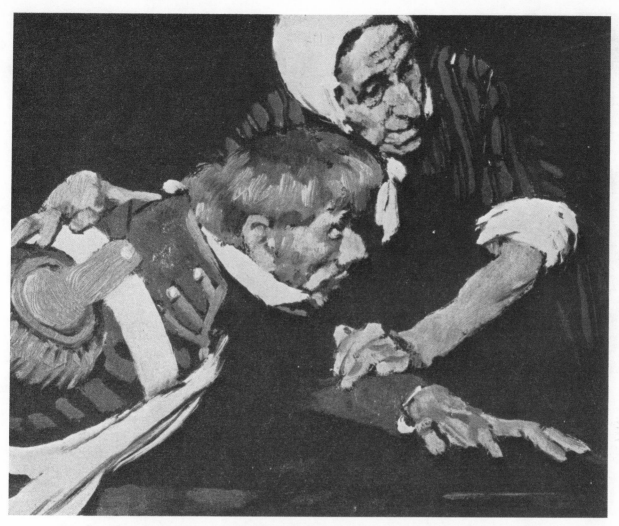

An exact-size reproduction in halftone of a color study made after the completion of the charcoal drawing shown opposite. Notice how the dark and light pattern, applied broadly here, is retained in the final canvas reproduced below.

257

The two subject pictures reproduced on this page represent the natural story-telling abilities of this illustrator. They show his unmistakable reverence for time-worn things and old age. Notice how the seemingly casual objects — the umbrella, the tipped picture and other minor properties — provide oblique accents and optical stepping-stones of light. Compare these with similar story-telling pictures by Vermeer, Abbey, Pyle and Rembrandt.

The
Old and Young
in a Bookshop
by
Norman Rockwell

258

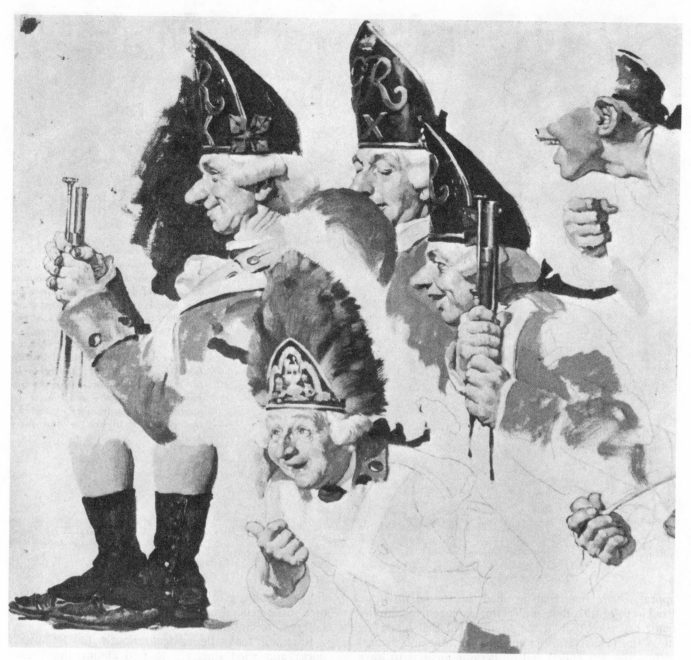

A group of studies for the mural, "Yankee Doodle"

For one blessed with a natural talent for mural decoration, Norman Rockwell has produced all too few. This one graces the Nassau Tavern at Princeton, New Jersey, an establishment that goes back to the period illustrated in the mural.

This comparison of reproductions of the final drawing (left) made on the canvas itself and preparatory to painting, with a miniature of the cover (made from a printed copy), shows how carefully every inch of the composition is planned. Notice how the spotting of the lights in the whole design (including the two panels) accent the movement in contrast to the stationary attitude of the principal figure in the foreground.

Illustrations on page 255 and pages 260, 261, courtesy of The Saturday Evening Post, and those on pages 256-258, courtesy of The Ladies' Home Journal.

appeal which more than justified the special privilege. Rockwell admits that under this arrangement his income *exceeded* that of the admiral, but that his rating of a "third-class varnisher and painter" did not change! When the war ended and he became anxious to leave the service and return to his studio, it was only through the loophole of his "inadaptability" as a third-class varnisher that he was able to gain an honorable discharge.

During the twenties and thirties, Norman Rockwell turned out a large volume of painting. Besides his work for the *Post* and *Ladies' Home Journal*, he contributed illustrations for other periodicals and executed paintings for national advertising accounts. His story-telling proclivity was exploited on all sides, and much that he painted was reproduced in full color.

By nature and tradition Norman Rockwell is a conservative. The artists he admires—Pyle, Rembrandt, the Dutch Little Masters, Degas, Breughel, et cetera—all belong to the rational and objective schools as opposed to the modernistic and subjective ones. This statement does not mean that Rockwell blinds himself to the work of more individualistic artists for he is constantly studying the paintings of artists like Eakins, Cèzanne, Manet and Renoir. Some of Rockwell's friends urged him to look into the new trends in easel painting. They

argued that his great popularity would fade in the face of a more general acceptance of new art forms, unless he began to embrace a fresh and "different style."

Rockwell took the advice seriously (as he usually does) and tried sincerely to find among the French Moderns a new way for himself. He even attempted to do a few covers for the *Post* that included some strange style-marks that resembled a weird, artistic cocktail. It was too much for his friend, the Editor, George Horace Lorimer, who called the artist in and gave him a fatherly lecture on the importance of being one's self. According to the record, Rockwell came away from the meeting considerably chastened, determined to improve his own style through a more complete assimilation of contemporary influences.

For the first twenty-five years of his professional career, Rockwell painted from living models. First, he made a number of rough drafts of his composition and then he sought out his models in the process already described. And more in the tradition of good mural decoration than illustration, a number of completely drawn studies in charcoal preceded his work on canvas. Often, studies in paint augmented these charcoal drawings leading up to the final plotting of his design on the canvas itself. Such procedure may be seen in the illustrations we have reproduced on pages 256-257.

Nostalgia

Contentment in Costume

The Antique Pitcher

Good Afternoon, Mrs. Smythe!

Patriotism Plus, 1944

Body Artist at Work

Observe that the detail is subordinated to the large pattern in the selected covers of The S.E.P. They give the lie to those critics who claim Norman Rockwell's art is primarily based on "photographic" detail.

Good solid drawing, anatomically correct, furnished the basis of his painting, in which no detail or expression was left to chance or sudden inspiration.

In surrounding his models with correct accessories and providing authentic background, this artist has been no less thorough. Over the years he has bought enough costumes to clothe all the inhabitants of a small town; many are the stories told about Rockwell's bargaining for time-worn articles of clothing from their startled wearers, gravely suspicious of the sanity of a man who would pay good money for an old pair of pants, or a battered felt hat. Articles of furniture—chairs, tables, bedsteads, rugs and bric-a-brac—have been carefully selected from antique shops and second-hand dealers. After being used for a given picture they have found their way into the artist's home, where, like a favorite old horse, they continue to serve. In other words, Norman has built his reputation, at least in part, on the *reality* of the *material* things in his pictures, with as much passion and love for their patina and detail as was lavished on those delightful interior pictures by the Dutch Masters themselves.

Finally the strain of working exclusively from *posed*

models became too much. Many of his colleagues had used photography as an aid in their work for years, though at first they were loath to admit it, even to one another. Rockwell says, "the wear and tear and strain that working with living models placed on me was awful. I would sit for eight hours yelling, 'Lift eyebrows!', 'Raise that arm a little!', and 'Make that smile bigger!' I would carry out all these gestures and facial expressions myself, and by the end of the day I was so tired and nervous that I was ready to drop."

So now Rockwell uses the camera, tempered, however, by his long experience as a draftsman. He continues to make the careful studies described previously. Commenting on the camera, especially to young illustrators, he has said, "I don't suppose anyone will follow my advice, but it is better *not* to use photographs until you have proved your ability to get along wholly without them."

Critics, Norman Rockwell has in great abundance. The most serious, he believes, are the millions who have followed his career emblazoned on the covers of the S.E.P. The 57th Street variety either ignores him completely or condemns him haughtily for what is termed story-telling Victorian stuff, unworthy of serious consideration. But for every detractor among professionals, there are others like painters George Grosz and Rockwell Kent (with whom he is sometimes confused) who have heaped enthusiastic praise on him for his art. His colleagues among illustrators hold him in high esteem—first, as a man and secondly, as an artist.

In order to gauge public opinion that will begin to function as soon as one of his paintings has been reproduced, Rockwell is wont to press unsuspecting critics into service. Many are the townsfolk who have passed severe judgment on his work in progress. While remarks are being made at the *insistent* invitation of the artist, Norman takes it all in and then when they have filed out, he sets about making the necessary changes and adjustments. When he reaches what appears to be an impasse, he calls in his friend and neighbor, the illustrator, Mead Schaeffer, with whom, says Jack Alexander, he operates "A Mutual-Admiration, Hand-Holding and Aid Society." Each helps the other in such cases, and if their combined efforts are not enough, their wives are called in and the four give the painting the benefit of their combined critical powers!

Rockwell makes no apology for his art direction. He holds his office of illustrator, despite the handsome five figured income it has earned him, to be an important trust. He says: "No man with a conscience can just bat out illustrations. He's got to put all of his talent, all of his feeling into them. If illustration is not considered art, then that is something that we have brought upon ourselves by not considering ourselves artists. I believe that if we would say, 'I am not just an illus-trator, I am an artist,' the work of all of us would show great improvement. I like to think that we can create another golden age of illustrators, like the one thirty years ago, when men like Edwin Abbey and Charles Dana Gibson and Frederick Remington and Maxfield Parrish were painting. Maybe they were not the greatest of artists, but they were conscientious. They worked hard and they had great talent. I believe that we could re-create the public interest in illustration that those men knew. This is important now, because there are a lot of things that need to be said about good will and good relations between nations and men. I think we illustrators ought to help say those things."

Today, Norman Rockwell is confining his labors to two commissions: painting for the *Post* and continuing to do his annual Boy Scout calendars for Brown & Bigelow—which he began in 1920, and has executed every year since, except two. These keep this slightly-built artist hard at work, protected against the onslaught of a heavy fan mail and the calls of the curious and well-wishers who seek him out—by his good wife, Mary. His trips to the city—Philadelphia or New York—are undertaken in haste, dictated by his work, or an occasional lecture at the Art Students League or the Society of Illustrators, where he speaks, modestly but knowingly, to packed houses. Most of the time he works away in his quiet studio, contented with his art, his simple New England way of life. His neighbors pay him the greatest compliment Vermonters can bestow—that of treating him as one of themselves, and by sharing soberly with him, the fame and fortune he has brought to his chosen home in Arlington, Vermont.

Martha Sawyers

*Martha Sawyers
in Bali in 1937*

MARTHA
SAWYERS *Illustrator of Oriental Lore*

AMONG THE BOOKS which fed the mind and imagination of Martha Sawyers when she was a tiny girl in Cuero, Texas, was one entitled "Religion of the Far East." A forbidding title to be found in a nursery! However, for the little Texan lass this volume became a magic carpet upon which one might journey at will— and that was rather often—into strange and exotic lands on the other side of the world. She learned very little about the religious philosophies of their inhabitants I imagine; but the pictures of their ceremonies, surroundings and ways of life convinced her that the people of the Orient were just about the most fascinating people on earth. She still thinks so, indeed so passionately that she is willing to be pigeonholed by art editors as an illustrator of Asiatic lore.

That does not narrow her field of action as greatly as one might imagine, especially in these latter years when, willy nilly, our interest in the Orient has become far from casual. As this is being written, Miss Sawyers has just donned the uniform of Army Correspondent and is off for the Far East to make pictorial records of the war for *Life* magazine.

The supply of artists with any kind of oriental background is severely limited and publishers are fortunate, when a Pearl Buck or a Mona Gardner feature comes along, to have Martha Sawyers in the offing. Dr. Roy Chapman Andrews found her equally useful for his treatise on *The Future Man* in *Collier's*. In her series of drawings for him she reconstructed the Java ape man and other types leading up to and including the Man of the Future as envisioned by the scientist-explorer. When China Relief looked about for a poster artist, there again was Miss Sawyers who had lived and painted in Peiping until the advancing tide of Japanese aggression all but shut off her escape to Shanghai. Indeed,

the war was raging at the Marco Polo bridge two weeks before her departure.

Life (January 24th, 1944, issue) reproduced, in color, several of her pastel drawings of oriental types in the British Merchant Navy. The originals of these were exhibited at the Ferargil Galleries in New York. F. N. Price, in the catalog foreword, gave the following thumbnail picture of the artist's colorful background:

"Martha Sawyers came out of the heart of Texas to New York (a cheer for the Art Students League). To paint in Paris, to work in Bali, where the men know pigs and rice and the natives dance and the women are beautiful. So on to Penang, Singapore, Sumatra, Java, Hong Kong, Shanghai, Peiping. So that now she is an ambassador of the Orient. Later there was Mexico and men in white pajamas, women with dark long skirts and a black shawl from which generally emerged a little brown baby. So she brings us a bright picture of the other sides of the earth, unbelievable peoples and places. Only a great love for these could have exacted the hundreds of paintings asiatic-oriental. Hard work that perfected a technique and color brilliant and authentic. To quote (in part) the dean of American art critics, 'Her line is as fluent as it is sure, and her color while giving exotic brilliance, its value is nevertheless restrained in good taste'."

Miss Sawyers never planned her career as an illustrator; she had it thrust upon her. Returning from the round-the-world tour that she and her husband made in 1937, she exhibited in the Marie Sterner Galleries drawings and paintings she had produced in the Dutch East Indies and in China. Her pictures were seen by William Chessman, art editor of *Collier's*, who happened to be in need of such an illustrator as Miss Sawyers certainly seemed to be. Since then, *Collier's*

China Relief Poster by Martha Sawyers
Painted in oil colors on canvas

Balinese Man. 19 x 24 inches. Drawn in pastel,
from life, in 1937. First reproduced in Collier's in color.

having discovered her has had first though not exclusive claim upon her brush.

Her study at the Art Students League was principally under the tutelage of George Bridgman and George Luks. She had greater sympathy for the teaching of Bridgman than for that of Luks, an understandable bias when we remind ourselves that although Miss Sawyers paints, her approach is that of the draftsman rather than of a painter such as Luks, an exponent of broad, luscious brush-work. She wields her brush pretty much as she uses her pastel sticks in her portrait studies; with these crayon-like strokes she builds up her forms on top of thin washes of color. And with a knife blade she often produces line technique by scraping through dried color tones to the canvas, handling the knife blade as though it were a stick of crayon. She paints with a medium—mineral spirits (refined kerosene)—that gives her work as rapid a drying quality as watercolor or gouache. Thus she is definitely a "dry worker," insisting that her canvas be dry at practically every point where she applies a brush stroke.

Her technical manner has been influenced by the very first professional work she did after leaving the Art Students League. This was in the studios of J. & R. Lamb, creators of stained glass windows. She says that her present method of work is really founded upon that which she employed in painting on glass with a "needle" in the Lamb studios.

Miss Sawyers' illustrations are invariably done in oil color on canvas. After she has developed a composition plan with her pencil she makes one or more small color studies in oil or pastel. Then she proceeds on her final canvas, first sketching the subject with a round sable

Chinese Woman. Pastel portrait 19 x 24 inches.
The head is done mostly in sanguine and black with
moderate use of cool colors.

brush and thin oil color. She employs impasto with reservation, much of the canvas being covered with a watercolor-like rendering of oil paint greatly diluted with mineral spirits.

Models have been something of a problem, though now she finds among her circle of acquaintances many oriental friends who are willing to pose for her illustrations. The Asiatic relief agencies also supply types on occasion. There have been times when she has resorted to "kidnapping" types encountered on the streets. An old Chinese actor from Chinatown has many times posed for her.

Martha Sawyers is the wife of William Ruesswig, the well-known illustrator. The Ruesswigs live in a New York apartment that boasts two studios which enable

Composition sketches in pencil for the Chinese Garden illustration. There is no intervening step between the accepted pencil study and work on the final canvas. The figures are first drawn freely on the canvas with a small round sable brush. Thin oil washes (oil color diluted with mineral spirits) are then applied, in much the manner of watercolor, before any impasto painting is done.

both artists to maintain professional independence.

Miss Sawyers is petite, vivacious and has a very disarming manner that must account for her success in overcoming the diffidence of native peoples of the Orient. One can scarcely imagine declining to pose for such a pleasantly persuasive and sympathetic person.

A chinese Garden. Oil on canvas, 24 x 32. Originally reproduced in color as an illustration for Collier's. Miss Sawyers' technique is demonstrated in the exact-size detail below. There is very little impasto on the canvas which is mainly treated with thin oil washes. Note the crayon-like handling — the result of applying the paint with relatively small brushes, and scraping the canvas with strokes of a knife blade.

By courtesy of Collier's

Howard Scott

AN INTERVIEW

with one of America's Top-ranking Poster Artists

I REMEMBER HOWARD SCOTT as a student at Pratt Institute in the days when I was a member of the Art School faculty. He was not, as I recall, considered a brilliant student. Nor was he altogether too popular with his instructors. Even then he had his own ideas and persisted in doing things more or less in his own way, refusing to fit snugly into any prescribed pattern.

By graduation time in 1925—perhaps even before—he had decided what he wanted to do. He wanted to be a poster artist. He *determined* to be a poster artist, and his determination brooked no opposition. In the years to follow, that purpose never wavered. He began at once designing posters; he has kept on doing posters. Today his work probably occupies more billboard footage than that of any other poster artist. He has done much to establish a definitely American type of poster design.

In his early years Scott was an ardent admirer of the European viewpoint of poster artists and of the impact their posters had. But he soon realized that the American public preferred in its posters the same brand of art that Norman Rockwell was giving it on magazine covers and in illustrations—good home-spun characterization salted with pithy Yankee humor. "Give them a nimble-witted one-act play," says Scott, "convincingly characterized with complete realism if you want to stop the crowds on Main Street."

Knowing this, Scott never bothered his head about "modern" art. He has not let the vogue for "modern" confuse him. Even in the field of fine art he has not failed to note that the visiting throngs always cast a popular vote for the "J. Frederick Waughs" after the jury of experts has pinned its gold ribbons on the "Braques." Scott is out for the popular vote.

The frontispiece, opposite, shows a detail of the Esso poster, "Long Distance Thrill," reproduced at exact size of Howard Scott's original painting from which the large 24-sheet poster was reproduced. This poster — as are indeed all of Scott's posters — was done in watercolor. Compare this finished painting with the "rough visual" shown on page 274. Scott's skill in the expression of human emotion is one of the factors of his success as a poster artist.

Scott's studio is located on the fifteenth floor of the Associated Press Building in Radio City, it looks out from the east windows upon Rockefeller Plaza; it commands a view of upper Manhattan and the Hudson from its three northern windows and the French doors which open upon the terrace of the set-back.

As we enter we find ourselves in a small entrance lobby not over seven feet square. This lobby and the reception room beyond—a fair-sized room—receive generous light from a large north window, without which the Pompeian-red wallpaper would doubtless be too sombre. The ceilings of both rooms are of laid silver leaf which contrasts smartly with the wallpaper, an importation from Switzerland. Against the dull red of the foyer walls, several of Alexander Iacoleff's marvelous Conte crayon drawings of African types repeat the red of the interior color scheme.

The door that connects with the studio is a massive paneled affair of English hairwood, a warm silver gray with a delicate feathery pattern. All the woodwork throughout the studio is fashioned from this rare imported wood.

And now we enter the studio itself. It certainly looks like no studio we have seen before. Were it not for the large adjustable drawing table near a north window we might believe we had entered the apartment of some swanky executive. It is decorated in the best modern style, without stint of expense and with the most thorough-going treatment of every practical and esthetic consideration. The furniture—cabinets for art materials and equipment—has been especially designed by Mr. Scott. The color scheme, with the English hairwood as motive, is warm gray—walls and carpet. Green-blue upholstered chairs and colorful books in the shelves flanking the east window complete the harmony. This evidently is a room for relaxation as well as for work.

Indeed it was designed to serve the double purpose of studio and reception room for consultation with clients. If at first it seems inappropriate for work, it soon becomes apparent that its practical use as a studio has really been studied to the last detail. It is completely functional, serving all purposes of social contacts, workshop and relaxation. In other words it is planned for the perfect organization of all factors that enter into the artist's professional life.

Scott emphasizes the importance of organization, states that it is indispensable in advertising work. Everything must be planned, and plans must be rigidly adhered to. "If I have to produce a poster in five days," he says, "I divide the job into five parts and insist upon completing each day's assignment on schedule."

From the first, Scott has favored watercolor as a medium for executing his posters. In fact, he has never painted them in oil. Occasionally he adds tempera white to secure effects required by an opaque medium. "The superiority of watercolor is apparent," says Scott, "when time is at a premium. The artist working in oil simply has to wait for his medium to dry at various stages. Sometimes that delay is serious, for the client often clamors for the finished work in three or four days after sketches have been approved. When using watercolor the artist can keep steadily at work until the job is completed."

Scott's mastery of his medium is well demonstrated in the large plain areas of his posters where no sign of the brush is visible—yet there is no airbrush in his studio.

Scott calls ideas for his posters "scenarios" and refers to the posters as "one-act plays." The scenario must be as direct as an arrow, aimed at a single idea; and it must reach its mark as unfailingly as a good cartoon gag. Considering that the advertiser may be spending $125,000 on a single billboard poster showing, his insistence upon a smart plot and brilliant casting can be understood.

It does not necessarily follow that a bright idea plus clever casting will result in a successful poster. There is the directing to consider. That, of course, is a matter of composition—the final test of one's genius as a poster artist. His problem here is not unlike that of the cartoonist. Cartoonists have told me that some of the most brilliant ideas keep them guessing for weeks before they find adequate graphic presentation.

So you will find Scott playing around with his pencil, making innumerable thumbnail sketches, trying to make the actors in the advertising drama behave so intelligently that the meaning of the poster will be revealed in a flash. The action must be so legible that not more than a few words are needed to complete the dramatization. Scott says, "Keeping the action in a single plane is a big factor in securing legibility; perspective in a poster, unless handled very cautiously, is apt to be confusing."

A rough visual, about 8 x 18 inches, follows the thumbnail sketches. It serves to test the selection of a design from the thumbnails and is a means of further developing the subject. Some artists submit such visuals to clients for approval but Scott prefers to make another sketch, larger—about 16 x 36 inches—which is usually the size of the final drawing. Often he carries these large sketches so nearly to completion that, when approved, very little more needs to be done to make a finished painting out of the sketch.

If we drop into Scott's studio a day or two after he has made his rough visuals for a series of posters, we shall witness something that suggests the filming of a scene on a movie lot. Professional models are the actors, Scott is the director, and the camera man is busy with his photography. The models understand the part they are to play, the artist instructs and exhorts them while the photographer takes one action shot after another. This goes on until Scott feels sure he has ample material to work with. Out of this performance come the photographic references essential for the final characterization. As a matter of fact, Scott's trained visual memory serves him almost as completely as pictures.

Asked to comment upon the opportunities for new recruits in the poster field, Scott said: "We could use twenty-five or thirty good realistic painters right now —if there were that many in the country. The trouble is that most of the schools do not seem to realize what the market demands. The vogue for surrealism and other modern tendencies in poster advertising has only a limited audience. Such work shown in exhibitions may impress the 'arty' person, but it is of little interest to most advertisers. I have mentioned Norman Rockwell as a fine example to follow, because of his tremendous skill as a portrayer of character and his good, sincere drawing and painting.

"Learn to draw well. It is the foundation of all successful painting."

What about photography in posters? Is the camera, particularly color photography, likely to compete with the artist on the billboards of America?

"So far as 24-sheet posters are concerned," replies Scott, "the camera is out. And for good reasons. Take the matter of color. The camera *reproduces* the colors of the subject; the artist *intensifies* them, makes them more brilliant than they are in nature. He does this to allow for the subtraction of intensity due to distance and conditions of poor visibility. Another thing. It's practically impossible to get models to act successfully for the camera in the portrayal of poster 'one-act plays.' Imagine, for example, getting two old ladies to act the scene in the Essolene poster, 'Starts quicker than gossip', even if the right types could be found. And this is a simpler problem than many poster ideas present.

"Again the artist can often be more dramatic by taking liberties with drawing. Figures may be shown in actually impossible positions to put over an idea that would stump the accurate camera. Sometimes anatomical distortions—not obvious to the observer— serve to make the action more legible or to give it greater emphasis.

"The camera most certainly cannot compete with the artist in this field."

It seems to me that the qualities of character that are responsible for Howard Scott's success as an artist are precisely those which promise success in any field. Singleness of purpose is one of these. In Scott's career there has been no vacillation. His objective has been clear from the beginning and his life has been completely organized for the realization of that purpose. He probably would have been equally successful as a lawyer, a doctor, or a chemist had he chosen one of those careers. Most art students overrate what is known as talent. They lean on it, rest secure behind it, and often discover too late that talent is, after all, but one ingredient of the success formula.

Howard Scott's studio, designed especially for him by Reinhard and Hofmeister, architects, is on the fifteenth floor of the Associated Press Building at Rockefeller Center. This view was taken from the door of the reception room. Windows at the left face the north, and a French door opens onto the terrace of the set-back. The room serves the dual purpose of work studio and office for consultation with clients.

Howard Scott at work on an Esso poster. The cabinet between the windows contains oil colors, brushes and other equipment used by the artist when he forgets gasoline and automobiles and drags his easel from the closet for a few hours of recreation with paint and canvas. The top of this cabinet lifts off, exposing a second top of oiled maple which serves as a palette.

Note the orderliness of Mr. Scott's work cabinet in the foreground — and it was not especially tidied up for this picture.

273

This is a reproduction of Howard Scott's "rough visual." The original was about 8 x 18 inches. A visual is a rapid sketch intended to try out the projected design. It expresses the general character of the advertisement, determines the size, position, weight and color scheme of the various elements. It also suggests the style of technique to be employed. A visual should never be carried so far as to invite criticism of details. Place a visual across the room — look at it from a distance and it gives a pretty good idea of the appearance of the future finished painting.

These thumbnail sketches may not suggest much to anyone but the artist. To him they are merely symbols of designs that doubtless exist quite fully developed in his mind. They represent the first steps he takes on paper in developing the design.

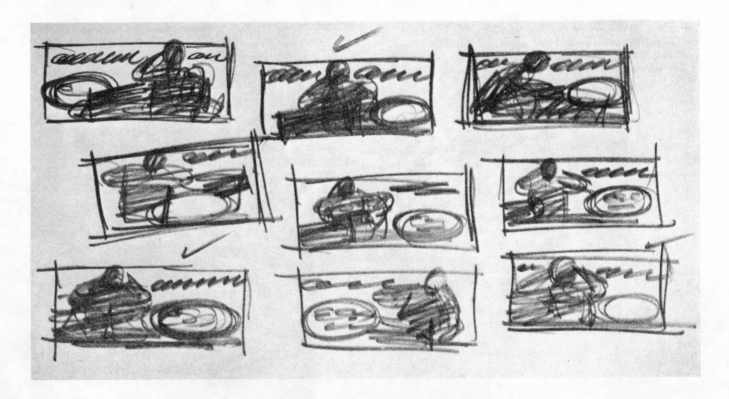

HOWARD SCOTT

Comments below on the "plots" of four of his 24-sheet posters.

FALL CHANGE-OVER

This is a combination product-and-human-interest poster. The "try on" feeling in the old character had to come off fast plus a bit of humor in the small-sized hat being tried on. Here was a swell chance to get a laugh from the audience. To keep the action wholesome and good natured is what to strive for.

CONNECT WITH POWER

A chance to make the "ideal" poster. One figure, short caption and a chance at strong lighting. The actual round-up of the batter was considered more powerful looking than any action showing a hit. The strong pattern of the figure said "baseball" long before you could read the caption as you approached the poster on the highway.

STILL TALKING ABOUT HER NEW FORD

Here was a chance to create an entire setting around a character without actually showing it. One look at the old lady — plus the old Bell party line telephone — gives the tip-off as to the locale. Here is an example of how important the facial expressions are in telling a "five second" audience a story.

STARTS QUICKER THAN GOSSIP

The inference that another person is the target of these two gossips had to be put over. The action had to be plotted carefully to convey this to the reader. The general flow of both picture and copy, plus quick understanding of both, is of the utmost importance in poster design.

Amos Sewell

Amos Sewell

THE TOWN OF WESTPORT, on Connecticut's southern shore, is one of the principal homing centers for New York's professional men and women. It is about an hour's ride by train from Grand Central Station, thus is near enough for frequent forays to the great publishing metropolis, while sufficiently remote to insure protection from unwelcome interruptions. You would not find it easy, for example, to ferret out Amos Sewell who lives about seven miles from the railway station, over a route which has many a turning before it finally leads along a narrow country road and passes a squarish old farmhouse. It is a gray, shingled structure with a large brick chimney which carries the flues from several fireplaces. Across the lane and opposite the Sewell front yard, a dozen cows stand in the shade of roadside trees in the heat of the summer's day. In a new high-raftered studio, built among the ancient apple trees in the rear, Amos Sewell stands at his easel drawing pictures which, in a few brief days, will be on every newsstand in America and poked into rural delivery mail boxes from Maine to the Mexican border—and far beyond.

Amos Sewell is indeed master of a popular art; painter to America's millions. Yet as recently as 1931 he came to New York from California, where he was born, with practically no professional background. His only formal art study was a brief course in the evening classes of the California School of Fine Arts; this while he was working as a teller in a San Francisco bank. He sketched a good deal and experimented with etching, but all his work was on an amateur basis—certainly an unpromising background for the kind of career that awaited him in the East.

Yes, a career awaited him in New York, but the publishers did not meet him at Grand Central Station with a brass band and the proffer of manuscripts. His arrival caused no unusual stir in art and publishing circles. And four or five years were to pass before fellow illustrators, seeing his first drawings in *The Saturday Evening Post*, would ask "Who is this guy Sewell?"

Sewell was indeed a long, long way from the *Post's* inner sanctum though he could have thrown a stone into it. He, more than anyone else, knew that somehow he must acquire the schooling he had missed in his earlier years. He turned his steps, not in the direction of the art schools, but toward the offices of the pulp magazines. For four years, with scarcely enough time out for sleep, he made pen and drybrush illustrations of hairbreadth escapes. He swam in a sea of graphic melodrama, barely keeping his head above water. Turn-

ing out two double-spread drawings a day became routine, and without models—there was no time to bother with models.

Four years of that! Yet Sewell, when I was comfortably seated in his studio, said, "Well, really I've never had any art training, no professional background of any kind to speak of." He had managed, to be sure, to attend some evening classes at Grand Central School of Art during this pulp period; he studied under Harvey Dunn there.

No illustrator likes to be pigeonholed, but all of them, inevitably, have a very special genius for expression in certain phases of life and experience. It is natural that art directors should make capital of these special aptitudes, and they do. Thus we find Sewell in the top ranks of character illustration, particularly in the field of homespun fiction. One of his first assignments for the *Post* was for illustrations of the "Babe" series of stories which has run for several years.

Through his graphic dramatizations of the adventures of Babe, Little Joe, Big Joe and Uncle Pete these characters of fiction have been made real to *Post* readers. He was so successful with that assignment, especially in his drawings of Babe and Little Joe, that the *Post* has kept him on that series ever since. Sewell is particularly fond of youngsters and draws them with great understanding of their emotional reactions to the crises thrust upon them by fiction writers.

My visit to Amos Sewell interrupted him in the reading of a *Post* manuscript. His desk was littered with penciled notes which he scribbled as he read. These jottings recorded descriptions of characters and what they were wearing, details of the scene or setting and references to incidental things which if not scrupulously observed by the illustrator will be quickly noted by a

ILLUSTRATION

BY AMOS SEWELL

FOR

WHEREVER THERE'S ANGELS

THERE'S HEAVEN

by R. Ross Annett

IN THE FEBRUARY 7, 1942, ISSUE,

THE SATURDAY EVENING POST

Ed Juvey hollered,
"We'll cut his heart out!"

Sewell with his back to the wall

Sometimes the artist, preferring to feel the desired action, takes the pose and is photographed in it.

hundred readers who love to write critical letters to the Editor. Noted also were the various picture possibilities in the story.

Illustrators are often asked, "Honestly now, do you actually *read the whole story?*" Even those too sophisticated to ask such a brainless question may be surprised to know how hard the illustrator works over his manuscripts. Sewell reads and rereads, often as many as four and five times. At his first reading he tries to visualize the characters, to make them real, living personages whom he can feel and draw with conviction. Obviously he cannot acquire that intimacy except through the most painstaking study of the manuscript. Sometimes the story's picture possibilities will be rather obvious, often the selection of the best episodes for illustration appear only after several readings.

Sewell never begins to draw until he has a clear mental conception of the pictures for the story in hand. Then he takes charcoal and begins to develop his composition on his tracing-paper pad. The two composition studies

Exact-size detail from Amos Sewell's illustration "Limbs Is a Flourish Word" by Lucretia Penny

herewith reproduced are typical of these preliminaries.

When this study reaches a satisfactory conclusion he lays it aside and begins to make drawings of the characters—with charcoal on tracing pad. He begins without models, though he makes much use of photographs, as indeed do most contemporary illustrators. After all, our splendid picture magazines bring into the studio such an array of types as formerly the artist had to roam the countryside to discover. When he has created his types he calls in models. He finds suitable children in the neighborhood and there are professional models in Westport. Some journey out from New York. Bill Cuff, pictured on page 282, is one of Sewell's favorite models. He poses for practically every male character the artist creates. Comparing him with the group of characters (on the same page) for which he posed it is evident that the model does not serve Sewell in any creative sense, but merely affords a structural basis for

Sewell's preliminary study for his illustration shown in two stages (here and page opposite). This charcoal study is about twelve inches square.

many diverse types. Also he serves for factual incidents of lighting and the action of drapery. No matter how intimately one may know the figure and how experienced in nature's accustomed appearances, no artist can readily imagine those unusual and accidental effects which, when observed, add conviction to the drawing.

"Actually," says Sewell, "I have never been able to work successfully on the final drawing while the model is there in front of me. I find his presence distracts me and keeps my imagination from working, and I am too prone to make a portrait of the model rather than of the character as I feel it. Instead, I work from the character sketches (like those mentioned) or from photographs." Occasionally the artist, eager to express the action he feels, becomes his own model, as shown on page 279. Here we see Sewell with his back to the wall as he is threatened by Pete and his gang. He was demonstrating for his model—the kind of pose he wanted. "Look," he said, "this is the action. Just imagine that gang coming at you." The photographer clicked his shutter and the professional model was dispensed with for that pose.

281

These character studies by Amos Sewell were all drawn from Bill Cuff, shown below

After the characters have been carefully studied in these preliminary drawings, Sewell begins his final picture. He works large—the illustration reproduced here is 28 x 30 inches. He is one of the few contemporary artists who employ the charcoal medium. In his hands it seems to give the broadest possible scope for delineation and dramatic effect. The exact-size detail demonstrates that and it reveals, I think, qualities which make Sewell's work so convincing. For that old man writing on the wall is a living, breathing being; you sense it in the intimately felt portraiture of his fine head. There is nothing casual about it. It is searching; the artist makes fullest use of every incident of form, texture and light to give us, not the representation of a man, but the portrait of a particular man. And he gives us something beyond the mere word picture of the author's text. Well, that is illustration at its best.

I have mentioned the importance of detail in illustra-

A drawing by Amos Sewell for The War Finance Committee used for the 4th War Loan drive

tration. It is not enough that the incidental objects be correct according to the text; unless they are rendered with as great a feeling for reality as the figures themselves the illustration will lack conviction. An illustrator once told me of an early experience. He submitted a drawing of a farmer setting out tomato plants. The art director looked it over critically. "A pretty good picture," he admitted, "but it's not an illustration." The young artist, puzzled, asked for a more specific criticism. "Just how does that farmer get his box of tomato plants along the row as he sets them out?" asked the critic. Then the youngster understood; the box of seedlings had left no path in the earth as it surely would do when pushed along the lengthening row.

That sense of reality in an illustration which gives us the feeling that the whole environment has been created and given character by human hands is one of Amos Sewell's particular claims upon our admiration. He makes us feel that the jug has been handled, the chair sat in, the table subjected to long years of wear; the whole interior has been made eloquent of its inhabitants. This is a subtle thing which cannot be taught or quite explained, but it is a very real factor in successful illustration.

Sewell's illustrative genius is fully expressed in black and white. Nothing that can be said of his color would add to it particularly. That probably would apply to nearly every illustrator, for no matter how good the color, it is the one element that may be considered superfluous from the standpoint of pure illustration.

While Sewell's color illustrations have all the good qualities of his charcoal drawings, color adds nothing to them except the attractiveness which is conferred by color *per se*. In a two-color job (black and one color) he combines a watercolor red or orange with charcoal, the burden of the picture resting upon the charcoal. He uses tempera for his full-color pictures.

Amos Sewell speaks the language of average Americans. They know and love the kind of people he draws and they respond to that homespun sincerity with which his art speaks to them. He is truly painter to America's millions.

Donald Teague

Donald Teague

illustrator of frontier and sea

The drawings on this page came from Collier's

CALIFORNIA, as everyone knows, is the land of heart's desire, the most favored spot for a man—even an illustrator—to live in and bring up his family.

But New York, so far as illustration is concerned, is the source from which all blessings flow.

It is taking a lot for granted to expect them to flow 3,000 miles from their headwaters, over mountain and plain, just to indulge the whim of an artist who prefers to live in Los Angeles rather than New Rochelle, Westport, or—heaven forbid—Danbury, Connecticut. Almost like asking the mountain to come to Mohammed. Yet it works! Donald Teague has maintained his studio on the West Coast for the past six years, thanks to air transportation which delivers his drawings to New York publishers in twenty-four hours.

As a matter of fact, Teague's predilection for the sunshine of the West Coast is no mere whim. While he was away on a world cruise the family hearthstone was transferred to Los Angeles by his father and brother who moved there from the East in 1937. Then there was the enthusiasm of Pruett Carter, who had already settled in "God's Country." California, to be sure, was a garden of Eden for Teague and his bride, Verna Timmins, in 1938—and it has been an ideal place in which to rear their two blond daughters. It is, moreover, a happy hunting ground for an illustrator of the out-of-doors; of horses, cowboys, and the romantic life of the forty-niners; a bounty of the moving picture industry which provides properties, color and action. "In twenty minutes," says Teague, "I can have access to any type of historical vehicle, with or without horses. I can ask 'Fat' Jones, nearby, for a McClellan saddle of 1870 and get it. Jones supplies horses, saddles, and all equipment including stage coaches

and other vehicles. At the Western Costume Company I can get authentic costumes of all periods.

"As to horses and horsemen, the country is full of them; and a cowboy is always at hand to cast a critical eye upon my drawings—which, believe me, he does! My favorite model and severest critic is Ted Wells, who doubles for Bill Boyd in the *Hopalong Cassidy* Series. Ted was brought up on a big cow ranch in Wyoming and knows every angle of a cowboy's life. Replicas of pioneer streets and buildings on the movie lots serve as settings for many of my illustrations. Then of course there are the mountains and the desert themselves."

There also is the ocean, another of Teague's special interests and the setting for many of his story illustrations. He was familiar with ships and the sea before he went to California. These he has sketched, painted, and photographed pretty much all over the world. Since 1920, and until the war, he has spent three or four months out of each year in travel; has made fifteen trips to Europe, and one, of longer duration, which took him around the world. (Incidentally, his journeys touched the edges of two wars: the Riff war in North Africa in 1925 and the Chinese-Jap war in 1937-38. In each, he barely escaped having his head shot off.) As a result—not of his narrow escapes—he has a large collection of pictorial travel data that might be the envy of any illustrator. This is of far greater value to him than any published travel pictures, because every picture is but a part of a larger scene well remembered.

Teague is an inveterate sketcher. His sketchbook and camera accompany him wherever he goes. First he sketches, then he makes photographs of the same subject. The sketch serves his creative intention; the photograph records factual information that may be needed if and when the subject becomes part of an illustration. But the sketch comes first.

Continued on page 291

POST ILLUSTRATION BY DONALD TEAGUE

This typical Teague "Western" appeared in the August 21,
1943, Saturday Evening Post as an illustration for "Bugles in
the Afternoon," a story by Ernest Haycox. In the Post it was
a bleed-page color reproduction. The title was printed in a
white panel mortised out of the picture at the bottom, cutting
off the picture as high as the wheel hubs.

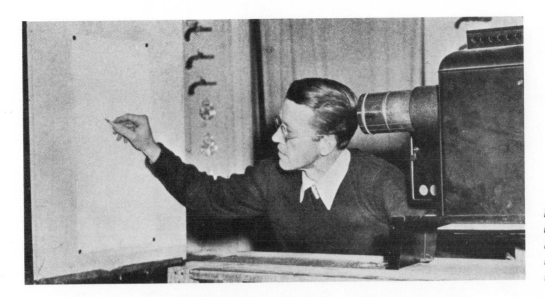

In this photograph Teague
is shown tracing the out
lines of photostated
sketches projected on hi
illustration board.

OVERHAULING GEAR

Halftone reproduction (one-hal
size) of a watercolor of sailor
overhauling gear outside Cape
town. The sailor at left wears
bright yellow slicker. The sea i
a deep ultramarine, the sky ligh
blue. Reds, browns and gray
predominate elsewhere.

This spirited ink drawing was
executed on scratchboard, for
American Magazine, about four
times the size of our reproduction.

*Wash drawing for Collier's,
about one-fifth the size of the original*

*Small color sketch for the illustration,
at right, for a Saturday Evening Post
story. The original watercolor for the
final painting is 30 inches high.*

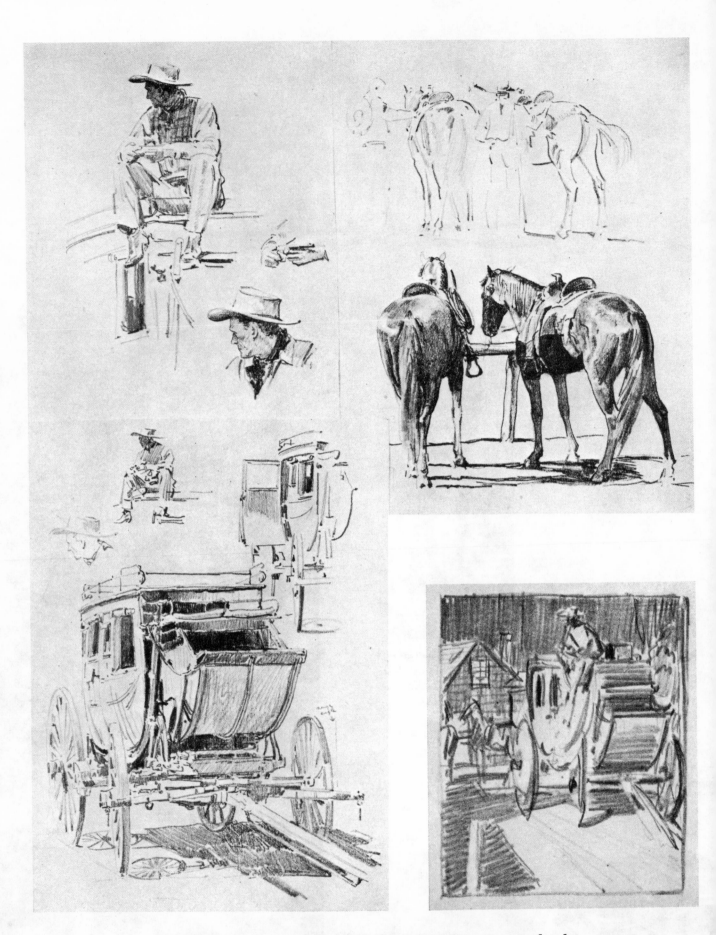

Pencil studies from models and objects for the Post illustration reproduced in color on page 287. The pencil composition above is one of many made by Teague for this picture. A color sketch (not shown) preceded the final painting.

In developing an illustration Teague begins with small pencil compositions. He may make a score, fifty, or even more of these before he takes up his brush for color studies—these also at small scale. "There is nothing I can add to this," Teague told us. "The preliminary sketches are just blood and sweat." After he has produced a satisfactory color comprehensive he goes out on location to sketch from models which he poses as they are to appear in the composition. There may be a dozen horses, three or four figures, and a vehicle or two in the picture. All will be sketched in pencil and afterwards photographed.

The next step is to have the sketches photostated down to size (six-inch maximum) to fit his projector—his originals are usually large. They are then projected, one at a time, upon a sheet of watercolor paper, and lightly drawn-in with a pencil. This insures a clean line. The surface of the paper is not spoiled by changes or erasures. Through proper adjustment of focus and distance the individual figures can be projected at the exact size called for in the comprehensive, and in their proper position in the picture. This is a great mechanical advantage over tracing or redrawing. What is even more important, the spirit of the first sketch, made from the model, is transferred to the final rendering.

Teague's illustrations are invariably done in watercolor or gouache; he prefers the former, delights in the crisp handling of direct brush work. It reproduces well too. He works at rather small size, twenty inches being the usual maximum dimension.

Donald Teague enjoys a reputation as a painter in the fine arts field. He is usually represented in the big national shows; wins prizes too.

The artist was born in Brooklyn in 1897. He studied at the Art Students League for two years under Bridgman and DuMond, then got a job under Ray Greenleaf for Ward and Gow. After a year of this he realized his need for more study and went back to the League. His next position was with the Frank Seaman Agency where he did advertising drawings and lettering for two years.

Following his service in the Navy in the first World War, he made his first trip to Europe and, returning, decided to be an illustrator rather than an advertising artist. His first commission came from *Everybody's* [now defunct]. It was the beginning of a continuing demand which brought him sufficient prosperity to provide for those annual visits abroad.

Teague says that an account of his career would be incomplete without a bow in the direction of Dean Cornwell for his aid and encouragement. "In those early days," he recalls, "Cornwell rarely failed to make time to look my stuff over, despite his own very busy days and the constant knocking on his studio door of young illustrators who sought his advice. He handed down the principles of illustration promulgated by Howard Pyle and demonstrated to him by Harvey Dunn, his teacher."

Aldren A. Watson

Illustration by Aldren A. Watson

from "Walden, or Life in the Woods," by Henry David Thoreau

Peter Pauper Press

Aldren A. Watson, one of our younger illustrators, is a great lover of wood. The stump of a giant tree displaying its pattern of annual rings and the torn, upstanding splinter that escaped the cut of the saw might appropriately be the "charge" on the shield of his professional coat of arms.

It is odd how a passion of this sort can color an artist's creative work. In young Watson's drawing it appears in a variety of manifestations. The sawed stump itself bobs up in a surprising number of illustrations. That, of course, is mere detail in a picture. More significant is the loving rendering of wood surfaces, wherever they appear. Wood grains decorate a floor, or give pattern to an article of furniture, as in the *Golden Summer* illustration here reproduced. Mortised and pegged timbers are favorite accessories that lend robust grace to many an interior. Growing trees are rendered with intimate knowledge of their idiosyncrasies and the accidents that befall them.

All this is a reflection of physical experiences with wood: from early boyhood he has had wood-working tools in his hands and one of his chief delights has been designing, inventing and constructing things of wood. Among the first achievements of his married life—he married Nancy Dingman in 1941—was the building of maple and ash furniture for their dining room.

In two books that I would like to mention, Watson's love of wood and the woods found fullest expression. *Christmas in the Woods*, a tiny volume of verse by Frances Frost and published by *Harper's*, contains ten paintings of forest interiors, the snowy habitat of familiar woodland creatures. The pictures are only 3½ by 5 inches, but they are big with affection. They come from the heart of a nature lover as well as from the hand of an artist. They would, I think, have de-lighted that great naturalist of Concord whose philosophy the artist has quaffed and whose book, *Walden or Life in the Woods* (Peter Pauper Press), provided him an enviable outlet for his arboreal predilections.

This second book that I refer to contains twelve full-page pictures and eighteen chapter headings—all printed in two colors, dark green and light gray-green. The illustration from *Walden*, shown on page 294, could not—for mechanical reasons—be reproduced in our book in its original color scheme.

These drawings were created under conditions that were ideal for their conception though difficult for their production. Watson, at this time, was himself a woodsman. He was in the employ of the American Friends Service Committee and was a resident worker in rural Southeast Missouri, on a project that involved companionship with evicted sharecroppers of the district. He spent his days on one end of a two-man saw and in the evenings, under a kerosene lamp, he translated his physical experiences into line and color. The following quotation from a letter outlines his arduous day: "Up at 5:00 A. M., breakfast, feed hog, split wood for kitchen range. Saw in woods from 7:30 to 5:00—supper, feed hog, put chickens up for the night. Then Walden!"

From a technical point of view Watson's principal claim to our attention is his design. Design is, of course, an indispensable ingredient in all works of art. But in some it is overshadowed, almost obscured by other qualities. In Watson's work it greets the appreciative eye at once and remains a chief source of esthetic delight. Design, with him, is purely instinctive: he never studied it or made conscious effort to master it. He simply cannot help it.

But design, after all, is chiefly a vehicle for saying something. In illustrating children's books what counts most is imagination, the ability to give eye-witness accounts of events that couldn't possibly happen, to make fantasy as plausible as reality. The artist must know

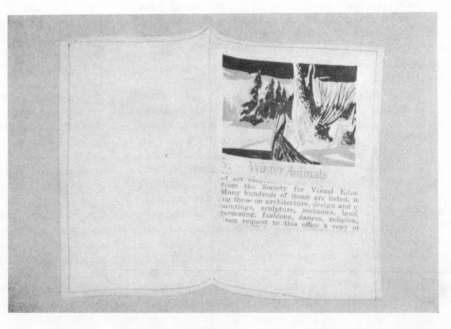

*In planning his illustra-
tions, Watson often makes
miniature sketches like
this with type clippings
pasted on to give im-
pression of entire page.
This reproduction slightly
reduced from original
sketch.*

Title Page for
THE BLUE HILLS
by Elizabeth Goudge
Designed by Watson

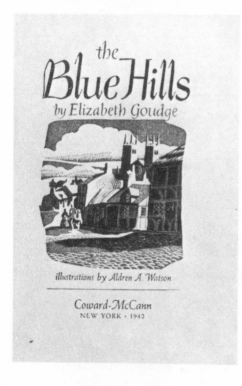

Illustration from
THE BLUE HILLS
Printed in black and green
Courtesy Coward-McCann

his way about in the realm of make-believe when he is painting pictures for juveniles. Watson in his drawings for Elizabeth Goudge's *The Blue Hills* exhibits this happy faculty, as he does in *Wonder Cat and Aesop's Fables*, to mention a few of his most successful titles.

Watson's output is about evenly divided between adult and juvenile books. His keen appreciation of all the factors that enter into the art of the book has invited commissions for adult books such as the *Walden* and *Shakespeare's Sonnets*, and has led to the designing of the book as a whole. He is indeed an all-round book man, with an affection for every detail of book production—he was doing hand-binding as a lad in his early teens. He has a fine flair for lettering, and although he has never set type he has considerably more than a speaking acquaintance with it.

Watson works almost exclusively with brush and ink or color, seldom employing pencil even for his first idea sketches. These idea studies fill the pages of sketchbooks that become fascinating records of an illustrator's

creative processes. His finished drawings are usually small, slightly larger than the reproductions.

Aldren A. Watson was born in Brooklyn, N. Y., in 1917, and received his early schooling at Friend's School. He began his formal art training at the Yale Art School, but finding this institution distasteful he remained at New Haven only one semester. The Art Students League of New York proved more congenial. There he studied under Charles S. Chapman and Robert Brackman. This was his only formal study but he took his education into his own hands, drawing and painting during every spare hour. His first year as a professional artist found him busy with commissions, including several double-page full-color maps for *Time*. In that year too, he produced his first book illustrations, and won a U. S. Maritime Commission competition for an overmantle mural for the S. S. *President Hayes*. He found time to paint fifty or so watercolors and produce some color woodcuts.

At the close of the War, Watson prowled around in

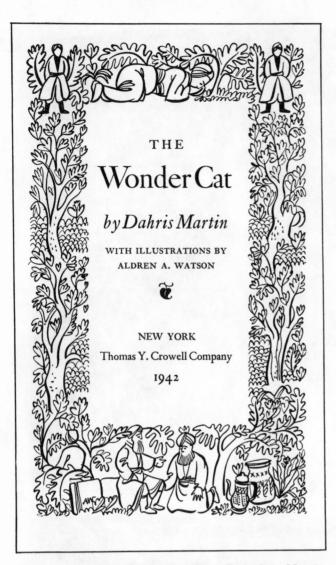

THE
Wonder Cat

by Dahris Martin

WITH ILLUSTRATIONS BY
ALDREN A. WATSON

🐛

NEW YORK
Thomas Y. Crowell Company
1942

Title page for "The Wonder Cat," by Dahris Martin
Designed in red and black by Watson

Illustration from "The Wonder Cat"
Printed in red and gray
T. Y. Crowell, Publisher

Vermont, looking for a home site. He vowed he would never again live in a city. He found and purchased a place in Putney, where, at this writing, he is busy doing work for the publishers, and painting the rural landscape. "I have my workroom rigged for a twenty-four-hour service," he wrote in a recent letter. "Whenever I get the chance," he continued, "I shall set up my Washington hand-press and play around a bit with type."

Watson has just been announced first prize winner ($3,000) in the Domesday Press Juvenile Book Illustration Competition, for which there were more than 700 entries. The illustrations which won the award were paintings for *Moby Dick*.

Sketch (exact size) for an illustration
for "Christmas in the Woods"—Harper & Brothers

298

SHAKESPEARE'S SONNETS

Designed and Illustrated by Aldren A. Watson

*The pictures are in two colors, red and gray. In them, design is
triumphant. It brushes aside all limitations of conventional illustrative method. It scorns perspective (in the realistic sense),
anatomy, scale and all the usual demands of picture making. In
so doing, it paints an atmospheric background for verses that
summon ideas rather than celebrate action. The pictures are
dream fragments—unreal, yet more suited to the text than
reality, in their power to reconstruct the spirit and color of
Shakespeare's time.*

Denys Wortman

Denys Wortman

Whose pencil smiles at the comedy and pathos of Metropolitan Life

ALL DENYS WORTMAN has to do for a living is to draw one of those famous *Metropolitan Movies* every day—only one a day! Day in and day out he delivers a drawing to the New York *World-Telegram* depicting an episode in the lives of Mopey Dick and the Duke, of the run-of-the-mill boarders that cross Mrs. Rumpel's threshold, and the heterogeneous assortment of humanity that makes New York one of the most amusing and pathetic spots on earth. This he does three hundred and twelve days each year; he has been doing it since 1924. If my arithmetic is correct that makes between —well, figure it out for yourself.

That is an impressive accomplishment. Yet, taking it day by day perhaps it looks easy. One may picture Wortman rising from a late breakfast, yawning and remarking to his attractive wife, "Ho, hum, my dear, I guess I'd better toddle into the studio for an hour or so and get that drawing off my conscience." Those cartoons, sketched with such evident facility, certainly do give the impression of having been tossed-off quickly and with little effort. So far as the final drawings are concerned that is doubtless true, just as Katharine Cornell's stage performance is easy, and Josef Hofmann's and Charlie McCarthy's. But the creative effort that goes into a completed masterpiece of whatever sort is often astonishing. The public is of course aware of the long hours of practice that precede a musician's appearance on the concert stage. There is less known of the preparatory work that occupies most of the cartoonist's waking hours.

In the first place there is the idea. Ask Wortman how he manages to think up so many ideas. The answer is, he doesn't. Ideas are supplied him by four or five collaborators. But they do not "think-up" ideas. Wortman doesn't want *made-to-order* lines for his cartoons. His are not "gag" cartoons or joke pictures. They are dramatizations of the little absurdities of life's give and take. They are not always funny, though Wortman can make us smile even when he is dealing with bitter ironies. Words actually spoken and overheard are the source and motive of his drawings, not imagined situations.

No artist ever went to greater pains to make his work authentic, and therefore convincing. Nothing is *faked* in *Metropolitan Movies*. The scenes are all familiar to the artist. Often they are sketched on the spot. The people are real flesh and blood if not actually portraits

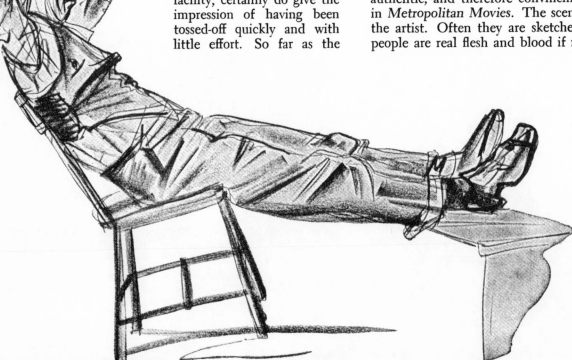

This is not a portrait of Denys Wortman though he posed for the figure (a study for the Duke) before the 5- x 6-foot mirror in his studio. Like many other artists, Wortman finds his own reflection one of his best models.

of individuals. They are the embodiment of definite types, personalized by an artist whose understanding of human character is as noteworthy as his skill with the pencil.

Take the caption of the cartoon reproduced herewith. That line, "Grandma's still in bed, but I'm keeping the window open so she won't miss the nice June smells and sounds," came from a collaborator in the East Side tenement district. Commenting upon that theme and its dramatization Wortman said, "That line would have no significance if it were picked up in the country where the fragrance of the fields naturally floats into a sickroom as a healing remedy. When the words are spoken in a tenement room looking out upon a narrow, dirty street, their irony is evident; they are good raw material for a cartoon. I say raw material because the caption is merely a starting point. The effective dramatization of the episode is really the part of my job that worries me. Drawing, composition, perspective are merely details of craftsmanship that every artist is supposed to have mastered. But many swell ideas are surprisingly hard to illustrate. While this story of Grandma and the June smells was not a particularly tough one—some ideas keep me guessing for weeks—it presents a typical problem. The only way to create those smells and sounds was to picture their source, the fish peddler with his pushcart, the garbage cans, the shouts of hucksters, the cries of playing children and the noise of traffic. It had to be a street scene. But what about Grandma? Somehow the sickroom and the street must be connected. Obviously it would not do to have the girl speaking her lines at the street door. But if she is leaning out of the open window as she talks with her sympathetic neighbor, the observer readily visualizes Grandma within. Where shall we put the neighbor, on the street looking up to the second or third story window? Not so good. Grandma would be too far away. She might be in a window of an adjoining flat, but better yet on a fire escape. So we arrive at a satisfactory setting. We have the smells and sounds of the busy street, insistent enough yet subordinated to the action which occupies the foreground."

All very simple and natural when we see the thing done and explained. But would you have thought of the flower pot with its forlorn bit of greenery? Would it have occurred to you to tell the time of day by the neighbor's curl-papers? Could you have managed so successfully to make Grandma's window the focal point in the busy composition? For that matter could you have managed the difficult perspective with such skill?

Mopey Dick and the Duke came upon the scene back in 1929. Their home was a shack in what was known as "Hoover Village," a community of hobos and unemployed veterans who settled on the east bank of the Hudson River above Seventy-second Street (in New York City) after being run out of Washington by order of the President. Soon after starting this series, Wortman left New York for his summer home on Martha's Vineyard, where he goes every spring for a six-months' stay. There he discovered a somewhat similar shanty which he decided to use as the setting for interior scenes. Although there were some discrepancies in both plans and details of the Hoover Village and the Vineyard shacks, they seemed trivial and not likely to be noticed.

Before using this interior in his cartoons, Wortman had made three very careful drawings of the room, from as many viewpoints. By this time they are quite shopworn from constant reference. If you compare all Mopey Dick interiors you will see that they are all faithfully consistent in plan and detail.

Let us now make a visit to *Mrs. Rumpel's Rooming House.* Far from being a fiction, a "typical" rooming house, it is a particular four-story brick structure in upper New York. As soon as Wortman had discovered this house and had been a welcome visitor there, he assured himself that no architect would have a single cause for complaint. He made drawings of every room in the house, including the basement; he drew the brick façade; he made a sketch plan. In his New York studio I saw dozens of these studies, including diagrammatic perspectives of the hallways and of the stairs, looking up and looking down. Every episode pictured in Mrs. Rumpel's Rooming House has an absolutely authentic setting. It happens in the northwest corner of the parlor bedroom or on the second floor stair-landing. It is just as it would be seen if you were looking in from the front hall or peering up the narrow flight of stairs, as the case may be. Even a detective couldn't catch the artist making a false step in that Bronx rooming house. No less real are the people: Mrs. Rumpel herself, her husband, and the very human strangers within their gates. Many of them have actually sat for their portraits. Of Mr. and Mrs. Rumpel, Wortman has made scores of sketches from life.

The very happenings which are pictured in this series

METROPOLITAN MOVIES — By Denys Wortman

"Grandma's still in bed, but I'm keeping the window open so she won't miss the nice June smells and sounds."

303

are based upon reality, the themes for the drawings have been supplied by one of Mrs. Rumpel's boarders with an exceptional nose for ideas: odd bits of scandal; trifling gossip; innuendos overheard through open transoms; the petty schemings of landlady and the complainings of roomers. Such is the raw material collected by this collaborator and delivered to Wortman—and paid for.

Thus you can be sure that whatever you see in Wortman's drawings is authentic. If the scene is a college boy's bedroom, it is a particular room, not a *typical* room; Wortman has been there and made sketches. If it is an East Side sweat shop, Wortman has somehow squeezed himself in between piles of clothing and perspiring workers to make his sketch.

It may occur to some to ask if such authenticity is important. Would less insistence upon correct detail weaken the cartoon? Let the artist answer. "Detail," says Wortman, "contributes more to the cartoon than is generally realized; that is, detail which is significant. The things one sees in a person's bedroom and the degree of taste or lack of it, give more than a hint of his character and personality. A half dozen photographs of boy friends on the girl's dresser is certainly a convincing biographical note. That of course is pretty obvious, but often I discover unusual details that I would never think of if I were faking the scene. Paradoxical as it may seem, an artist is less likely to clutter his drawing with unimportant detail when he sketches the room on the spot. I think that is because

MOPEY DICK AND THE DUKE

"Say, Mopey, what was it you wanted me to remember not to let you forget?"

"Yes, over the phone you seem willing enough to kiss me — but when I meet you . . ."

Exact-size detail of a drawing by Wortman

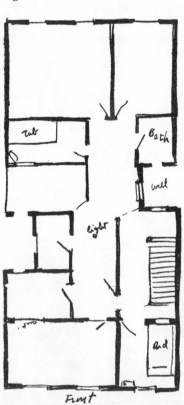

Sketch Plan of Mrs. Rumpel's Rooming House, an actual boarding house in the Bronx, New York

MRS. RUMPEL'S ROOMING HOUSE

"Miss Brown, I wish you'd close your door and transom while you're cooking that stew. The smell makes the others hungry and it all runs up my gas bills something terrible."

his practiced eye, roving over the scene, is attracted by detail that is significant and relates directly to the theme, items that even the most imaginative mind would never think of. Lacking such significant detail when faking, the artist introduces meaningless items, since detail there must always be in any setting."

In faking, Wortman explains, one easily weakens the result by being too much absorbed with detail. The necessity of making it up means concentration upon it which is not required when sketching from the objects. In one of his drawings of an interior there appeared a very small transom hook over a door.

"Why did I introduce that hook in the scene?" asked Wortman. Answering his own question, he continued, "Because it was there and I saw it. It didn't occur to me at the time to ask why. But several people noticed that hook and spoke of it. Then I realized that this transom hook which something told me was significant must have a meaning. Perhaps it started an unconscious chain of memories and emotions dating back to childhood time when wolves and tigers and burglars might come through that transom if the hook were not securely fastened! Perhaps I, and my public as well, had at some time had similar experiences with transom hooks—perhaps we, with quaking hearts, had stood on high chairs and fastened a hook like that as a protection against the terrors of an outside world. At any rate the incident may serve to illustrate what we have been saying about detail."

After Wortman has decided how he will dramatize the idea suggested by the caption line, he experiments with very rough sketches that look more like diagrams than drawings. These diagrams indicate the placing of persons and objects. This decided, he poses models in the desired attitudes and makes careful drawings for all figures in the cartoon. Of course he sketches very rapidly. He seldom employs professional models. He frequently acts as his own model, posing as Mopey Dick and the Duke before an enormous mirror. His wife generously impersonates shop girls, Mrs. Rumpel's maid, even the landlady herself, undergoing a remarkable metamorphosis under the magic of Wortman's pencil. Wortman's friends are likewise willing models.

The artist also summons the camera to his aid; not as a substitute for living models but as a record of facts that one cannot always sketch on location. Perhaps the scene is laid at a busy street crossing. The photograph is a great help here. It notes the relative heights of persons and postal boxes or lamp posts. It gives the detail of street signs, shop windows, passing traffic, and a thousand and one necessary details. It is just another resource of an artist who insists upon authenticity as the essential background for his pictorial commentaries on the life of a metropolis.

Wortman draws with square lithographic crayons, and a black carbon pencil and ink on a rough-surface board. The originals, measuring about 11 x 13 inches, are reproduced by line engravings. They are usually reduced to 6 x 7 inches for insertion as *Metropolitan Movies* in the New York *World-Telegram* and *Everyday Movies* when syndicated by United Feature Syndicate, Inc.

As we bid Denys Wortman goodday we catch a glimpse of a chessboard beside a comfortable chair in his studio. When the day's work is done, kings, knights and bishops, apparently awaiting the resumption of an interrupted play, will help the artist close his mind's door on Mopey Dick and Mrs. Rumpel. Perhaps it is characteristic of the man that his intellect must be active even when it seeks relaxation. For he takes chess seriously; his friends tell me he is a thoroughgoing student of the game, has even sat opposite national champions in handicap matches. So we leave Denys Wortman lighting his cigarette as he contemplates the next move, losing himself in this exacting hobby that makes him forget tomorrow's *Metropolitan Movie.*

Mrs. Rumpel's hired girl. Detail of a cartoon by Wortman

Pencil sketch by Wortman actually made in Mrs. Rumpel's Rooming House

306

MRS. RUMPEL'S ROOMING HOUSE

"With his armchair so near the window he don't need a cuspidor."

"At the store a specialist tells yer what type beauty yer are, and sells yer the make-up for yer individuality. It's marvelous!"

N. C. Wyeth

GIANT ON A HILLTOP

N. C. Wyeth

IN EXPLORING any career of great distinction we inevitably turn from the tangible product of a man's genius to its fountainhead in his nature. Drawn to him at first by what he does, we end up in contemplation of what he is. If he is great in his work we are not likely to be disappointed in what we discover in the man; there can be no Niagara without inexhaustible waters to sustain the grandeur of its spectacle.

We journey to Chadds Ford, Pennsylvania, preoccupied with the brilliance of a performance; we retrace our steps meditating upon the man who stands behind the magic brush, having learned, of course, that the magic lies not in a brush but in a life.

Thus we find ourselves talking first not about N. C. Wyeth's illustration and his painting, but about a man, a giant on a hilltop, an ardent American who has spent his days and employed his genius in objectifying the great traditions upon which his nation was founded and has prospered.

No artist in his work has so fully encompassed the cosmic spirit of his native land. This is not due to fortuitous circumstance: from student days, when Wyeth sat at the feet of Howard Pyle in Wilmington and Chadds Ford, he has studiously shaped his life to achieve a well-defined purpose. In the region of the historic Brandywine the young artist was inspired to consecrate his brush to whatever expressed the spirit of America—historical pictures and the romantic life of American Indians, adventurers, pioneers, trappers, woodsmen and farmers.

To accomplish this, Wyeth began to soak up all the historical fact and folklore he could lay hands on. But, although a great reader, he has not relied overmuch upon books. His philosophy of illustration is that the artist should be an experiencer rather than a mere observer. He likes to express this by a saying of the French painter Eugène Carrière. Carrière had painted a portrait of his wife, and a friend had complimented him upon its superlative qualities. The artist replied, "No wonder: like repoussé it was beaten out by blows from the inside."

Wyeth has indeed beaten out his pictures by blows from the inside. It is his firm belief that in order to paint a particular subject one must first become thoroughly versed in all its ways. He must sense deeply of the fact and substance of the object he intends to portray in form and color and—to express it more profoundly—must live the very life that he intends to perpetuate in pictures.

Thoroughly imbued with this philosophy, and eager to have first-hand knowledge of frontier life, Wyeth set out for Colorado in 1904. For a period of four months he spent most of his time in the saddle, taking an active part in the autumn round-ups, joining in the rugged social life of the plains people, embracing every phase of the many and colorful duties of ranch life, and otherwise exercising his extraordinary vitality.

Then, later, he went to the Navajo Reservation in New Mexico where he was, for a time, employed as a mail-rider in the Government service, making lengthy trips on horseback between stations and settlements. He fraternized with the Indians; filled his notebooks with sketches.

These adventures formed an honest background for his numerous illustrations of pioneer life on the western plains, but they were no more constructive than the quieter days spent on farms—where, in his teens, he worked as a "hand"—and at his home in Chadds Ford. His knowledge of the sea and of men who go down to the sea in ships has its source in many seasons at Port

Illustration by N. C. Wyeth

from "DRUMS"
by James Boyd

**This illustration painted in 1928 represents
Johnny Fraser and John Paul Jones standing on
the sea wall overlooking the Harbor of Brest.**

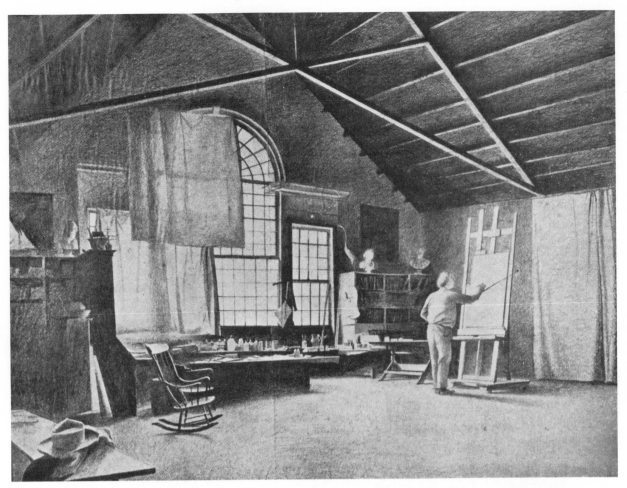

N. C. Wyeth in his Chadds Ford Studio   *Reproduced from a 22 x 28 pencil drawing by son Andrew*

Clyde on the Maine Coast, where the Wyeths have their summer home. In all these activities he has been in constant touch with nature. His hands have accustomed themselves to the "feel" of tools of rugged labor. He has followed the plow, swung the woodsman's axe, and raised livestock, partaking of any sort of experience from which he might extract the essence of life. These physical contacts with nature justify his declaration that everything he has done is fundamentally autobiographical. He says, "In every illustrative problem I must first find something that echoes within me. In my research for the picture I look for those things that have come within the range of my experience. Scholarly research and the marshaling of correct details in a picture are of little avail without such a procreative basis. This does not necessarily mean that the artist needs to visit China in order to illustrate a Chinese story. But he will be wise to search the narrative for a common denominator in his own experience and that of his oriental subject theme."

Wyeth spends as much time as possible with his books, favorite among which are Thoreau—of whose work he owns a complete library—Tolstoi and Romain Rolland. He believes that most artists do not read enough books that might play a vital part in the unfolding of themselves to their art.

He stresses the importance of honest association with people, becoming widely versed in the vagaries of human character. He is an intimate of the fisher-folk

on the Maine Coast, and a friend of the farmers in the Brandywine countryside, is equally at home among the great and the humble.

N. C.—by the way, how many know that the initials stand for Newell Convers?—loves simple living, caring little for formal society. He is a hard worker, is in his studio every morning at 8:30, including Sundays; allows himself a half hour for lunch and remains at his easel till four or five o'clock. Although he is now sixty-two, he continues to do considerable work on his twenty-acre homestead. He still impresses one as a man of tremendous vitality and creative force.

His home, a substantial brick structure designed by him in a style native to the Brandywine country, is half way up the side of a hill, on the top of which is his studio, a huge interior, 38 x 70 feet. Folding doors divide the room in half except when a mural is on the east wall and the painter requires that 70-foot vantage point for the inspection of his work.

That wall is seldom bare. Mural commissions throughout the years have competed with contracts for illustrations. Noteworthy among these are two panels in the Missouri State Capitol at Jefferson City; eight panels in the Metropolitan Life Insurance Building in New York; panels in the Federal Reserve Bank and the First National Bank, both of Boston; altar panels for the National Episcopal Cathedral in Washington, D. C., and a panel in the Wilmington, Del., Savings Society. This is but a partial list of wall paintings

THE LITTLE SHEPHERD
OF KINGDOM COME
by JOHN FOX, JR.

A random collection of N. C. Wyeth illustrations

which have given scope to a brush that refuses to be held down to 7 x 9 inch reproductions between the boards of children's books.

This is not to belittle the magnitude of Wyeth's contribution as a book illustrator; we cannot over-estimate the greatness of his service to two generations of young Americans in putting the breath of life into the history and romantic tradition of their country. These volumes are too well-known to need listing here—they fill many five-foot bookshelves. They are so important to all growing Americans that parents should make an immediate run on bookshops to buy up whatever titles may still be available.

But, however glorious Wyeth's career in this realm, we cannot conceive of his being entirely absorbed by book illustration. An illustrator, as conceived by Wyeth, is *incidentally* a painter of pictures for publications: he is first of all an artist, that is, a creator, whose only limitations are those within himself.

Wyeth has always painted pictures for the sheer love of painting and, of course, as a means of perfecting his art. He has painted several hundred still lifes, portrait studies, and landscapes in the last two decades. These were not made for exhibition purposes, but in 1939 Wyeth did become a gallery exhibitor at Macbeth's. Peter Hurd wrote an introduction to the exhibition catalog that I want to quote because it reveals a less-known side of a many-faceted genius:

"These works introduce for the first time publicly a new aspect of the art of N. C. Wyeth. They are the product of revolt against the inevitable limitations of that art of illustration which Mr. Wyeth has long served with sincerity and grace. For two generations he has shown a magic world to youngsters—in itself a rewarding achievement. But as the spiritual maturing of the man has demanded a freer and more personal expression he has descended within himself to find its terms. In his mind he lives on an heroic plane, the humble familiar, as all men may be, of the poet Homer, of Beethoven and of Thoreau. Without trying to measure a near man against far titans, you feel that he is of their kind; and, secured in his spirit by their common honesty of creative life, he is free to acknowledge any means to his painter's purpose. Of the illustrator's heritage he takes freely and consciously those components which may relate to painting: a strongly dramatic presentation but one delivered of the paraphernalia of archaeology; an ability to establish vividly the quality of a certain moment in which he enfolds the observer and causes him to see, to hear and, above all, to feel. He compels us to stop and ponder with him the surrounding vision of form and color, of radiance and shadow. This world of his is at once grave and lyric.

"It seems to me that in these works is implicit and essential character of the man, the gauge of truth which confirms victoriously Robert Henri's remark that 'A work of art is the trace of a magnificent struggle.'"

Now let us see what kind of pictures come from Wyeth's studio when he takes up his brush for that "freer and more personal expression" that Peter Hurd refers to. As he brings his canvases out to show us, and talks about each one, we see that he has indeed "descended within himself," that each picture is autobiographical in a very literal sense.

War Letter, for example. In this canvas the artist's father and mother are painted in the orchard of the Wyeth homestead on the banks of the Charles River at Needham, Massachusetts. The mother sits on a wheelbarrow reading the letter; the father, pitchfork in hand, stands attentively at her side. Smoke from a bonfire—it is autumn—ascends in the frosty air. The family cow stands in a meadow near by.

In another canvas, *Island Funeral*, we look down upon a tiny island on the Maine Coast at the moment when the neighbors have come in all manner of small sea-craft to bid their last farewell to Captain Teel, one of Wyeth's friends among the rugged Maine fishermen.

Not all of his pictures are episodal by any means. Pure landscapes and marines are among his recent productions. But even when devoid of human interest his pictures usually reflect some deeply felt and personal relationship to the chosen subject. *Summer Night*, for example. Let me quote Wyeth's own account of the origin of this painting.

"One summer's night several years ago, during one of my familiar walks along the broad stretches of the Brandywine Meadows, I passed among a herd of dairy cows quietly standing and lying down in the bright moonlight. It was sultry, and great threatening clouds moved and lifted in majestic patterns across the sky line like the silent shifting of scenery on a celestial stage.

"The full moon threw shafts of clear mellow light through the cloud openings which slowly swung across the dark terrain like beams from a beatific searchlight.

"As I watched the impressive spectacle before me, I became conscious that one of the cows, standing apart from the main groups of reposing animals, was in labor and about to drop her calf.

"I watched the progress of this miracle of birth for a long time, in fact until the new bit of life on earth finally struggled to its feet, cast its own new shadow, and wobbled and fumbled its way to its mother's teats and drenched itself in warm milk.

"Many times since then I have attempted to express the mood of this impressive experience in pattern and color. The one you see printed is, I think, the best I have done with it.

"Incidentally, the Jersey cow portrayed in the painting represents my recollection of our family cow at home, one I helped care for, and milked, as a boy. She was an old but magnificent animal and has always symbolized to me the great mother of all cows."

Wyeth, asked for an account of his technical procedure, gave me the following: "This painting was made entirely from memory, which is my customary practice in creative painting. It is painted in egg tempera on gesso ground, and the method used in painting it strictly conforms, I believe, to directions handed down to us from the time of the Renaissance.

"The preparation of a gesso panel is an exacting performance. I make most of my panels which are of whiting and glue built upon sheets of pressed wood. The many details of this procedure cannot be gone into here.

"After weeks—or months, as the case may be—have gone into the intensive preliminary phases of compositional effort and the motive has been completely realized in black and white cartoon (charcoal perhaps) then, by means of a lantern slide, a careful map-like tracing is made directly upon the prepared panel. This pat-

SUMMER NIGHT

Egg Tempera Painting (22 x 36) by N. C. Wyeth

*The color plate below is an exact-size repro-
duction of a detail at lower left of the canvas*

Caldwell's Island   (24 x 48)   A recent egg tempera painting by N. C. Wyeth

Corn Harvest   (31 x 34)   N. C. Wyeth

Lobsterman   (42 x 52)   N. C. Wyeth

tern is carefully drawn in with brush and india ink to such a degree of completeness that an excellent and complete tonal drybrush drawing results. This is all imperatively necessary in order to give the over-painting in color full body and power—it can make the shadows deeply rich and luminous and will give the over-all pattern in its finality a unified and richly fabricated surface.

"Following the completion of the ink rendering, the entire surface is evenly coated with a thin solution of egg yolk and distilled water. This makes for an adhesive ground for the color.

"Painting in egg tempera is strictly a process of building one color over another, seeing to it that, in the end, every inch of surface carries a faintly equalized weight of pigmentation. Opaque painting must be observed throughout, depending upon transparent glazing over the opaque to achieve glowing depth or luminous brilliance.

"The method of applying color, or the sequence of color overlays or glazes, is something for the individual to find out for himself through patient and incessant practice.

"True tempera painting is not a fortuitous procedure, but on the contrary is very painstaking and methodical. Accidental flourishes of the brush do not count, and one achieves only so far as he feels and sees things definitely.

"The making of the panels, the safe methods of preparing dry color, and its application is a precise affair, but once grasped, it is all very simple.

"Every illustration or painting I have made in the last thirty years has been done from the imagination or the memory. However, I have constantly studied from the figure, from animals and from landscape, and have especially stressed the training of my memory. This I've done from the time I was seventeen. An early and greatly valued teacher of mine, one Charles W. Reed of Boston, insisted that the faculty of memory had become a lost function among American artists and he blamed much of the lack of mood and imagination in their work to this fact."

Pencil Study for an illustration
by N. C. WYETH

Mention has not yet been made of Wyeth's advertising illustrations, but no outline of his career would be complete without at least a reference to the considerable volume of work he has executed in this field. It would, indeed, have been surprising if he had escaped the clamor of business for the persuasions of his magic brush. It is characteristic of Wyeth that these commercial assignments have received the same conscientious study that goes into his other work.

It would be pleasant—if space allowed—to fill a page with talk about the more personal and domestic life of N. C. Wyeth. His years have been filled with many satisfactions, among which is a devoted and talented family, doubtless the largest-sized family of artists in America. Besides father Wyeth and Andrew, there are sisters Henriette and Caroline, both painters; and sister Ann, whose symphony was performed by the Philadelphia Orchestra before she was twenty. Henriette married Peter Hurd, famous painter of New Mexico. Ann is the wife of John McCoy, a young Chadds Ford painter. Brother Nathaniel is an inventive engineer. Nor should we omit the predominant importance of a mother whose love and energy have, over the years, supplied a rich background of domestic completeness incalculable to an artistic family. All fit companions for a giant on a hilltop!

*   *   *

This chapter was written in the late fall of 1944. The book is on its way to press, a year later, only a few days after news was received of N. C. Wyeth's untimely death. The author, quite naturally, questioned whether it was advisable to rewrite some of the passages which quote Mr. Wyeth in the present tense. To do this, it was decided, would impair rather than strengthen the biographical interest of the story. So the text has been printed without change from its original appearance in *American Artist* in January 1945.